n University at the
ope.

the better advance- Preamble.
amongst all classes
Colony, to establish
t the Cape of Good
se with the services
Examiners : Be it
Cape of Good Hope,
of the Legislative
embly thereof, as

of a chancellor, a Of whom university
graduates, shall be to be established
shall consist.
Hope, and shall be
the name of " The
Hope," and by such Its name and powers.
ccession, and shall
nd shall be capable

Unisa 1973

MAURICE BOUCHER

SPES IN ARDUIS

a history of
the University of South Africa

Photographs, accompanying
biographical descriptive texts
J. J. BRITS

UNIVERSITY OF SOUTH AFRICA
PRETORIA 1973

ISBN 0 86981 001 4

Designed, printed and bound in South Africa by
Wallachs Printing Co Pty Ltd,
Pretoria

Contents

Foreword

The University of South Africa has compiled this record of its history as part of its centenary celebrations.

It is really more than just its own history. The University of South Africa, formerly the University of the Cape of Good Hope, is the oldest degree-conferring institution in the Republic and until 1918 was in fact our only university. Its early history is thus to a great extent the history of higher education in South Africa as a whole. It will not therefore surprise the reader if the first chapters of this account reflect a wider view of educational developments than those which follow. On the other hand it must be remembered that as a modern university with a unique method of teaching the University of South Africa is of very recent date. For that reason considerable emphasis has been placed upon the rapid expansion of facilities in the last few decades.

It was our good fortune to have in Professor Boucher someone who had carried out exhaustive research at home and abroad into our history to 1946 for his D.Litt. et Phil thesis, *The University of the Cape of Good Hope and the University of South Africa (1873–1946). A Study in national and imperial perspective.* The early chapters here are largely based on this study. For the additional chapters a great variety of official and unofficial sources have been used, enlivened by the personal reminiscences of past and present members of the teaching and administrative staffs. Mention must also be made of the generous co-operation of other people and other bodies. A special word of thanks is due to the Department of National Education for permission to consult the files in the government archives.

As this work is not primarily intended for the specialist, foot-notes and bibliography have been dispensed with. The earlier thesis, which has now been accepted for publication in the *Archives Year Book for South African History*, contains a comprehensive list of sources for the period to 1946. Professor M.J. Posthumus is responsible for the excellent translation of the present text in the Afrikaans edition.

Professor Boucher was also fortunate in having Mr J.J. Brits as his collaborator. Mr Brits, through his long association with the University of South Africa and his deep interest in its history, particularly in the day by day events and human aspects, was able to provide biographical and other details, photographs and information otherwise difficult to track down. His knowledge and research have enriched a number of university publications.

For both, this study has been a labour of love. "Labours of love," Professor Boucher has written, "are sometimes uncharitably described as acts of piety, uncritical panegyrics in praise of those who make up a small society. It is indeed difficult to be dispassionately objective when events are seen from the inside and without the perspective which time alone can lend them. However, if approbation is the keynote of the story of this university since 1946, it can at least be said that the view is widely shared, particularly among the many students who have, over the years, enrolled for its courses. For whatever the shortcomings of the federal university and that at the Cape before it, the modern foundation has never lost sight of its duty to the peoples of South Africa. The long battle for full recognition has been waged solely in the interests of those for whom it was created."

This history of a university is offered with pride, and also with humility.

Theo van Wijk,
Principal and Vice-Chancellor

1 *The prelude*

University education in South Africa is only a century old. Through the years of Dutch East India Company rule at the Cape from 1652 until the first British occupation of 1795, higher educational development extended no further than the creation of a few private secondary, or "Latin" schools. Population growth was slow and the need for educated leaders could easily be supplied by the motherland itself. There had also been a steady drift into the interior of men and women who, by the close of the century, were living in areas remote from Cape Town, the main centre of colonial life. Before the Cape of Good Hope could begin to think of founding a university, a firm groundwork of elementary and secondary schooling would have to be constructed.

Not until the brief period of rule by the Batavian Republic from 1803 until 1806 were there signs of advance in this direction. Real progress had to await the resumption of British control. Improvement came slowly, but by 1839, a government education department had been established with a Scottish-born teacher, James Rose Innes, at its head. The new Superintendent General of Education inaugurated a system of state and state-aided schools throughout the colony. By this time, the movement which would at length open up the rest of southern Africa to white settlement was under way. It would, however, be long before adequate educational facilities became available to youth in coastal Natal or in the inland regions beyond the Orange and Vaal Rivers.

Even before the colonial government assumed a measure of

1

responsibility for education, there had been some who had dreamed of the provision of more advanced instruction than that which could then be obtained at the Cape. In 1817, a future Dutch Reformed *(Nederduitse Gereformeerde)* Church minister, Abraham Faure, who was at that time studying in the Netherlands, made suggestions for higher educational development in his homeland. A decade later, he was to take a leading part, with other prominent colonists, including James Adamson of the "Scotch" Church, in founding an "Athenaeum" in Cape Town – the South African College. The courses which this new institution proposed to offer gave promise of high standards of attainment and its staff were accorded professorial rank. The opening of the college in 1829 added new lustre to a small colonial capital. For Cape Town, though remote from the cultural centres of Europe, could at least boast a public library, an observatory and one or two promising schools, among them the academy of the *Tot Nut van 't Algemeen* society.

The example of the founders of the South African College inspired the Anglican Church to promote similar schemes. These culminated twenty years later in the establishment of a rival Diocesan Collegiate School. Sir John Herschel, one of the architects of the government education system of 1839, saw in the inclusion of more advanced studies in the Cape school curriculum the beginnings of future university development in South Africa.

The South African College was at best a secondary school in its early years and, in many respects, no more than a primary school. The reverend professors who presided over its first classes – Adamson, Faure and the Anglican, Edward C. Judge – discovered that before they could initiate their charges into the mysteries of metaphysics, trigonometry and astronomy promised in the prospectus, they had to teach many of them to read! A stimulus to further achievement was also lacking. The public oral examination which brought courses of study to a close was no doubt a dignified ceremony, but it was no searching test of a student's ability.

Already in distant Britain, the formal ritual of oral disputation had begun to give way to written examination at the ancient universities of England. Soon, the idea gained ground that society was obliged to seek impartial means to select the best man for each post in an increasingly competitive world. The written test was found to be an excellent way of doing this and its suitability was clearly demonstrated in the work of the purely examining University of London. This institution was founded in 1836 to combat the religious exclusiveness of Oxford and Cambridge and to prevent continued hostility between rival colleges in the capital. At length, the system of written examination was introduced into the civil service, where patronage had long governed recruitment. The new tests were speedily extended to other fields and, after mid-century, came increasingly to dominate the school curriculum at all levels. Charles Kingsley wrote feelingly in 1863 of the unfortunate citizens of "the Isle of Tomtoddies", who were "all heads and no bodies". They worshipped the idol Examination with such devotion that only water on the brain could secure for their children a merciful release from ceaseless cramming!

Public opinion at the Cape of Good Hope was not unaware of these developments. Indeed, the introduction of written examinations in the colonial civil service coincided with British experiments in that direction. In fact, by extending the new method of recruitment to the entire service, the Cape was in advance of Britain. The efficacy of the system also led to its adoption in other educational fields, as was the case in the mother country.

The administration of the civil service examinations was placed in the hands of a Board of Examiners of Candidates for Government Service which was established in 1850. The schools of the colony were improving and the time had come, as the Government Secretary, John Montagu, observed, for the Cape "to exact higher qualifications, even for clerkships, than the mere discharge of clerical duty would require". In addition, therefore, to a simple test for the lowest class of recruits to the service, two further examinations were instituted, the more advanced one requiring a

3

knowledge of "Classics, Mathematics, and the Elements of Physical Science". In such manner was young South Africa launched upon the deep waters of written examination which were to engulf many an aspirant to intellectual honours in the years ahead.

The board consisted of three members and a part-time clerk, F.R. Jervis. The Superintendent General of Education, Rose Innes, an indefatigable committee man, was an obvious choice. His colleagues were the Auditor General, William Hope, and the Master of the Supreme Court, John Steuart. Hope, quiet-spoken and friendly of manner, seems to have taken precedence at early meetings, but fades from the picture some time before his death in the last year of the board's brief existence. The Cape judge, A.W. Cole, has left us a description of Steuart. Cole tells us that he was "a man of ancient Scottish lineage, polished and courteous", although somewhat reticent, except with his friends. He was, we learn, often convulsed with inward laughter, so that his face turned crimson, giving him the appearance of "a dissipated old Punch".

That these men grappled with novel problems appears from the minutes of their meetings and from their correspondence. They were given what today would seem quite superfluous instructions upon the way in which they were to carry out their duties; they also found it necessary to explain to government the method which they had adopted to mark scripts. Although it had been designed to do away with patronage in the selection of officers, the board evidently found difficulty in convincing the public that a new era was dawning. Indignant parents, among them the Rev. William Robertson of Swellendam, had to be pacified; disappointed candidates sought explanations. Robertson, a former teacher, should have known better, but there seems to have been a feeling that the new scheme operated with unnecessary severity. The members of the board would not make concessions, however, and stressed that under no circumstances could they be influenced "by the Birth or descent of the Candidates", but would be guided entirely by the results of the examinations. Patronage was on its way out at the Cape, although not

4

all newly appointed members of the public service in the fifties of the last century took the board's examinations.

The Board of Examiners was nevertheless a step forward in the direction of efficient administration for a colony which, in 1854, received the gift of representative government. It took its duties seriously, was prepared to conduct examinations at centres far from the colonial capital and provided an opening for many who would subsequently make their mark in the public service or in the wider world beyond. One whose name appears in the board's final list of successful candidates was Charles Bletterman Elliott. He was to contribute his services to the further development of higher education at the Cape before he began his long association with the government railways. The board deserves to be remembered in another connection. Although its members advocated no radical change in an exclusively English examination system, they stressed the need for a test in Dutch for those whose work would take them to the country districts. The suggestion fell upon deaf ears. It would be many years before the language of the white majority would receive fair treatment at the Cape.

The examinations of the Board of Examiners clearly demonstrated the value of such tests in determining academic ability, but they were not designed to meet the requirements of schools and colleges in the colony. Neither did the board issue certificates to successful candidates, while its highest test of learning found little favour. Few were the locally educated men at that time who could have attempted it. There was a call for a series of examinations specially designed to attract the interest of those responsible for the instruction of younger people. A new controlling body which would absorb the existing board and extend its functions was also needed. The Cape of Good Hope was fortunate in having as Governor between 1854 and 1861 Sir George Grey, an energetic supporter of educational progress. His interest encouraged others to press for a different approach in higher education and in 1857 a government commission was appointed to investigate the possibility of establishing an examining board

5

L A N G H A M D A L E was born on 22 May, 1826 at Kingsclere, Hampshire, England. He was educated at Christ's Hospital, London and Queen's College, Oxford and after graduating, was appointed Professor of English and Classics at the South African College, Cape Town.

He succeeded James Rose Innes as Superintendent General of Education for the Cape Colony in 1859 and became President of the Board of Public Examiners in 1867. In 1859, he received an honorary LL.D. degree from the University of Glasgow.

A leading promoter of the university ideal, Dale was Chairman of the government commission which recommended the establishment of the examining institution of 1873. Although he saw the advantages of a teaching university, his subsequent plan to create one was frustrated.

Langham Dale achieved much in his efforts to improve the colonial educational system and was knighted for his services in 1889. He did, however, clash with those who suported the use of Dutch in the schools. He retired as Superintendent General of Education in 1892.

Vice-Chancellor of the university for all but four years of the period from 1873 to 1889, Langham Dale was unanimously elected Chancellor by Convocation in 1890.

He died on 12 January, 1898 at his home, Montagu Cottage, Mowbray, Cape Town.

Sir Langham Dale, M.A., LL.D. (h.c.), K.C.M.G.
Member of Council 1873–1892
Pro Vice-Chancellor 1890–1892
Vice-Chancellor 1873–1877; 1879–1882; 1884–1889
Chancellor 1890–1898

with wider powers. Rose Innes was, not unnaturally, a member. He was joined by Langham Dale, the English-born professor at the South African College who was rapidly becoming one of the colony's leading educationists, and by Egidius Benedictus Watermeyer, a writer of distinction and early Cape historian who had recently been raised to the bench. Watermeyer, although born in Cape Town of Dutch-speaking stock, was thoroughly at home in an English environment and was keenly interested in the provision of improved higher educational facilities.

The commission reported in 1858 and proposed the appointment of an enlarged board with examiners in arts, science and law. Certificates were to be issued in two classes upon the results of examinations modelled upon those for degrees in British universities. Special attention was also to be given to examinations in civil engineering and in other professional fields. The carrot of bursaries, prizes and scholarships was to be dangled before the eyes of candidates for academic honours, as it was felt that the certificates proposed might not provide a sufficient inducement to further study. It is clear that the members of the commission were aware of developments in the British academic world, for they had in mind the eventual founding of a colonial university, "corresponding in powers and functions to the London University and the Queen's University in Ireland".

The examining institution of this kind had become a model for export. It had taken root in Dublin at mid-century and had since made its appearance at Toronto, Upper Canada, in 1854 and at Bombay, Calcutta and Madras in British India three years later. The cheapness of such a course carried much weight; moreover, all these foundations had been created on a non-sectarian basis in an endeavour to overcome the often bitter wrangling among colleges maintained by competing religious bodies. Already, an Anglican institution had been founded at the Cape in opposition to the South African College; other denominations might follow this example. A religiously neutral, or as some would have it, a "godless" examining board might lead the colony away from denominational strife in the field of education.

8

One proposal which could bring the day of full university status nearer was made by the commission. It was suggested that when the number of certificate holders reached fifty, they might form a sort of convocation, having the privilege of sharing with the Governor the right to elect a triennial educational council which would have the power to select examiners.

The findings of the commission were embodied in a draft bill which, with the support of Governor Grey, came before the colonial legislature in 1858. There was inevitably opposition from those who considered that the Cape needed to place more emphasis in education upon the three R's and less upon the classics. Certificates in technical subjects were felt by some to be quite unnecessary, since it was to the efforts of the self-made man that Britain owed her industrial supremacy. The measure was nevertheless passed with few changes. The Cape's first representative assembly refused, however, to institute the Queen's scholarships which had been proposed for study abroad. These would have involved a permanent grant and there was a strong desire to retain parliamentary control over the operations of the board by means of an annual vote.

The members of the Board of Public Examiners in Literature and Science were elected for five-year terms of office. Watermeyer, Dale and Rose Innes could not be overlooked for membership of the first board. Watermeyer was the law examiner and President until his untimely death in 1867. Had he survived, he might well have attained high office in the future university, which was to adopt the motto, *Spes in Arduis,* attributed to him. Rose Innes continued to examine in science after his retirement as Superintendent General of Education in 1859. His successor in that office, Langham Dale, examined in arts and became President on Watermeyer's death. Two other former South African College professors served on the board : the Rev. Edward Judge, then chaplain and private tutor at Simonstown, and A.N.E. Changuion, an early champion of higher education for the colony and at that time the proprietor of an excellent private school in Cape Town.

9

WILLIAM PORTER, the son of a Presbyterian minister who later joined the Unitarians, was born on 15 September, 1805 at Artikelly, County Londonderry, in the north of Ireland. He received his early education at schools in Limavady and Londonderry.

He was apprenticed to a Dublin merchant in 1819, but was unfitted for a business career. He therefore turned to the law and after studying in London and Dublin was called to the Irish bar in 1831. Eight years later, he was appointed Attorney General of the Cape Colony, where he also built up an extensive private practice.

Porter was closely involved in the constitutional struggle at the Cape between 1848 and 1872. In 1866, he resigned as Attorney General and three years later, was elected to parliament, of which he had previously been an *ex-officio* member. He also served on the Board of Public Examiners from 1867 until 1871 and vested a generous annuity in it which was subsequently transferred to the university. In addition to this fund, he has given his name to a reformatory and the village of Porterville.

A convinced Unitarian and a kindly, generous and unselfish man, Porter was keenly interested in the progress of the colony. He was awarded the C.M.G. for his services in 1872 and in the following year helped to pilot the university bill through the House of Assembly. He was nominated a member of the university Council and in 1876, after he had left the Cape, was elected by Convocation as the first Chancellor.

William Porter spent his declining years in the land of his birth and died in Belfast on 13 July, 1880.

The Hon. William Porter, C.M.G.
Member of Council 1873–1874
Chancellor 1876–1880

10

CHARLES ABERCROMBIE SMITH was born on 12 May, 1834 at St Cyrus, Kincardineshire, Scotland. He had a brilliant scholastic career at the Universities of Glasgow and Cambridge, specializing in physics, with particular emphasis upon the fields of heat, light and electricity.

He came to the Cape for health reasons in 1860, where he practised as a surveyor. In 1866, he entered parliament as the member for King William's Town and rose to be Commissioner of Crown Lands and Public Works in the Molteno administration. In 1875, he accepted the post of Auditor General and served the Cape government in that capacity for 28 years. He was knighted for his outstanding services on his retirement.

A member of the Board of Public Examiners from 1868 until 1873, he was appointed to the first university Council, retaining his seat until 1916. Smith was Vice-Chancellor from 1877 until 1879 and for successive terms between 1905 and 1911. In 1917, the honorary degree of Doctor of Laws was conferred upon him by the university.

He made important contributions as a member of Council to the advancement of scientific studies and was for many years a moderator and examiner in science and mathematics. He also took a leading part in the affairs of the Diocesan College in the colonial capital.

Sir Charles Abercrombie Smith died on 1 May, 1919 at St Cyrus, his Wynberg, Cape Town home.

The Hon. Sir Charles Abercrombie Smith, Kt, M.A., LL.D. (h.c.)
Member of Council 1873–1916
Pro Vice-Chancellor 1892–1897
Vice-Chancellor 1877–1879; 1905–1911

Among the law examiners was another promoter of the university ideal. This was the Ulsterman, William Porter, whose generosity in vesting in the board the additional pension granted him on his retirement as Attorney General led to the creation of a major South African scholarship. Two men who distinguished themselves at the board's examinations, C.B. Elliott and Charles Abercrombie Smith, later became science examiners. Elliott also took over the secretaryship from Rose Innes in 1863. It was said of Smith, a Cambridge wrangler, that his answers in the survey examination showed that he was "a better man than his Examiners". Both were subsequently appointed to the Council of the future university, Smith serving as Vice-Chancellor for a number of years. The Rev. Professor G.F. Childe of the South African College, a brilliant mathematician, was a member of all three boards between 1858 and 1873, while the Diocesan College provided two examiners. One was the Rev. F.G. White, a descendant of the famous naturalist, Gilbert White; the other was the Rev. George Ogilvie, a much-travelled member of that breed of muscular Christians who figured so prominently in nineteenth-century British education. Ogilvie, like Smith, would later become Vice-Chancellor of the Cape's first university.

The Board of Public Examiners in Literature and Science assumed control of the public service examinations conducted by its predecessor and added to them first-class and second-class certificates. These corresponded closely with the M.A. and B.A. examinations of the University of London. Examinations in law, civil engineering, land surveying and navigation were also provided. The engineering syllabus was based upon that of the University of Glasgow, but in those days before large-scale industrial development in South Africa, the test only attracted two candidates! Navigation certificates were never issued. Examinations were at first held only in Cape Town, but were later extended to other centres. It is perhaps superfluous to add that, in an age of almost unchallenged British supremacy, English was the only language permitted for examination purposes.

Schools and colleges soon began to see in the board's tests a convenient method of determining the ability of their pupils. There was therefore an early demand for examinations of secondary school standard, similar to those which were becoming popular in England. The board decided to introduce a Competition for Schools in 1864 and added a third-class certificate examination, not unlike the Matriculation examination of the University of London, into which the schools' competition was ultimately merged. The new certificate took the place of the main public service examination and a few years later the preliminary examination for the public service, designed to prevent the incompetent from attempting any further tests, was abolished.

Although there was some criticism of the emphasis upon mathematics and classics in the board's tests for schools – and many found compulsory Greek a difficult hurdle – teachers soon began to prepare their better pupils for the new examination. In this they were spurred on after the passing of the Education Act of 1865 by a combination of financial aid and inspection which had much in it of the English system of payment by results. Good instructors were in demand and Scotland continued to supply many of them. These dedicated men strove to raise standards and to give students a sufficiently thorough grounding to enable them to tackle more advanced work without trying, as a board report put it, to erect "a Corinthian capital upon a pillar of dust and ashes".

There was, it may be added, no bar to prevent either women or non-Europeans from attempting the examinations of the Board of Public Examiners. Girls' schools were being established at this period, but our Victorian ancestors were by no means certain that young ladies were strong enough to support the strain of prolonged intellectual activity! Girls did not come forward for the board's tests and it was not until the early seventies, when the Rev. Andrew Murray's enthusiasm led to the founding of the Huguenot College at Wellington, that a move was made towards providing higher educational facilities for women. As for the coloured races of South Africa, they had a longer road to travel. There were, however, some promising signs. The Lovedale mis-

GEORGE OGILVIE was born at Calne, Wiltshire, England on 30 June, 1826 and was educated at Winchester and Wadham College, Oxford, obtaining the M.A. degree in 1855.

He took Holy Orders and became Vice-Principal of Bradfield College in Berkshire before accepting a similar post at Buenos Aires in the Argentine Republic, where he was also chaplain to the British community.

He came to South Africa in 1858 as Precentor of St George's Cathedral, Cape Town and Principal of St George's Grammar School. In 1861, he moved to the collegiate school, soon to be known as the Diocesan College ("Bishops"). Under his able guidance, this foundation rapidly rose to the front rank. Ogilvie was also appointed a member of the Board of Public Examiners in 1868, served on the university Council from 1873 until 1903 and was Vice-Chancellor for two terms in the period 1893 to 1897. His valuable contributions to Cape education were recognized by the university in 1906, when the honorary D.Litt. degree was conferred upon him.

In 1885, he succeeded Badnall as Rector of St Paul's, Rondebosch, where he remained until he retired in his seventy-sixth year.

George Ogilvie, who introduced "Winchester rules" football to the Cape, will long be remembered as a pioneer of South African rugby.

He died on 1 May, 1915 in Cape Town.

The Rev. Canon George Ogilvie, M.A., D.Litt. (h.c.)
Member of Council 1873–1903
Vice-Chancellor 1893–1897
President of Convocation 1890–1894

16

sionary institution was considering future expansion and, in 1867, the Board of Public Examiners also received an enquiry from the Anglican school, Zonnebloem College, about the possible admission of "a few Kafir lads" to the preliminary examination.

The third-class certificate was regarded by many as the pinnacle of intellectual achievement, but a few set their sights on higher things. The examinations of degree standard thus began to influence the teaching in the upper classes of the colleges in Cape Town. At the South African College, where written examinations finally replaced the surviving oral tests, academic work prospered under the direction of such able teachers as the versatile Roderick Noble, the Professor of English, James Cameron, and the mathematician, Childe. In 1859, J.H. Brand, later President of the Orange Free State, began law classes for the board's certificate. At the Diocesan College, no longer designated a school after 1867, Ogilvie reorganized the entire course of study so thoroughly that the Anglican institution became a serious rival to its older Cape Town neighbour.

The influence of the Board of Public Examiners was not, however, confined to the colleges of the colonial capital. Other institutions came into being – some of them inspired by Grey's interest in higher education. These began to prepare students for the new advanced examinations. Although not all of them lived up to the high hopes entertained at their birth, there is no doubt that, as Cameron was to say at a later date, "the scattered rays of intellectual light throughout the Colony were, to a great extent, concentrated and focused by the establishment of the Board".

Grey's influence is remembered in the Port Elizabeth and Bloemfontein schools which bear his name. Grey Institute in Port Elizabeth failed to make a success of its advanced work, but the Free State college at length became the nucleus of the present university there. In the Eastern Province, the Anglicans were active in the field of higher education and St Andrew's, Grahamstown was destined to retain its upper classes until the early years of this century.

In the Cape midlands, local action led to the founding of

Graaff-Reinet College in 1860. This institution made rapid strides in its early years under the guidance of James Gill, a classics teacher of considerable attainments, and Francis Guthrie, lawyer and scientist, promoter of railway development and inventor of a flying machine. The college, however, failed to maintain its position. Another foundation which, after strenuous efforts, was finally forced to withdraw from the higher educational scene was Gill College, established at Somerset East in 1869. It also owed much of its initial success to an excellent professorial staff. This included the Scotsman, John Brebner, a former teacher at Burgersdorp who was later to head the Free State educational services, and the eminent Yorkshire-born botanist, Peter MacOwan.

In the western Cape, the Dutch Reformed *(Nederduitse Gereformeerde)* Church realized a long-deferred dream by establishing a theological seminary at Stellenbosch in 1859, with Andrew Murray's brother, John, and N.J. Hofmeyr as its first professors. The Board of Public Examiners expected that some of its students would seek its higher qualifications, but the development of university education in the district came not from the seminary, but from the founding in 1866 of an Undenominational Public School at Stellenbosch. Within a few years, students there were to achieve success in the board's second-class examination. From this modest beginning the Victoria College, today the University of Stellenbosch, would arise.

Finally, the Reformed *(Gereformeerde)* Church opened a theological seminary in 1869 at Burgersdorp. Making little immediate impact upon the educational scene, this foundation was destined to develop an Arts Department, ancestor of Potchefstroom University for Christian Higher Education.

Langham Dale regarded the South African College as the intended "cope-stone of a public system of education in the colony". Although he came to accept that the college at Graaff-Reinet, remote from the colonial capital, served a useful purpose, he regretted the proliferation of small institutions. They, in turn, were jealous of the two Cape Town "giants", particularly as both of them had representation on the board after 1867. There

JAMES CAMERON, born on 19 July, 1831 at Tananarive on the island of Madagascar, was the son of a Scottish missionary. He came to the Cape at an early age and attended Dr A.N.E. Changuion's school and the South African College.

As a young man, he went to Manchester in England, where he trained for the Congregationalist ministry at the Lancashire Independent College and later studied at Owens College. In 1852, he obtained the London B.A. degree.

From Manchester, Cameron moved to Bournemouth in Hampshire, but soon returned to the Cape, where he taught under Dr Changuion and Langham Dale. He succeeded Dale as professor at the South African College in 1859. An excellent teacher, gentle and courteous in manner, he earned universal respect.

He was appointed to the university Council in 1873 and at its first meeting was chosen as Registrar, a position he occupied for 22 years. In 1878, he acted as Superintendent General of Education for several months. After his retirement, he again became a Council member.

Cameron received two honorary degrees: the LL.D. of the University of Glasgow in 1870 and a D.Litt. from the University of the Cape of Good Hope in 1901.

Long a regular Sunday evening preacher, he ministered to the Congregationalists of Sea Point from 1895 until 1902, when he left for England. His last years were spent at Bournemouth, where he died on 2 October, 1906.

The Rev. Dr James Cameron, B.A., LL.D. (h.c.), D.Litt. (h.c.)
Registrar 1873–1895
Member of Council 1873; 1896–1897; 1897–1902
Pro Vice-Chancellor 1897
Secretary of Convocation 1873–1876

was, at this time and later, widespread opposition to a system which permitted a teacher to examine his own students. Childe's appointment as an examiner had met with some disapproval on this ground, despite his acknowledged superiority in his field. A minor crisis arose when Ogilvie was appointed by Governor Wodehouse. It was alleged that the Diocesan College Principal had deliberately insinuated himself on to the board because the rival Cape Town institution had a member. Moreover, it was said with some justice that he had done so at the expense of another candidate for the honour, the Stellenbosch Public School Principal, W.E.W. Braid. The dispute hastened the end of the Board of Public Examiners and the university which was erected in its place was compelled to appoint, as far as was possible, "external" examiners. This, too, was to cause problems in days to come.

As the 1860's drew to a close and the colony emerged from a period of economic stagnation to move towards responsible government and new prosperity, the future course of higher education became increasingly a subject of earnest debate. Whatever shortcomings may have become apparent in its constitution, the Board of Public Examiners had undoubtedly helped to raise educational standards at the Cape. It was also attracting attention in Natal, where the Superintendent of Education, T. Warwick Brooks, considered that the younger colony should forge close ties with the board, since political federation with the Cape would probably be Natal's destiny.

On the other hand, the board lacked the standing of a full university and had largely failed in its quest to gain recognition for its examinations overseas. The University of London, for example, refused to contemplate the idea that other bodies could maintain the undeviating high standard of examining upon which it prided itself. The English institution, after acceding to a request from Mauritius in 1864, had transformed itself into an imperial university in the fullest sense, accepting individual examination entries from candidates in many distant territories. By 1871, its influence had extended to the Cape. In that year,

Josiah Slater, educationist of note and future newspaperman, began the series of examinations which would lead to a London B.A. degree. In 1872, F.C. Kolbe, in years to come a leading figure in South African life, both educational and spiritual, won the coveted Gilchrist Scholarship for further study in Britain. The award was made on the results of the University of London's Matriculation examination. Confusion was already beginning to arise between the English university and the local board, whose officers seemed likely to become reluctant agents for the greater London body.

When the creation of the Board of Public Examiners had first been discussed, there were some who had felt that the best course for the Cape to pursue would be to transform the South African College into a full teaching university with a medical faculty as well. It was then without doubt the Cape's leading academy and had that plan been adopted, the colony might have succeeded in avoiding the introduction of an examining university on the London pattern, as New South Wales had managed to do after the founding of the University of Sydney some years earlier. However, by the time the number of certificate holders approached the fifty needed to reconstruct the board, the college position was not so assured. It no longer enjoyed a monopoly and although its competitors were, like itself, simply secondary schools with a handful of mature students, they were fairly numerous and well supported.

There were, however, other reasons for refusing to entertain the idea of a teaching university. The Board of Public Examiners had done good work and had never been a drain upon the colonial exchequer. If it could be converted into a degree-conferring institution with a complete separation of the examining and administrative functions, it would, at low cost, enhance the prestige of a colony which in 1872 at last achieved responsible government. The London model had been a success in other lands and would soon be introduced into New Zealand and further extended in Canada. If the Cape of Good Hope did not found its own university of this type under charter from the

Queen, the University of London itself would probably secure an even firmer foothold in southern Africa. It would be regrettable if a self-governing colony were to remain subservient to the mother country in matters of higher education.

The old board had been a useful asset. Its examinations had set a high standard and its bursaries and awards had encouraged many to further endeavour. Its value was beginning to be appreciated by the general public and in the last year of its life it became the guardian of a special fund bequeathed by a wealthy widow, Sophia Jamison. This sum had been donated to enable students at the South African College who passed the second-class certificate examination with distinction to continue their studies in Europe. Many capable men had succeeded in the board's higher examinations; more still had obtained the third-class certificate. In addition to Elliott and Smith, others who would give their services to the administration of the future university had satisfied their examiners at various levels. These included E. A. Buchanan, J. H. de Villiers, J. I. Marais and J. X. Merriman. Holders of the higher certificates had to wait for more than twenty years before their academic successes were accorded degree standing in the University Incorporation Amendment Act of 1896. They may justly be called, however, South Africa's first home-produced graduates, worthy to be remembered beside those who qualified at a later date, when the Board of Public Examiners in Literature and Science had surrendered its powers to a greater examining machine.

2 *The examining university*

The campaign for a university opened in March, 1873. At the beginning of that month, the editor of the *Argus* newspaper in Cape Town, Thomas Ekins Fuller, discussed the question with two leading figures, the Attorney General, J. H. de Villiers, and the man who had earlier held that post, William Porter. This meeting in the newspaper's offices was followed by an editorial calling for speedy action to create "a Cape university, with power to grant degrees under charter from the Crown".

The appeal was immediately taken up by the South African Teachers' Association, whose President, Langham Dale, the Superintendent General of Education, was by that time in favour of something better for the colony than a reformed Board of Public Examiners and an educational council. The governing bodies and professors of the Cape Town colleges also gave strong support to the idea. Within two weeks the Molteno government had set up a commission to report on the form which the new university should take, for there was no suggestion that the Cape should have any less dignified an institution at the apex of its educational pyramid. Dale was selected as President and was joined by Fuller and Porter, two of the original sponsors of the scheme, and by three leading educationists, Cameron and Ogilvie of the Cape Town colleges and John Murray of Stellenbosch. The other members appointed were the President of the Colonial Medical Committee, Henry A. Ebden, and the Astronomer Royal, E. J. Stone.

The Dale Commission sought the opinions of prominent teachers in the colony and the answers received indicated a general preference for an examining university on the London model. A draft bill was drawn up and presented, with the blessing of the Governor, Sir Henry Barkly, to the colonial parliament. The proposed measure met with little hostility. A few grumbled about the expense, but it was demonstrated that an expanded examining board would not be costly to run. Eastern Province members of the House of Assembly were surprisingly conciliatory and were quite prepared to accept Cape Town as the university seat. There was some disappointment that government had decided against a teaching institution, but J. H. de Villiers, who introduced the bill, and Porter, who moved the second reading, effectively countered any dissatisfaction. Both emphasized that the new venture was just a beginning. "Let us have", said Porter, "first the blade, then the ear, and then the full corn in the ear", for the colony should "not despise the day of small things, when the day of great things will follow". The millennium would be long delayed.

The Cape parliament was content to pass the bill with little further argument and it is a measure of the general approval that one of the longest debates concerned nothing more significant than a point of grammatical usage. After some discussion, it was decided that the indefinite article should precede the word "university" in the phrasing of the legislation!

Act 16 of 1873, creating the University of the Cape of Good Hope, received the royal assent on 26 June and in due course was approved by the mother of parliaments. The university was to be governed by a Council of twenty members, appointed initially by proclamation of the Governor for a period of six years. Convocation, however, which would consist of the qualified certificate holders of the former board, graduates by examination and admitted graduates of other universities, was to elect a member to fill every second vacancy and one-half of the members of subsequent sexennial Councils. The governing body was to choose from its own members a Vice-Chancellor to hold office for two years, appoint a salaried Registrar and select the examiners. With regard to this last duty, Council was to "avoid, as much as may be, appointing any person to be an examiner of any candidate who shall have been under the tuition of such examiner at any time during the two years next before the examination".

Council was empowered to admit graduates of other universities to degrees and to confer similar distinctions after examination to all comers in arts, law and medicine. It could also issue certificates in civil engineering, land surveying, navigation and law, although it never availed itself of its powers so far as civil engineering and navigation were concerned. Attempts were made from the beginning to introduce a full medical course at the Cape, but although many members of that profession became admitted graduates, no degrees in medicine by examination were ever conferred by the University of the Cape of Good Hope. A link with the board of 1850 was maintained by the insertion of a clause authorizing the university to conduct entry tests for the public service. However, the introduction of a Matriculation examination, which came to be regarded as both a school leaving test and a necessary preliminary to university study, made it unnecessary to institute special examinations for government employment.

Convocation was intended to be an influential body, but it could only act in an advisory capacity and never made a big impact upon university life, except at election times. Its Presidents, with the exception of J. H. de Villiers from 1874 until 1880, were always admitted graduates. Three of its six Secretaries, however, held qualifications obtained at the Cape. Two of them were to have distinguished legal careers in South Africa : Sydney Twentyman Jones, Secretary from 1876 until 1879, and his successor, Victor Sampson, who retained the position until 1881. Charles Murray of the Department of Education, a Cape M.A., was elected Secretary in March, 1901. He remained in office until the examining university was no more.

The body of graduates had, in addition to the privilege of

27

CHARLES THOMAS SMITH was born on 20 November, 1823 in Fulham, England. He received his early education locally and at Wiesbaden in Germany. On his return to Britain, he studied law in London and was also a student at Caius College, Cambridge. He obtained his M.A. in 1850, was admitted to the bar in 1857 and was awarded an honorary LL.D. in 1875.

A fine sportsman, he coxed the Cambridge crew in the University Boat Race of 1854. He was also an excellent marksman and has been called the father of shooting associations in South Africa.

His legal career began in England, but in December, 1868, he was appointed a Cape Puisne Judge, joining the Eastern Districts Court at Grahamstown. In 1880, he moved to Cape Town, retiring from the bench in 1892. On three occasions, he acted as Chief Justice for the colony.

Deeply interested in social questions and particularly in education, he served on the university Council from 1880 until 1897 and as Vice-Chancellor from 1889 to 1893. In 1898, he succeeded Langham Dale as Chancellor. He also did much to promote advanced studies in Grahamstown and at the South African College.

Mr Justice Smith died on 10 February, 1901 at his home in Rosebank, Cape Town.

The Hon. Mr Justice Charles Thomas Smith, M.A., LL.D. (h.c.)
Member of Council 1880–1897
Vice-Chancellor 1889–1893
Chancellor 1898–1901
President of Convocation 1883–1890

choosing members of Council, that of selecting the titular head of the university. The Chancellor, unless he decided to resign, held the appointment for life. The first election took place in 1876, when Convocation's membership reached the required figure of one hundred. Several names were suggested on that occasion, but the final and unanimous choice of William Porter, then living in retirement in the Irish city of Belfast, was widely acclaimed.

The university was in receipt of a modest grant voted each year by the Cape assembly. This ranged from R3 000 in 1873 to rather more than twice this sum in the last year of colonial rule at the Cape. The amount allocated was seldom considered sufficient for administrative purposes, but an early move to obtain a permanent endowment proved unsuccessful. The accumulated funds of the Board of Public Examiners were also made over to the new Council, which was required to account for its actions and to justify its expenditure in an annual report to parliament. Finally, the new institution was to be entirely non-sectarian, imposing no religious tests upon its officers or upon those who sought to pass its examinations.

While the Board of Public Examiners was winding up its affairs in July, 1873, the Governor was considering the appointment of its successor's first governing Council. The final list gave due recognition to the professions and although the colleges were not automatically represented, their interests were adequately safeguarded. The number of clergymen chosen is an indication of the close links then existing between the various denominations and the world of education. All the members of the Dale Commission were appointed, with the exception of Fuller, who had become the Cape's emigration representative in London. However, on his return in 1878 as General Manager of the Union shipping line, he was elected by Convocation to fill a vacancy. Brebner and Guthrie were selected to represent the colleges at Somerset East and Graaff-Reinet, although the former was soon compelled to resign on appointment to the Free State education department. Not until the election of Peter MacOwan in 1876 did Gill College again have a representative, while Guthrie did not remain long at Graaff-Reinet.

Chief Justice Sydney Smith Bell and his successor in that office, Attorney General J. H. de Villiers, were both members of the first Council; so, too, was the former Secretary of the Board of Public Examiners, C. B. Elliott. Others chosen included Abraham Faure's brother, Philip Eduard, minister of the Dutch Reformed *(Nederduitse Gereformeerde)* Church at Wynberg and Moderator of Synod, the former board examiner, E. C. Judge, and his colleague in that office, C. Abercrombie Smith, in 1873 Molteno's Commissioner of Crown Lands and Public Works. Not all the members of this, or subsequent Councils were noted for regular attendance at meetings; some, too, were connected with the university for a short period only. Five of the first members, however, gave the University of the Cape of Good Hope long and devoted service: Cameron, Dale, De Villiers, Ogilvie and Abercrombie Smith.

Convocation early showed a disposition to choose active professors as Council members. In 1874, it found a seat for Roderick Noble and two years later it not only elected MacOwan, but also Paul Daniel Hahn of the South African College, a member until his death in 1918 and a pioneer of the modern, scientific approach in higher education. The emphasis upon professorial appointments at Convocation elections led, from 1879, to the compilation of tickets by rival factions. This would be a feature of Council elections throughout the life of the Cape University and for many years during that of its successor.

One of the most important tasks confronting the Council of 1873, when it met for the first time on 1 September in the offices of the Superintendent General of Education, was to select a Vice-Chancellor. Langham Dale was, by common consent, the most suitable choice and the University of the Cape of Good Hope was thus from the outset closely linked with the entire colonial educational system. It has been said that Council often found it difficult in the early days to persuade anyone else to fill the office; certainly, in the period to 1889, Dale dominated the

31

GENERAL FUND OF THE UNIVERSITY.

RECEIPTS.	£	s.	d.
The Colonial Government:			
Allowance to the University for Sixteen Months from 1st Sept., 1873, to 31st Dec., 1874, at the rate of £1,500 per annum ... £2,000 0 0			
Interest on Debentures ... 15 15 0	2,015	15	0
Fees received from Candidates for examination ...	359	0	0
,, ,, for Registration ...	14	0	0
Cash lodged in Cape of Good Hope Bank by Executors in the estate of the late J. B. Ebden, Esq. ...	200	0	0
Debentures purchased ...	500	0	0
,, ,, (for J. B. Ebden Fund) ...	200	0	0
	3,288	15	0

PAYMENTS.	£	s.	d.
Fees to Examiners ...	575	0	0
Salaries ...	588	13	4
Extra Attendance and Petty Expenses ...	9	14	9
Fees to Commissioners and Petty Expenses at centres of Examination ...	28	13	4
Travelling Allowances to Examiners and Members of Council ...	43	14	0
Bursaries on account of the late Board of Examiners ...	150	0	0
Exhibitions ...	15	0	0
Paid Messrs. S. Solomon & Co. (Printing and Stationery) ...	146	11	8
,, ,, Bruce & Co. (Academical Robes) ...	15	0	0
,, ,, Lawton & Co. (Strong Box)...	3	3	0
,, Mrs. Bowler (desk) ...	10	0	0
,, Proprietors of *Cape Argus* (Advertisements) ...	1	7	0
,, ,, *Graham's Town Journal* do. ...	5	13	6
,, Mr. W. Torbet (Debentures)...	510	0	0
,, Mr. J. Wiley ,, for Ebden Fund ...	202	0	0
,, Mr. P. J. Stigant (Furniture, &c.) ...	31	14	0
,, Mr. N. H. Marais (Binding) ...	0	6	0
,, Mr. A. Espic (Furniture and Fittings) ...	40	0	0
,, Consistory of Dutch Reformed Church (Rent) ...	66	13	4
Cheque Book, 8s. 4d.; Fee returned, £12... ...	12	8	4
Debentures lodged in the Treasury... ...	700	0	0
Balance in Cape of Good Hope Bank on 31st Dec., 1874 ...	133	2	9
	3,288	15	0

JAMES CAMERON, Registrar.

University Chambers, 15th January, 1875.
Examined and found correct,
C. B. ELLIOTT, } Auditors.
L. MARQUARD, }

18th January, 1875.

THE FIRST FINANCIAL STATEMENT issued covered a period of 16 months and was submitted with a report of university activities required in terms of the Incorporation Act.

The university began its career with the assets of the Board of Public Examiners. Its annual income, however, was very small and the new institution was largely dependent upon a modest government grant and the fees of candidates for its various examinations. In this period there were 49 entrants for the Matriculation examination, 11 who sought certificates in law or surveying and 10 who hoped to obtain graduate qualifications.

The main items of expenditure were examiners' fees, the Registrar's salary and wages for the messenger.

It is interesting to compare the position today with that obtaining when the university was young. Almost 100 years after the compilation of the first financial statement, the university's annual income from government funds and other sources (Matriculation fees excepted) had reached the figure of R7 265 663. Expenditure then amounted to R7 220 726. The total number of candidates in 1971, including those for the Matriculation and music examinations, was approximately 40 000.

First financial Statement

THE FIRST MEETING OF THE UNIVERSITY COUNCIL on Monday, 1 September, 1873 was a significant event in the history of South African higher education.

Of the members chosen by the Governor, 14 were present when the meeting began in the Cape Town office of the Superintendent General of Education. Four of them – James Cameron, Langham Dale, George Ogilvie and Charles Abercrombie Smith – were destined to play a large part in the development of the examining university; a fifth, the future Chief Justice, J.H. de Villiers, also gave many years to the service of the governing body and was the first President of Convocation.

The presence of three medical practitioners – Henry A. Ebden, J.Z. Herman and P.G. Stewart – indicates a desire on the part of the founders to introduce degrees in medicine, for which provision had been made in the Incorporation Act. Medical degrees were never conferred, however.

The close connection between the various religious bodies and the world of education is seen in the appointment of such men as the Moderator of the Dutch Reformed *(Nederduitse Gereformeerde)* Church, P.E. Faure, the Anglican priest and educationist, Edward C. Judge, the Stellenbosch seminary professor, John Murray, and the Scottish teacher and minister, David Smith. The others present on this occasion were the former Secretary of the Board of Public Examiners, C.B. Elliott, and the Astronomer Royal, E.J. Stone.

Absent from the meeting on 1 September were Sir Sydney Smith Bell, the Rev. John Brebner, the Venerable P.P. Fogg, Professor F. Guthrie, the Rev. W. Impey and the Hon. William Porter.

First Page of the first Council Minutes

34

1873.

At a Meeting of the Council of the University of the Cape of Good Hope, held at the Office of the Superintendent General of Education, in Cape Town, on Monday, the 1st day of September, 1873, at 11 o'clock, a.m., in conformity with His Excellency the Governor's Proclamation No. 77, of the 30th July. 1873, were present:

Rev. James Cameron, B.A., L.L.D.
Langham Dale Esq., B.A., L.L.D.
Hon'ble John Henry de Villiers Esq.
Henry Anderson Ebden Esq., M.D.
Charles Bletterman Elliott Esq.
Rev. Philip Edward Faure, D.D.
Johannes Zacharias Herman Esq., M.D.
Rev. Edward Judge, M.A.
Rev. John Murray.
Rev. George Ogilvie, M.A.
Hon'ble Charles Abercrombie Smith Esq., M.A.
Rev. David Smith, M.A.
Peter Gordon Stewart Esq., M.D.
Edward James Stone Esq., M.A., F.R.S.

On the motion of the Hon'ble Mr. de Villiers, seconded by the Hon'ble Mr. Smith, Dr. Dale was unanimously elected as Chairman.

Dr. Dale proposed that Mr. Elliott should fill the Office of Acting Registrar. Carried unanimously.

The Chairman read the Governor's Proclamation No. 77, of the 30th July. 1873, appointing the University Council and convening this Meeting.

Hon'ble Mr. de Villiers proposed that Dr. Dale be Vice-Chancellor of the University. Rev. Dr. Faure seconded the proposal, which was carried by acclamation.

Dr. Dale signified his acceptance of the Office.

The Vice-Chancellor proposed that the functions and Salary of the future Registrar should be defined.

This proposal was agreed to.

Hon'ble Mr. de Villiers proposed that the Salary of the Registrar should be subject to the approval of Government.

Hon'ble

scene. Only twice was another Vice-Chancellor chosen: Abercrombie Smith in 1877 and the Anglican churchman, Hopkins Badnall, in 1882. When Langham Dale retired as Superintendent General of Education in 1892, he was Chancellor of the University of the Cape of Good Hope, a position he held from 1890 until his death eight years later.

The other office which Council had to fill was that of Registrar. The position was given to the South African College representative on the governing body, James Cameron. This choice created the first vacancy in Council membership and provided the Governor with the opportunity of appointing Cameron's colleague on the college staff, the former board examiner, G. F. Childe. Cameron was a popular Registrar. A good classical scholar and a useful addition to the examining panel, he brought to his new post valuable gifts of kindliness and patience. Chosen also as Secretary of Convocation between 1873 and 1876, he was to remain as Registrar until 1895. He served again on Council after his retirement and retained his interest in the university even after his departure for England, where he died in 1906.

In August, 1877, the University of the Cape of Good Hope became a full member of the select band of British and imperial universities. The Royal Charter which Queen Victoria was pleased to bestow upon the Cape institution was modelled closely upon that which had recently been granted to the examining University of New Zealand. As it was the Queen's duty and desire to promote the advance of education among "all classes and denominations" of her subjects, the degrees of the Cape University were afforded full recognition throughout the British world. They were not to be considered in any way inferior to those conferred by the universities of the United Kingdom.

English was the language of the University of the Cape of Good Hope and the majority of its Council members were drawn from the English-speaking section of the community. A number of representatives of the Afrikaner group in Cape society were chosen, however. Several were closely associated with education at Stellenbosch and among them may be mentioned the three seminary professors, J. I. Marais, Adriaan Moorrees and C. F. J. Muller. Marais and Moorrees gave many years of service to the examining university and were not forgotten by the institution which at length took its place. Muller was specially selected during the dark days of the Anglo-Boer War as a man who knew and understood the feelings and aspirations of the Afrikaner people.

All the Chancellors and Vice-Chancellors, however, were English-speaking and none was South African-born. For examination purposes, candidates were obliged to use English until the last years of the university's life brought some relaxation in this hitherto inflexible rule. When the first Council drew up regulations for examinations, Dutch was treated as a foreign accomplishment and was made an optional subject, together with French and German, in the Matriculation and B.A. examinations. Some years later, "Kafir" (Xhosa) and Sesuto were added to the list of alternative modern languages at Matriculation level.

Much time was spent at early Council meetings in drawing up rules and by-laws. There was considerable discussion on the question of pass marks for the various examinations. Abercrombie Smith was not in favour of this method of judging scripts, since "competent knowledge", he said, "cannot be strictly defined by marks". However, his objections were overruled by a narrow margin and the usual method of assessment adopted. At first, the marks a candidate was required to obtain for a pass were not divulged in the annual *Calendar*. They were surprisingly low and remained so for many years. One-fifth of the total was sufficient in most subject papers, with an aggregate of one-third in the examination as a whole.

The M.A. degree was initially divided into three departments : language and literature, mathematics and natural philosophy and physical science. Other groups were added later. The B.A. was a composite arts and science degree in the early years, but after the introduction of an Intermediate B.A. examination in 1883, during Hopkins Badnall's term of office as Vice-Chancellor, the finals could be taken in literature and philosophy or in mathe-

HOPKINS BADNALL, the son of a silk manufacturer, was born on 21 September, 1821 at Leek, Staffordshire, England. He received his early education at home and under the guidance of an uncle in Liverpool.

After graduating at the University of Durham, Badnall took Holy Orders and became a curate at Stockton-on-Tees under the future Bishop of Cape Town, Robert Gray. He accompanied Gray to the Cape as his chaplain, reaching Table Bay early in 1848. He officiated at Claremont and was also Vice-Principal of the Diocesan Collegiate School from 1849 until 1853.

He then ministered in England for some years, but returned to the Cape in 1862 as Archdeacon of George, where he remained until 1869. In that year, he was appointed Archdeacon of Cape Town and Rector of St Paul's, Rondebosch.

His skill as an ecclesiastical jurist enabled him to play an important part in the establishment of the Church of the Province of South Africa. A churchman of moderate views, he was also involved in the Anglican controversies of the period. Badnall was a scholar of repute and in 1862, obtained a doctorate in divinity from his old university.

He served on Council in 1875 and 1876 and again from 1879 until 1885, being chosen as Vice-Chancellor for the period from 1882 to 1884.

The Venerable Hopkins Badnall returned to England in 1885 to take charge of a parish near Doncaster in Yorkshire. Poor health soon compelled him to retire to London, where he died on 27 September, 1892. He was buried at his birthplace.

The Ven. Hopkins Badnall, M.A., D.D.
Member of Council 1875–1876; 1879–1885
Vice-Chancellor 1882–1884
President of Convocation 1881–1882

Once the University of the Cape of Good Hope had been established, its governing Council sought to increase the standing of the new institution in the British academic world by applying through the Governor of the colony for a ROYAL CHARTER. This was granted by Queen Victoria in 1877.

The degrees of the university were recognized as "Academic Distinctions" and were "entitled to rank, precedence and consideration in Our United Kingdom, and in Our Colonies and possessions throughout the world, as fully as if the said Degrees had been granted by any university of Our said United Kingdom".

Full recognition, however, was long in coming and it was many years before the university examinations were accepted – and then often with reservations – by British universities.

Royal Charter, 1877

Victoria by the Grace of God

By Warrant under the Queen's Sign Manual

matics and natural science. A candidate could either read for a pass or an honours degree. In the last years of the Cape University's life, a considerable expansion of the groups and subjects offered took place and a mixed degree once again became an acceptable alternative. The fees decided upon in 1873 ranged from R4 for a Martciulation examination to R60 for a complete LL.B. They remained at a moderate rate throughout the history of the university. No candidate was permitted to enter for an examination without presenting a certificate of good conduct.

With the passing years, the university greatly extended its functions and the growing complexity of Council's work led to the setting up of a Standing Committee as early as January, 1883. There was a large increase in the number of law examinations provided and the University of the Cape of Good Hope ultimately became responsible for testing the civil service law candidates of all the territories of southern Africa. In 1896, a School of Mines was opened in Kimberley, under the general supervision of Gardner F. Williams of De Beers and with Professor J. G. Lawn in charge. This took students who had begun courses in mining engineering at one of the major Cape colleges and provided them with advanced training, including practical work on the Witwatersrand. Examinations in this field were conducted by the Cape University.

Degrees in music were added in terms of the Amendment Act of 1896, but were never instituted. Music examinations of a general kind, however, became an important feature of the university's work. In 1892, Council commissioned the distinguished physician and composer, J. H. Meiring Beck, long a member of the university's governing body, to approach the recently established Associated Board of the Royal Schools of Music in London in order to see whether it would extend its examining function to the colony. The suggestion was favourably received and the visit of the first music examiner, Franklin Taylor, in 1894 inaugurated the world-wide expansion of the board's activities. A long association between the university, its successor and the

42

London body followed. It was not without its vicissitudes, but it provided many South African musicians and vocalists with an opportunity to study further.

Plans by the Anglican Church to establish a Faculty of Divinity at the Cape at the end of the nineteenth century brought to the fore the need for theological examinations under the auspices of the university. Students at the Stellenbosch seminary had earlier been able to obtain external degrees in theology from the University of St Andrews, but the Scottish institution had been forced to abandon this scheme. In 1902, the University of London let it be known that candidates would be able to write its new divinity degree examinations externally. This facility once again gave the Stellenbosch students an opportunity to graduate in their own land. If a non-sectarian university like that in the imperial capital could provide theological examinations, there seemed no reason why the University of the Cape of Good Hope should not do so. The subject was debated at length and brought before parliament in 1907. There, it had a rather stormy passage. Merriman, at that time a member of the university Council, was strongly opposed to divinity degrees and his views enjoyed considerable support. However, their introduction was permitted in terms of a further Amendment Act in 1908. The first B.D. by examination was a future Union Member of Parliament, Nicolaas J. van der Merwe. He obtained his degree in 1911.

Soon after the founding of the University of the Cape of Good Hope, it was being pressed to institute elementary examinations for school children. The first of these, the examination for Certificates of Proficiency in Elementary Subjects of Instruction, was launched in 1875 and was followed by the introduction of an examination designed to appeal to girls as well as to boys. This was the School Examination for Honours, a leaving certificate. These tests were to become the School Elementary and School Higher examinations, later replaced by Junior and Senior Certificate examinations of superior standard. The university thus early became a vast examining machine to test the products of Cape education at every stage. A further link with the teaching pro-

HENRY HOWARD MOLYNEUX HERBERT was born in London on 24 June, 1831 and was educated at Eton and Christ Church, Oxford. He inherited his title at the age of 18 and took his seat in the House of Lords.

A Conservative in politics, he became Under-Secretary of State for the Colonies in the Earl of Derby's second administration in 1858. When Derby became Prime Minister again in 1866, Carnarvon was appointed Colonial Secretary. He introduced the bill for Canadian federation, but before the British North America Act became effective, he resigned in protest against proposed measures of parliamentary reform at home.

He again became Secretary of State for the Colonies in 1874 under Benjamin Disraeli (the Earl of Beaconsfield), but resigned four years later over the Eastern Question. As Colonial Secretary, he tried hard to federate South Africa along the lines which had proved successful in Canada. In this, however, he failed.

Chairman of the Commission on Imperial Defence (1879–1882), he was appointed Lord Lieutenant of Ireland in the Marquess of Salisbury's first administration of 1885. Somewhat indecisive as a politician, he was nevertheless courteous and conciliatory. A man of literary tastes, he published translations from the Greek classics.

Chosen as Chancellor in 1884, he touched at the Cape three years later on his way to Australia. On 29 September, 1887 he became the first Chancellor to attend a Cape graduation ceremony. An Oxford M.A., with honorary doctorates from that university and from Dublin, he was admitted to the degree of M.A. (Cape) on the occasion of his South African visit.

He died in London on 28 June, 1890 and was buried at his country home, Highclere Castle, Hampshire. The town of Carnarvon in the Cape bears his name.

Henry Howard Molyneux Herbert, M.A., D.C.L.(h.c.),
LL.D.(h.c.), F.S.A.,
the Right Hon. the 4th Earl of Carnarvon
Chancellor 1884–1890

Year	M.A.		B.A.		LL.B.		Matriculation		Intermediate		Law Certificate		Survey Certificate		C.S. Law		School Elementary		School Higher		Tot.	Tot.
	Ex	Psd	Ex	Psd	Ex	Psd	Ex	Psd	Ex	Psd	Ex	Psd	Ex	Psd	Ex	Psd	Ex	Psd	Ex	Psd	Ex	Psd
1874 ..	1	1	9	6	0	0	49	31	0	0	9	8	2	1	0	0	0	0	0	0	70	47
1875 ..	1	0	16	12	1	1	58	34	0	0	7	7	3	0	0	0	158	97	0	0	244	151
1876 ..	4	2	9	8	1	1	80	60	0	0	3	3	5	3	0	0	154	117	0	0	256	194
1877 ..	3	1	11	6	1	1	74	49	0	0	3	2	7	3	0	0	182	130	0	0	281	192
1878 ..	2	2	15	8	1	1	100	73	0	0	3	3	13	7	0	0	213	141	0	0	347	235
1879 ..	0	0	15	8	1	0	109	46	0	0	5	5	12	8	0	0	240	150	0	0	382	217
1880 ..	1	1	14	7	1	1	118	62	0	0	8	7	17	8	0	0	281	204	24	17	464	307
1881 ..	0	0	14	10	2	2	109	61	0	0	3	1	22	10	0	0	333	242	40	32	523	358
1882 ..	0	0	10	7	0	0	116	84	0	0	10	10	24	14	0	0	414	256	45	21	619	392
1883 ..	0	0	16	13	1	1	144	88	38	32	4	4	20	14	0	0	419	293	42	33	684	478
1884 ..	2	2	13	10	0	0	185	118	38	20	15	14	21	10	0	0	475	379	37	18	786	571
1885 ..	0	0	16	10	4	2	228	118	52	23	14	9	13	5	0	0	755	526	88	42	1170	735
1886 ..	2	1	21	15	3	3	215	121	56	53	18	16	15	10	7	5	986	603	112	85	1435	912
1887 ..	0	0	24	16	4	2	216	122	45	25	29	13	4	3	31	13	892	530	203	145	1448	868
1888 ..	3	2	33	29	2	1	202	133	66	43	28	24	6	3	36	21	892	523	232	197	1500	976
1889 ..	1	0	22	13	3	3	188	109	40	31	21	16	6	5	17	11	915	610	193	162	1406	960
1890 ..	1	1	27	18	5	4	193	101	38	22	16	11	13	6	23	12	1295	930	284	233	1895	1338
1891 ..	2	1	21	14	8	5	228	142	43	35	21	11	12	8	35	12	1614	972	370	279	2354	1479
1892 ..	1	1	20	14	10	7	282	207	56	39	24	21	14	9	50	33	1813	1276	423	333	2693	1940
1893 ..	0	0	25	21	6	6	304	214	76	40	19	15	25	11	54	41	1897	1287	525	439	2931	2074
1894 ..	1	1	41	25	2	2	336	214	76	37	21	16	28	18	56	37	2148	1592	564	430	3272	2371
1874 to 1894	25	16	392	270	56	43	3534	2187	624	400	281	216	282	155	309	185	16076	10858	3182	2466	24760	16795

THE EXAMINATIONS of the University of the Cape of Good Hope soon came to dominate the lives of students in schools and colleges and the critics of the examining institution referred to it unkindly as a "factory of certificates".

Examinations were first held in Cape Town only, but were later arranged in Grahamstown as well, under the supervision of the Registrar. This officer used to travel by ship to Port Elizabeth and from there by mail-caoch to Grahamstown, carrying the papers with him.

Local representatives have long since relieved the Registrar of this arduous duty and today there are some 1 400 centres throughout the world for the many examinations for which the university is responsible.

Examinations: the first 21 years

HENRY BARTLE EDWARD FRERE, descended from an old East Anglian family, was born on 29 March, 1815 at Clydach, Brecknockshire, Wales. Educated at Bath and Haileybury College, he joined the Indian civil service, rising to the governorship of Bombay in 1862. He played a leading part in the early history of the university in that city, of which he was Chancellor from 1862 until 1867. On his return to Britain, he was appointed to the Council of State for India.

Frere was created a baronet in 1876 and in the following year arrived in Cape Town as Governor of the colony, a position he held until 1880. The new Governor and High Commissioner in Southern Africa became a controversial figure, especially with regard to his policy towards the tribes and his attitude over the British occupation of the Transvaal by Sir Theophilus Shepstone. He was, however, popular among many colonists, although this did not prevent his recall. His publications include a defence of his policy and actions.

Sir Bartle Frere held honorary degrees from the Universities of Oxford, Cambridge and Edinburgh. He was elected Chancellor of the University of the Cape of Good Hope in 1880 and retained this position until his death, which took place on 29 May, 1884 at his home, Wressil Lodge, Wimbledon, England. He was buried in St Paul's Cathedral, London.

The Right Hon. Sir Henry Bartle Edward Frere, Bt, D.C.L.(h.c.),
LL.D.(h.c.) (Cantab.), LL.D.
(h.c.) (Edin.), G.C.B., G.C.S.I., P.C., F.R.S.
Chancellor 1880–1884

fession was forged in the mid-eighties, when James Reid Whitton, head of the Cape Town Normal College of 1878, became a Council member. His connection with the university would be a long one and his services were later honoured by its successor.

As an encouragement to further endeavour, the Cape University was able to offer, in addition to the Porter and Jamison awards with which it began its career, many scholarships and prizes. Some were provided by the university itself; others by government, public subscription or through the generosity of private benefactors. The Cape government instituted scholarships commemorating Sir George Grey and Queen Victoria; other awards included scholarships in memory of the shipowner, Sir Donald Currie, the Cape surveyor, J. M. Maynard, and bequests from Mr Justice J. W. Ebden, Alexander Croll of Port Elizabeth and the wealthy Cape Town lawyer, Willem Hiddingh. An exhibition was also founded in honour of Porter's successor as Chancellor of the university, the former Cape Governor, Sir Bartle Frere. Prizes recall the names of the Cape merchant, J. B. Ebden, the Presbyterian missionary, J. A. Chalmers, and another Chancellor and his wife, the Duke and Duchess of Cornwall and York, later Their Majesties King George V and Queen Mary. Alfred, Lord Milner, the British Governor and High Commissioner in a stormy period of South African history, is remembered in the Milner Art Scholarship for women students, founded in connection with the university. This award was first gained in 1913 by the Cape artist, Dorothy Barclay.

A complete list of all scholarship and prize winners would contain the names of many distinguished South Africans. They include such prominent figures as the politicians W. P. Schreiner, Jan C. Smuts and his colleague, Jan H. Hofmeyr, judges Reinhold Gregorowski, William Pittman and J. W. Wessels and the scientists P. J. du Toit and Basil Schonland. Among churchmen who won awards were Monsignor Kolbe of the Catholic Church and the Dutch Reformed *(Nederduitse Gereformeerde)* Church minister and campaigner for the Afrikaans languge, T. B. ("Tobie") Muller, son of the Rev. Professor Muller of the Stellen-

50

bosch seminary and father of the present head of the Department of History at the University of South Africa.

The close connection between the University of the Cape of Good Hope and the colonial educational system kept that institution firmly in the public eye, particularly when examination results were published. It was often under fire in the press and it is possible that the attacks might not have been so frequent had the university agreed to suggestions that reporters be permitted to attend Council meetings. Summaries of deliberations were, however, issued for the newspapers and were later published in the university's own *Gazette*, founded in 1903. It was said, too, that one member, the Dutch-born journalist, J.W.G. van Oordt, was first appointed by the Governor as a representative of the press.

Newspaper comment was sometimes virulent. The system which prevented college professors from examining advanced work led to complaints about the qualifications of the "recurring decimals" who were appointed year after year to set Matriculation and degree examination papers and to mark the scripts. The university's reputation was not enhanced when it fell victim in the early nineties to the spurious qualifications of an examiner in French, R. A. van Angelbeek. As for the stranglehold which the university held on the school curriculum through its examinations, many regretted that it had ever extended its function in this manner. Dale's successor as Superintendent General of Education, the Scottish mathematician, Thomas Muir, was, despite his membership of the university Council and election as Vice-Chancellor from 1897 until 1901, strongly opposed to the Cape University's influence over the schools of the colony. The university cannot be held responsible for all shortcomings in the examination system. It was regrettable, but unavoidable, that the Matriculation examinations had to be delayed in 1877 when the papers, printed in England, were held in quarantine aboard the mailship, *Taymouth Castle*. Two decades later, the fault lay with the postal authorities when papers despatched from the university to nearby Wellington in the Cape set off on a longer journey to New Zealand!

THOMAS MUIR was born on 25 August, 1844 at Nemphlar, near the Falls of Clyde, Lanarkshire, Scotland. He received his early education at Wishaw before proceeding to the University of Glasgow, where he showed outstanding ability as a mathematician. He trained as a teacher and graduated with distinction in 1868, studying further at Berlin and Göttingen.

He began his career as a tutor at the University of St Andrews, returned to his old university as assistant to the Professor of Mathematics in 1871 and three years later, became chief mathematical master at Glasgow High School.

In 1892, Cecil Rhodes persuaded him to come to the Cape as Superintendent General of Education in succession to Langham Dale. He held this post until his retirement in 1915, doing much to advance the training of teachers and to promote the introduction of new subjects into the school curriculum.

Muir was highly esteemed as a scholar, educationist and administrator. A Fellow of the Royal Society, the Royal Geographical Society and the Royal Society of Edinburgh, he also became President of the Edinburgh Mathematical Society and the South African Association for the Advancement of Science. He received an honorary LL.D. from the University of Glasgow in 1882 and a D.Sc. *(honoris causa)* from the University of Cape Town in 1921. A C.M.G. in 1901, he was knighted in 1915. He devoted himself to mathematics after his retirement, writing many papers and completing his monumental work on determinants.

Muir was associated with the university as a member of Council from 1892 until 1913, serving as Vice-Chancellor from 1897 to 1901. He died in Rondebosch, Cape Town on 21 March, 1934.

Sir Thomas Muir, Kt, M.A., LL.D. (h.c.), D.Sc. (h.c.),
C.M.G., F.R.S., F.R.G.S., FR.S.E.
Member of Council 1892–1913
Pro Vice-Chancellor 1901–1905
Vice-Chancellor 1897–1901

It cannot be denied that the University of the Cape of Good Hope gave a tremendous impetus to educational progress. Its influence may be seen in the education of girls and of non-Europeans. Girls began to attempt the lower examinations of the university in the seventies and a decade later, Dr Jane Waterston, the Cape University's first admitted female graduate, noted a change in the climate of opinion concerning education for women. By that time, Professor Hahn and others were encouraging girls to attend advanced classes. From the last decade of the nineteenth century onwards, young ladies no longer had to follow in the footsteps of the Cape's first woman graduate by examination, Agnes Ellen Lewis, who was compelled to study privately for the B.A. which she obtained in 1886. In the university's silver jubilee year, the first graduates from the Huguenot College received their certificates. This institution, under its American Principals, A. P. Ferguson and Anna E. Bliss, would soon attain university college rank as a foundation primarily for women.

Education for non-Europeans made a slower start. Facilities were lacking in the multiracial missionary colleges and it was not until 1880 that the future Congregational minister, Simon Peter Sihlali, surmounted the Matriculation hurdle. It was unfortunate that his name had inadvertently been included in the list of passes from the Graaff-Reinet College. That institution would not, Sihlali wrote in a letter to the *Argus,* thank the university "for having increased to three its number of successful candidates by adding the name of a nigger"! The second African matriculant, John Tengo Jabavu, newspaper editor and educationist, obtained his Matriculation pass three years later while studying at Lovedale. Towards the end of the century, African girls began to matriculate in the annual examinations.

In the early years of the twentieth century, a drift of non-European students to universities abroad made evident the need for better facilities in South Africa. There was by then a thirst for knowledge among them which the admission of an occasional student to one of the colleges for Europeans did little to assuage. Not until 1915, when Alexander Kerr arrived as Principal of the South African Native College at Fort Hare were the doors to future advance partially opened.

At degree level, the main problem confronting the university was the relation of the teaching colleges to the examining body. Private, or external students could write the examinations of the university, but at this period it was the embryo university colleges which provided most of the teaching and entered the greatest number of candidates. At the founding of the Cape University, only the South African College and that at Graaff-Reinet enjoyed government recognition of their status, reflected in the provision of grants for professorships. Other colleges were, however, active rivals, and although there was much support for the idea that two widely separated colleges would suffice for the needs of the colony, it soon became evident that government aid would have to be offered to all. Accordingly, a Higher Education Act was passed in 1874 which extended the provision of grants to those colleges which the Superintendent General of Education considered were performing a useful service. Dale hoped that this stipulation would allow him powers of inspection, but in this he was disappointed. He did succeed in gaining a view of the colony's teaching at higher levels in 1884, when J. H. Brady carried out an inspection. This was, however, greatly resented and never repeated.

Government support for advanced work served to draw a line between undergraduate and school classes in the colleges, although a complete break did not begin to take place until the end of the century. Some of the grant-aided college departments of the seventies were soon struggling. All, except the South African College and the school at Stellenbosch, which Dale had unwillingly decided to assist, eventually gave up the fight. By 1885, the Grey Institute conceded that it had failed to overcome an apparent lack of interest in higher education at Port Elizabeth. At the same period, Graaff-Reinet College agreed that it, too, could no longer consider itself a university institution. There, Brady had poured scorn on the titles of "Professor" and "Senate". It was not enough that good men should devote their energies to the instruction of five little boys! Gill College had begun with a flourish, but by 1877, the *Argus* newspaper described it as "on the highroad to nowhere", with three professors and eight students. It ceased to draw grants soon after, but enjoyed a brief revival in the nineties when Dale, nearing retirement, gave it a second chance. It did well for a few years, producing a number of graduates, including Minnie E. Drummond, the first girl to win the Porter award. By 1903, however, there were only two matriculated students in attendance. New regulations for university colleges called for at least seventy-five and Dale's successor, Muir, brought the experiment to a close. There was considerable local protest, but Gill College henceforth restricted its activities to school courses.

The Anglican institutions fared better. At Grahamstown, post-matriculation work did not begin for some years after the founding of the examining university. Dale and Charles Thomas Smith, an energetic eastern Cape judge who was to become both Vice-Chancellor and Chancellor of the Cape University, tried hard to amalgamate competing schools to found a "Union College" for advanced studies. The attempt failed, however, and St Andrew's emerged in the eighties as the only higher educational centre in the town. It made great strides under Canon J. Espin – also for some years a member of the university Council – and retained its college department until the opening of Rhodes University College in 1904. Its four full professors were Arthur Matthews of survey fame, the scientist-historian, George E. Cory, Dutch-born G. F. Dingemans of the Chair of Modern Languages and A. Stanley Kidd, who undertook to teach everything not comprised in the other professorships! These men formed the nucleus of the university college staff. They were soon joined by others, among them Selmar Schönland of the Albany Museum as Professor of Botany.

The older Diocesan College flourished until the retirement of Ogilvie in 1885. Thereafter, it began to lose ground, despite the good work of such excellent teachers as A. A. Bodkin, G. W. Vipan and J. Martin. Attempts were made in the first decade of the present century to help this Anglican institution to regain its old pre-eminence. Funds were raised and lady students reluctantly admitted, but the task of competing successfully with its Cape Town neighbour proved too difficult. In 1910, "Bishops" handed over its university classes to the South African College and followed the example of its Grahamstown sister by concentrating upon school work.

Dale continued to regard the South African College as the colony's leading institution and in 1875, suggested that it become the teaching arm of the university. It was by then too late, however, to single out one college for this honour. The only change in the relationship between it and the examining body came three years later, when the university Council was permitted to nominate three members to the governing body of the college.

The South African College continued to prosper. Before the end of the seventies, Francis Guthrie of Graaff-Reinet had joined the staff and Charles E. Lewis, a distinguished Welsh-born Old Boy, was promoted from the school department. Lewis was the half-brother of the Cape University's first woman graduate and had helped her in her studies. The decline of the more distant colleges brought MacOwan from Somerset East in 1880 and William Ritchie from Port Elizabeth at the beginning of 1882. Ritchie, who became Professor of Classics, was to serve as university Vice-Chancellor from 1913 until 1916 and as President of Convocation between 1904 and 1914. Henry Eardley Stephen Fremantle, the politician and journalist who was long a member of the university Council, was appointed to the Chair of English and Philosophy in 1899. Two earlier arrivals who would do much to transform the college into a teaching university were the physicist, John Carruthers Beattie, and the mathematician, Lawrence Crawford. Such a transformation was then no more than a dream of the future. However, by 1900, the South African College at last became a true university institution by banishing its Matriculation classes to the separate school department.

In this change, however, it had been anticipated by a flourishing rival. Few in 1873 could have guessed that the Stellenbosch

Born on 21 September, 1847 at Leith, Midlothian, Scotland, T H O M A S W A L K E R attended the Royal High School in Edinburgh and the university in that city. A brilliant student, he gained an M.A. *cum laude* in classics in 1870. He studied further at Owens College, Manchester and at universities in Germany and the Netherlands, became proficient in Dutch and entered the ministry of the United Presbyterian Church.

In 1876, he was appointed Principal of the Boys' High School, Paarl and two years later accepted a professorship at the Stellenbosch Public School, which then had a flourishing Arts Department, later to become the Victoria College. He lectured in philosophy and, for many years, in English as well. His personality and teaching exercised a lasting influence on several generations of students.

As a member of the university Council from 1881 until 1916 and as Vice-Chancellor from 1911 to 1913, he did much to further the cause of higher education in South Africa. He played a valuable part in the long debate on university reconstruction after Union, but did not live to see his own college become the independent University of Stellenbosch.

Walker's scholarship earned him recognition overseas. An honorary doctorate in literature was conferred upon him in 1892 by the University of Edinburgh and in 1909, he received an honorary LL.D from Harvard University in the United States.

The Rev. Thomas Walker died in Stellenbosch on 8 June, 1916.

The Rev. Professor Thomas Walker, M.A., LL.D. (h.c.), Litt.D. (h.c.)
Member of Council 1881–1916
Pro Vice-Chancellor 1909–1911
Vice-Chancellor 1911–1913
President of Convocation 1894–1904
(Photo: University of Stellenbosch)

WILLIAM THOMSON was born on 31 December, 1856 at Kirkton of Mailler, Perthshire, Scotland. He matriculated at Perth Academy and continued his studies at the University of Edinburgh, where he obtained the M.A. and B.Sc. degrees and was appointed assistant to the Professor of Mathematics in 1878.

In 1883, he joined the staff of Stellenbosch College (later the Victoria College) as Professor of Mathematics, remaining in that post until 1895. His students included Senator F.S. Malan and Generals J.B.M. Hertzog and J.C. Smuts. He also examined in his subject for the University of Edinburgh in 1887 and 1888.

Thomson succeeded Cameron as Registrar in 1895 and held the position until his retirement in 1922. He played a prominent part in the negotiations to establish a "General University of South Africa", an ideal which was realized in 1918, when the federal university was opened.

Careful and methodical, Thomson served the university well. He prided himself on his excellent memory and could unhesitatingly quote the complete examination record of any well-known public figure whose name had appeared in the annual university lists.

A Fellow of the Royal Society of Edinburgh, Thomson was knighted in 1922. In that year, an honorary doctorate was conferred upon him by the University of Cape Town, a distinction which he had received from his old university in Scotland 18 years earlier. In 1924, he accepted the principalship of the University of the Witwatersrand, an office which he held until 1928.

A member of Council from 1883 to 1895, Sir William again gave his services to the governing body from 1924 until 1947. His death occurred at his home in Glencairn, near Cape Town, on 6 August, 1947.

Sir William Thomson, Kt, M.A., B.Sc., LL.D. (h.c.) (Edin.),
LL.D. (h.c.) (Cape Town), F.R.S.E.
Registrar 1895–1922
Member of Council 1883–1895; 1924–1947

61

Undenominational Public School would achieve greatness as a university foundation. It had, it is true, formed an Arts Department with the coming of the examining university and the Principal, Charles Anderson, soon had as colleagues on the first academic Senate four professors of note. George Gordon came from the school department to teach mathematics and physical science and Nicolaas Mansvelt was similarly promoted as the Professor of Modern Languages. They were joined by two new arrivals from Scotland: Archibald Macdonald for classics and Thomas Walker for English and philosophy. Mansvelt's name is better known in connection with education in the South African Republic; Gordon, a member of the university Council, died in 1882. Macdonald and Walker, however, gave the Stellenbosch institution many years of devoted service. Walker was long associated with the Council of the University of the Cape of Good Hope and was Vice-Chancellor from 1911 until 1913. He was also chosen as President of Convocation in 1894 and held that office for ten years.

The Arts Department became a collegiate foundation which, in 1887 – the Queen's jubilee year – was designated the Victoria College. The institution prospered. Inspector Brady had commended it in 1884 for insisting upon an entrance examination from prospective students; in 1899, the college became the first to abandon all work for the Matriculation examination. Scientific studies were introduced, plans for further expansion were laid and, as with the major Cape Town college, a number of staff members took part in the work of the examining university. William Thomson, who arrived from Scotland as Professor of Mathematics in 1883, followed Cameron as Registrar of the university in 1895 and was to serve the Cape institution and its successor for many years to come. Two other mathematicians, J. T. Morrison and A. H. Mackenzie, served on the university Council, as did H. C. Notcutt of the Department of English and W. J. Viljoen, who first held a combined Chair of History and Modern Languages. Viljoen would play a leading part in the early development of the University of South Africa.

62

Despite the provision of degree courses at the Cape, many parents continued to send their children abroad, particularly to Britain, for their entire university education. The ties of "home" were strong and in such subjects as medicine, the South African university offered no degrees. Cape graduates, too, often left the country for advanced studies, since the University of the Cape of Good Hope did little to foster scientific research. Nor can it be said that it gained wide recognition overseas for its courses of study. The University of Edinburgh, however, early gave partial acceptance to a Cape Matriculation certificate for prospective medical students and in 1885, through the good offices of Van Oordt, the Intermediate examination, with Greek and Latin, was accepted by Dutch universities. Further concessions were granted in course of time by other universities and professional bodies.

Despite the attractions of degrees earned at older and more distinguished institutions in other countries, Cape degrees were in demand. In the lifetime of the first Council, over fifty were conferred after examination in arts and law; by 1918, the total number of graduates exceeded two thousand. The University of the Cape of Good Hope also sought to extend its usefulness through extension lectures, although parliament refused to countenance what it felt was a misappropriation of funds on the part of an examining university.

Whatever its shortcomings, the University of the Cape of Good Hope made its mark in Cape society. It was never able to secure, on the British model, parliamentary representation as a university seat, but it did, towards the end of its life, come into possession of a building worthy of a university. For many years, the examining institution was housed in rented accommodation in Bureau Street, Cape Town. The offices were dingy and inconvenient, but it was not until after the death in 1899 of Willem Hiddingh that a move could be contemplated. Hiddingh left the university a plot of land in Queen Victoria Street and the sum of R50 000; the Cape government made a substantial contribution to the available funds and construction of a new building began. The first stage was completed in 1907.

WILLEM HIDDINGH was born in Cape Town on 29 May, 1808, the son of a Dutch lawyer who had come to the Cape in 1802 with Governor Janssens.

He was sent to the Netherlands for his education at the age of 11, obtaining a doctorate in laws in 1830. Meanwhile, however, British legal training had become necessary for Cape lawyers and Hiddingh was obliged to qualify in Scotland, where he studied for some time at the University of Edinburgh.

He returned to the Cape in 1833 and soon made a name for himself as a leading advocate, appearing regularly in the circuit court until 1850. He also played an active part in the cultural life of Cape Town, serving on the committee of the South African Public Library and as a trustee of the Grey collection.

He died, a wealthy man, at his home in Queen Victoria Street, Cape Town on 10 December, 1899. In his will he left £25 000 (R50 000) to provide a hall and suitable office accommodation for the university and a further £5 000 (R10 000) as a bursary fund. He also bequeathed land in Queen Victoria Street to the examining institution and sums of money to the South African Public Library and the South African College.

Dr Hiddingh's generosity, together with government assistance, enabled the University of the Cape of Good Hope to carry out the first stage of a building project by June, 1907. Further gifts – notably that from Sir Donald Currie's daughters – led to the completion of the scheme in 1913.

Dr Willem Hiddingh, LL.D.

DONALD CURRIE, one of the ten children of a barber, was born on 17 September, 1825 in Greenock, Renfrewshire, Scotland. His childhood was spent in the Irish city of Belfast.

He began work at an early age in the sugar industry, became a clerk in the Cunard line and 18 years later, founded his own shipping company.

By 1872, he had switched from sail to steam and had entered the Cape trade, where his "Castle" ships soon became popular for their speed and efficiency. His company amalgamated in 1900 with its chief rival to form the Union Castle line.

Currie had wide South African interests and visited the country on a number of occasions. He became a well-known public figure and his political activities brought him into contact with such statesmen as Brand, Burgers and Kruger. The Currie Cups for cricket, rugby and other sports were donated by him.

A member of the British parliament for some years, he received the K.C.M.G. in 1881, the G.C.M.G. in 1897 and an honorary LL.D. from the University of Edinburgh in 1906.

He is first mentioned in the university records on 31 March, 1888, when he gave £100 (R200) "to be used as the Vice-Chancellor may consider best in promoting the interests of Education in the University".

In 1910, his three daughter donated £25 000 (R50 000) to the university in memory of their father. The money helped to finance the completion of a university building and to establish a bursary. At a later date, the interest on this gift was used for a publication fund which commemorated his name and that of another benefactor, Willem Hiddingh.

Donald Currie died on 13 April, 1909 at Sidmouth, Devonshire, England and was buried in Scotland at Fortingall in Perthshire.

Sir Donald Currie, LL.D.(h.c.), G.C.M.G.

Further financial assistance was hard to come by and much of the credit for obtaining it must go to Sir John Buchanan of the university Council, who was Vice-Chancellor from 1901 until 1905. The daughters of Sir Donald Currie – Margaret, Lady Mirrielees, Elizabeth Molteno and Maria Wisely – donated R50 000 in 1910 and smaller sums were received from the mining magnates, Otto Beit, Solly Joel, Max Michaelis and Sir Julius Wernher. Government assistance was also obtained and the completed structure was officially opened in 1913. "Stone walls, however fine", as the *Cape Times* reminded its readers, "do not make a University any more than they make a prison". By then, the examining university was doomed and the new building would soon become its successor's white elephant.

Degree Day was the one annual function when the examining university was able to display itself before the general public as a corporate body. In its last years, it used its own hall for the ceremony, but for long it was forced to find other accommodation. The Huguenot Hall of the Dutch Reformed *(Nederduitse Gereformeerde)* Church was used on occasion; so too was the Good Hope Hall, with its incongruous theatrical backdrops. For many years, however, the South African Public Library was the scene of the annual presentation of degrees. The first ceremony of this kind took place there on 12 December, 1874 before the Governor, Sir Henry Barkly, and the cream of colonial society. It was an occasion more solemn than those of later years, when student rowdyism reached disquietening dimensions. Although not all the university's first seven graduates by examination were present, the spectacle seemed more impressive to Barkly than had the University of Melbourne ceremonies which he had attended as Governor of Victoria. The *Argus* felt sure that the university's future historian would not pass the function by "as a *dies non*". Gill College had reason to be proud that day, for three of the B.A.'s had been educated there : James Rose Innes, the future judge and grandson of the colony's first Superintendent General of Education, and the Postma brothers, Petrus and Marthinus, later ministers in the Reformed *(Gereformeerde)* Church. Two

B.A.'s were from the South African College : F. C. Kolbe, long to be associated with the university as examiner and member of Council and to be honoured by its successor, and another student who would one day rise to the defence of the examining institution, B. P. J. Marchand, the future Dutch Reformed *(Neder-duitse Gereformeerde)* Church minister. From Stellenbosch came Johannes A. Joubert, who subsequently gained a Cape M.A. degree. The M.A. on this occasion was a Diocesan College student, Robert Sheard, later an Anglican minister at Worcester in the Cape.

It was not only the graduates by examination who were · received on these occasions; the admitted graduates of other universities were also accepted as full members of Convocation. Council took its duty of selecting those who had applied for such recognition with due seriousness, for prospective members were expected, in the words of the relevant by-law, to "exercise the privilege to the honour and advancement of this University". It was, presumably, on the assumption that a hack journalist on the diamond fields would not promote the university's best interests that the application of F. Y. St Leger, future editor of the *Cape Times,* was refused. The successful approach made by the Rev. C. Maurice Davies, however, brought the university into unexpected contact with an unsavoury court case and with schism within the Anglican Church in South Africa.

Some applicants had insufficient qualifications and the university had no hesitation in rejecting the rather vague claims of the Rev. M. S. A. Looney of Durban and the M.A. and Ph.D. of the American Anthropological University submitted by another Anglican, the Rev. P. J. Oliver Minos of Pretoria. Degrees in music were not conferred by the University of the Cape of Good Hope in 1879, but it is doubtful whether any of the Council members at that time were qualified to express an opinion on the work of the authority on Hindu music, Rajah Sourindro Mohun Tagore, who sent six parcels of books and a letter asking for recognition of his ability in his field! In the period up to 1918, over eight hundred graduates of universities in several

DEGREE DAY was first held in the South African Public Library, Cape Town and it was not until the last years of the University of the Cape of Good Hope that it was able to make use of a hall of its own. The ceremony of 1901 was specially arranged to coincide with the visit of the Duke of Cornwall and York.

The early functions were decorous enough, but they soon became excuses for student rowdyism on the grand scale and the university authorities tried repeatedly but in vain to curb these annual outbursts of boisterousness. In 1908, the *Cape Times* reported that "the din created by the use of tin whistles, bagpipes and other musical instruments was such as has not been heard on Degree Days of the last few years". South African College students were on home ground and their war-cry often rang out clearly above the general clamour. Speakers, it need scarcely be added, had a hard task to make themselves heard. Today's ceremonies would seem tame affairs indeed to the undergraduates and their friends of an earlier age!

Programme, Degree Day, 1901

University of the Cape of Good Hope.

GRADUATION CEREMONY

AND

STALLATION OF H.R.H. THE DUKE OF CORNWALL AND YORK

AS

CHANCELLOR OF THE UNIVERSITY,

21st August, 1901.

Born on 8 March, 1844 on the island of Tahiti in the South Seas, E B E N E Z E R J O H N B U C H A N A N was the son of a Scottish missionary. The family returned to Britain in 1850, but soon left for Natal.

The boy attended school in Pietermaritzburg and later joined the *Natal Witness,* a newspaper founded there by his uncle in 1846. Further journalistic work in Natal and Cape Town followed, but he also began legal studies and in 1868, obtained the Second-class Certificate in Law and Jurisprudence of the Board of Public Examiners. He then went to London, where he continued both his newspaper work and his legal training. Called to the bar on 27 January, 1873, he returned to the Cape and was admitted in the May of that year as a colonial advocate.

He soon built up a big practice, became a member of the House of Assembly and saw active service during the Ninth Frontier War of 1877-1878.

A man of wide reading and author of a valuable legal reference book, he made rapid progress in his profession. In 1879, he acted as Attorney General for Griqualand West, soon moving to Grahamstown as an acting judge. This post was made permanent in 1881 and in 1887, he was transferred to Cape Town as a Junior Puisne Judge. He became a Senior Puisne Judge in 1892 and also acted on occasion as Chief Justice. He retired in 1920.

Buchanan was knighted in 1901 and six years later, received an honorary LL.D from the University of Cambridge, a distinction which was also conferred upon him by the University of South Africa in 1925. A Council member from 1888 until 1918 and Vice-Chancellor from 1901 to 1905, his enthusiasm did much to hasten the completion of the university building in Queen Victoria Street.

Sir John died on 11 October, 1930 in Claremont, Cape Town.

The Hon. Sir Ebenezer John Buchanan, Kt, LL.D. (h.c.) (Cantab.),
LL.D. (h.c.) (S.A.)
Member of Council 1888–1918
Pro Vice-Chancellor 1897–1901; 1905–1909
Vice-Chancellor 1901–1905

countries were admitted to Cape degrees. Their names, together with those of the board's certificate holders and the graduates by examination, constitute a valuable register of the academic qualifications held by many residents of South Africa in the lifetime of this country's first university.

Power to confer honorary degrees was granted by the Amendment Act of 1896 and the first awards were made three years later. The Herero philologist, P. H. Brincker, and the historian, George McCall Theal, received doctorates in literature on that occasion and a doctorate in science was awarded to the astronomer, Alexander W. Roberts. Many famous men – and one woman, the Bushman expert, Lucy C. Lloyd – were subsequently awarded honorary doctorates. Among the Doctors of Laws were King George V, then the Duke of Cornwall and York, his successor as Chancellor of the university, the Duke of Connaught and Strathearn, the High Commissioner before Union, Lord Selborne, and the Governors-General, Viscounts Gladstone and Buxton. The Union's first Prime Minister, Louis Botha, also received this honorary degree.

Doctors of Science included Sir Arnold Theiler, the veterinary bacteriologist, and Robert Broom, celebrated in the field of palaeontology. Several who were closely connected with the examining university obtained honorary awards. Four former members of Council – Sir Henry de Villiers, J. X. Merriman, C. Abercrombie Smith and Jan Smuts – became Doctors of Laws; so, too, did a future Council member, Mr Justice J. G. Kotzé. James Cameron, the first Registrar, received a doctorate in literature in 1901 and some years later, similar awards were conferred upon the well-known educationists and former Council members, Andrew Murray and George Ogilvie. Another member of the university Council, the botanist, Peter MacOwan, became a Doctor of Science. When a number of honorary degrees were awarded to visiting members of the British Association for the Advancement of Science in 1905, one of the recipients was Sir David Gill, who as Astronomer Royal at the Cape, had been appointed to the second university Council in 1880.

74

Throughout its career, the University of the Cape of Good Hope had to face the hostility of those who disliked it because it was not, in reality, a university at all, but merely "a factory of certificates", as W. J. Viljoen of Stellenbosch once described it. Although the university's examinations set a standard which raised the level of education in the Cape Colony, the institution which set and marked them left teaching to others. It was, as Professor J. W. Hales once said of the old examining University of London, just " a rigorous and many-voiced catechist, a keen spirit of interrogation". Demands for a teaching university would become increasingly insistent.

Another criticism which was levelled at the examining university was that it was not a South African institution, but an alien, English import. Nevertheless, the University of the Cape of Good Hope did try, from the outset, to foster a greater South Africanism within a British framework. It is evident from the names put forward at the election of Porter as Chancellor, as well as from the choice of his successors in that office – Sir Bartle Frere and the Earl of Carnarvon – that there was much sympathy for political federalism in some university circles. Equally significant was the reaction to the interest shown in the Cape University beyond the colonial borders. In Natal, the Barter Commission on education recommended in its report of August, 1874 that the colony should forge a link with what it described as "the South African University".

Similar desires were expressed in the Orange Free State. There, Johannes Brill, the Rector of Grey College, his assistant, Josiah Slater, and the Anglican Bishop of Bloemfontein, Alan B. Webb – all of whom would one day become members of the university Council – sought from the end of 1874 to arrange a connection with the examining institution in Cape Town. Such a step would be greatly to the advantage of both Grey College and the Anglican diocesan foundation in Bloemfontein, St Andrew's.

The result of the interest displayed by leading men in two neighbouring territories was the passing of the University Extension Act of 1875. This legislation enabled the Cape University to

(a)

(b)

Graduation Ceremony

February 27th, 1909

The Annual Address to Graduates was delivered by

The Right Honourable the Earl of Selborne, P.C.,
G.C.M.G.

The following Honorary Degrees were conferred.

Doctor of Laws:

The Right Honourable the Earl of Selborne.

Doctor of Divinity:

Professor N. J. Hofmeyr.

Selborne

N.J. Hofmeyr

C. Murray Smith
Vice Chancellor

W. Thomson
Registrar

HONORARY DEGREES were first conferred by the university in 1899, in terms of the University Incorporation Amendment Act No. 6 of 1896.

At that time, the following honorary degrees could be awarded: masters' degrees in arts, science and music, and doctorates in literature, laws, medicine, science and music. The university confined itself, however, to the award of honorary LL.D., D.Litt. and D.Sc. degrees until 1908, when further legislation enabled it to confer honorary doctorates in divinty. Other degrees were added to this list after 1918.

Special ceremonies were held in 1905 and 1929 to honour certain visiting members of the British Association for the Advancement of Science. In 1959, degrees *honoris causa* were awarded on the occasion of the fiftieth anniversary of the *Suid-Afrikaanse Akademie vir Wetenskap en Kuns*.

(a) Cover: Book of Honorary Degrees

(b) An LL.D. and the first Honorary D.D., 1909

See other side:
(c) 50 Years later: three Honorary Degrees awarded to mark the fiftieth Anniversary of the Suid-Afrikaanse Akademie vir Wetenskap en Kuns, *1959*

(d) Recipients in 1959: T.H. le Roux, M.W. Woerdeman and T.E.W. Schumann

Spesiale Gradeplegligheid
by die
Engelenburghuis, Pretoria, hoofsetel van die
Akademie,
op Saterdag, 11 Julie 1959 om 11:30 vm.

Met die oog op die halfeeufeesviering van
die Suid Afrikaanse Akademie vir Wetenskap en Kuns

en gehou by wyse van waardering vir die
werk wat die Akademie in die afgelope 50
jaar gedoen het.

Die graad D.Litt. et Phil. aan
Prof. Dr Thomas Hugo le Roux
gewese hoogleraar in Afrikaans-Nederlands
aan die Universiteit van Pretoria.

T. H. le Roux

Die graad Ph.D. aan
Prof. dr. Martinus Willem Woerdeman
rector magnificus van die Gemeentelike
Universiteit van Amsterdam, en Voorsitter
van die Koninklike Nederlandse Academie
van Wetenschappen.

M. Woerdeman

Die graad Ph.D. aan
dr. Theodor Eberhard Werner Schumann
gewese direkteur van die Brandstofnavorsings-
instituut, gewese direkteur van die Weerburo,
Staatsdienskommissaris, en fans ondervoorsitter
van die Raad op Atoomkrag.

T. Schumann

Prinsipaal
en
Visie kanselier

Registrateur

(c)

(d)

operate beyond the colonial borders in an undefined region of southern Africa and to frame regulations for the award of bursaries to successful students living outside the colony. If the University of the Cape of Good Hope could bring about unity in the world of South African education, this might be a prelude to wider political federation. The claim of the examining institution to be truly representative of the white races and the separate states and colonies of South Africa requires to be examined more closely.

3 A clash of ideals

The Extension Act of 1875 seemed to many a logical step, for a united South Africa under the British flag must soon be created. Then, the University of the Cape of Good Hope would play a greater role than that of an examining board for a single colony. When, two years later, it received its Royal Charter, the question was raised at the Colonial Office in London "whether Confederation might not soon render it preferable to enlarge the title and scope of the University, and to make it the 'University of South Africa' ". Many problems, however, would have to be surmounted before the suggested re-baptism could take place.

Co-operation in the educational field proved as difficult to achieve in the seventies as it did in the political. Students living outside the colonial borders came forward in increasing numbers to take the university's examinations, but governments in nearby territories showed little inclination to make the contribution of R400 a year which would enable their own candidates to enjoy the same bursary privileges as those who lived in the Cape Colony. In Natal, it was a question of standards. Plans to establish a Royal College there in connection with the university in Cape Town were shelved and for many years the smaller British colony stimulated higher education by providing financial assistance for those who wished to attend universities abroad. The Home Scholarships, as they were called, came to be awarded on the results of Cape University examinations. Education north of the Vaal River was still, when the Cape University was young, in an undeveloped state, as appears from the report of the Superintendent of Education, J. Vacy Lyle, during the first British occupation which began in 1877. Cape influence showed itself, however, in the setting up of a Board of Examiners in Law and Jurisprudence. It was in the Orange Free State that the University of the Cape of Good Hope might be expected to make its greatest impact.

The Extension Act had attractions for the Cape's northern neighbour and if the university authorities had adopted a more conciliatory attitude over the language question, close relations might early have been established. While Dutch continued to be regarded in Cape Town as inferior to English, however, men like Brill of Grey College would continue to see in affiliation with the Cape University a possible threat to Free State independence. As Brebner, the Inspector of Education in Bloemfontein, realized, the Cape institution would never become truly South African until it placed the two langues on equal terms. This, regrettably, was never done and the Orange Free State began to think of other possibilities for providing higher educational facilities. Relations with the Cape University remained cordial, nevertheless. In 1882, President Brand and Vice-Chancellor Badnall exchanged friendly letters on the subject of bursaries for deserving students.

It is not surprising that the Free State and, later, the South African Republic looked with so much suspicion upon the Cape University as an English institution. Even in the old colony, it was increasingly under attack on the language issue. English was a foreign tongue to many who came forward to attempt the university's examinations and the neglect of Dutch was regarded by most Afrikaners not only as an affront, but also as a real handicap to national progress. From 1890 onwards, the sporadic shots which had earlier been fired in the language battle became a barrage of steadily growing intensity, mounted at first by the Dutch Reformed *(Nederduitse Gereformeerde)* Church and the *Taalbond.* These were joined in the early years of the present century by dissidents who left the South African Teachers' Association because of its language policy and formed the *Zuid-Afrikaansche Onderwijzers Unie* of 1905.

81

In the early nineties, not much was asked of the Cape University. Most critics would then have been satisfied with compulsory Dutch at Matriculation level and in the School Elementary examination, a Dutch paper and the opportunity to answer questions in other subjects in that language. All that the university Council was prepared to do, however, was to make Dutch an optional subject in the Elementary examination. At this, even English speakers were disgusted. "It is not right", announced the *Argus* in May, 1891, "that, in a country in which Dutch plays so important a part, the language should be bracketed with German as a mere foreign accomplishment". As the tragic end of the century approached, however, and relations between Boer and Briton began to worsen, the language struggle merged into the greater conflict between the two white races. Fewer English voices were heard in defence of Dutch, the Cape University remained unsympathetic and the Superintendent General of Education, Thomas Muir, displayed even more hostility to Afrikaner aspirations than had his predecessor, Langham Dale.

If the Dutch-speaking section in the Cape Colony was dissatisfied with the Cape University, those who lived in the Orange Free State and the South African Republic were understandably far less inclined by the nineties to advocate closer relations with the examining institution in Cape Town. In Bloemfontein, where Grey College was emerging as the probable major centre for higher education in the state, there was so much disappointment with the University of the Cape of Good Hope that President Reitz warned in 1893 that, unless it were prepared to devote itself whole-heartedly to South African interests, the Free State would ultimately be forced to create a rival institution.

In the South African Republic, the Cape University enjoyed no official approval. It had its supporters, however – particularly among the immigrant English speakers who had flocked to the gold mines of the Witwatersrand and whose presence there contributed in so large a measure to the deteriorating relations between Britain and the Boer republics.

In 1892, Nicolaas Mansvelt had made legislative provision for

82

a Pretoria Gymnasium which might become for the northern republic what Grey College already was for the southern. At that stage, however, the government of the South African Republic looked to the Netherlands for university training. The assistance of the *Nederlandsch Zuid-Afrikaansche Vereeniging* was enlisted to help deserving students and bursaries were awarded for further education. By September, 1896, Mansvelt had also succeeded in obtaining recognition in the Netherlands of early qualifications obtained in the republic. This cancelled the advantage the Cape University possessed in the acceptance by Dutch universities of its Intermediate B.A. examination with Greek and Latin.

Only in Natal, where the population was largely British in origin and therefore in favour of an English language policy, did desire for closer association with the University of the Cape of Good Hope grow. Proposals to this end were made by the Natal Council of Education and were welcomed by Vice-Chancellor Ogilvie and the Cape University Council. Natal's first Prime Minister, Sir John Robinson, was in "full sympathy with any movement to secure common university privileges to both colonies and to South Africa at large". Accordingly, the Amendment Act of June, 1896 was passed. This not only widened the range of degrees offered by the Cape University and increased the size of its governing body, but also made provision for the representation on the university Council of the governments of the neighbouring territories of Natal, the Orange Free State and the South African Republic, on payment of an annual contribution to university funds.

Natal accepted the conditions immediately and decided to give the sum of R800 per annum to the Cape University. In 1897, therefore, Robert Russell, the Superintendent Inspector of Education, joined the Council, together with two Cape men who were asked to represent the smaller colony. These were J. X. Merriman and Professor Roderick Noble's brother, John, who was replaced later in the year by the former Registrar, James Cameron. Russell, as the *Witness* of Pietermaritzburg described him, was to be the "special messenger" for important debates; the other two would ensure that the colony's interests would not be lost sight of at regular meetings.

This connection proved to be a valuable one for the colony and a great deal of interest was aroused there on the subject of higher education. University work would not be centralized in one institution for some time, but an increasing amount was being undertaken from the last decade of the century onwards in various Natal schools. Of these, Durban High School and Maritzburg College stood high in public estimation. Among the successful candidates for the B.A. examination at the Durban institution was a future South African Governor-General, E. G. Jansen, who graduated in 1901. The rival school in the colonial capital had been developed to collegiate level by one of South Africa's great Headmasters, R. D. Clark, and was considered by many to be the obvious choice as the basis for a Natal university.

The Amendment Act of 1896 was received with less enthusiasm in the northern republics, already beginning to co-operate in the face of renewed fears of British imperialist expansion after the recent ill-fated Jameson Raid. The University of the Cape of Good Hope had, however, a good friend at Bloemfontein in John Brebner. He was, it is true, no admirer of the existing policy which gave pride of place to the English language, but he could see the advantages of the university connection. He pinned his hopes on those at the Cape, among them Sir Henry de Villiers, who favoured a more representative body.

If the fifth Council, due to be selected in 1897, were to prove more reasonable over the language question than had its predecessors, there was a good chance that the Orange Free State at least would be prepared to accept the university. Perhaps the South African Republic might also be persuaded to join a higher educational federation. To this end, Brebner stressed to Mansvelt the need for South African unity, for the peoples of the colonies and states of the sub-continent were really one "van de Kaapstad tot de Zambezi, met gelijke aspiratiën en behoeften". He would have to face much scepticism, although he could count on support from W. A. Macfadyen of the Pretoria Gymnasium staff and of Chief Justice J. G. Kotzé. His efforts were, however, in vain. The new and enlarged Council showed no inclination to favour the Dutch language.

The South African Republic was not, in any case, particularly interested in an examining university, for such an institution was quite foreign to those who looked to the Netherlands for their models in the field of higher education. The movement in the last tense years before the outbreak of the Anglo-Boer War was therefore in the direction of a Dutch language teaching university, as soon as the number of qualified entrants should be sufficiently large to meet the expense. In that connection, the Pretoria Gymnasium, under the rectorship of H. T. Reinink, was beginning to show promise of greater things to come. Hopes of reconciliation between Britain and the Boer republics continued to recede and the Free State and its northern neighbour drew close in defensive alliance. The Cape University remained obstinately English and as the Bloemfontein *Express* put it, experience had shown that "mooie praatjes te beginnen met John Bull" on that subject would be a waste of time. In March, 1899, the Council of Delegates representing the two republics recommended the establishment of a joint university, with teaching colleges in each country. A Dutch-language institution, in competition with the University of the Cape of Good Hope, was close to realization when the long war began which would put an end to dreams of political independence and educational autonomy.

If problems of language and nationality prevented the University of the Cape of Good Hope from expanding effectively into the Boer republics, similar differences of outlook hindered the transformation of the examining institution in Cape Town into a teaching university. For at the Cape, as in Britain itself, the examining university was under heavy fire in the last years of the nineteenth century. It was, as the *Zuid-Afrikaan* observed in 1887, a great pity that the colony had chosen an English model to crown its educational system, "en wel van een soort die geheel afwijkt van hetgeen men in bijna alle landen met den naam van Universiteit bestempelt". Moreover, the English tradition was foreign to the Afrikaner section and "een oprecht Afrikaner die zijn zoon of dochter aan inrigtingen van onderwijs toevertrouwt waar een beslist Engelsche of andere niet Afrikaansche zin heerscht, zal dikwijls bedrogen uitkomen".

Perhaps a teaching university might take Afrikaner sentiment into consideration; those institutions which offered courses for the examining university's degrees were all too often hostile to it. The nucleus of such a university was, as Professor J. I. Marais pointed out in June, 1889, to be found in the Victoria College, Stellenbosch. Was it not possible that one day a separate foundation would come into existence there, "onafhankelijk van examens namens den Universiteitsraad, en waar men een waar nationaal gevoel voor taal en vaderland zou zien oprijzen"? What, however, was lacking were the funds to carry out such a transformation.

Nevertheless, financial assistance was soon to be forthcoming, although not for the exact purpose suggested by Professor Marais. Cecil John Rhodes, who had become Prime Minister of the Cape Colony in July, 1890, attended an alumni dinner at Grey College, Bloemfontein towards the end of that year. He was greatly impressed by the work carried out there for the youth of South Africa and soon made it known that he planned to do something on a grand scale for higher education at the Cape. In March, 1891, Rhodes publicly announced at the Kimberley Congress of the *Afrikaner Bond* that it was his intention to create a residential teaching institution "under the shadow of Table Mountain", where the youth of South Africa, both English-speaking and Dutch-speaking, would be able to work and to play together. From this intermingling, Rhodes insisted, would spring a united country. A site for the proposed institution was made available at Groote Schuur and the profits of the De Beers diamond mining company would help to finance the scheme.

Rhodes evidently had in mind a new residential college, restricted, as the existing colleges were not at that time, to matriculated students. The new institution, together with those already preparing students for the Cape University examinations, would form an affiliation, with the University of the Cape of Good Hope at its centre. The new college at Groote Schuur would bear some resemblance to Oriel College, Oxford, which Rhodes had attended in his youth. A teaching function might perhaps be added to the examining university so that the scheme, in its entirety, would transform the colonial higher educational system into something resembling Oxford and Cambridge with their associated colleges.

Interest was immediately aroused; so, too, were misgivings. Langham Dale, in his last report as Superintendent General of Education, spoke of the intention to encourage "the necessary agencies for providing the highest modern appliances of a fully equipped University"; Merriman approved of the esprit de corps which Rhodes hoped to foster at Groote Schuur; T. E. Fuller hoped to see the new scheme embrace advanced technical studies, similar to those provided at Edinburgh's Heriot-Watt College; William Ritchie felt that the core of any subsequent development in university education must be the South African College.

On the other hand, some wondered whether there was yet at the Cape a sufficiently large leisured class to justify a residential university, or, if it did prove a success, whether the standing of the existing colleges could still be maintained. Moreover, Ritchie's remark touched a sensitive nerve among Dutch speakers. Was not the Rhodes scheme merely a way of improving the status of the South African College by moving it to another site and giving it a greater role to play in Cape education? Not surprisingly, such an idea, as the *Zuid-Afrikaan* put it, "vond bestrijding . . . van Stellenbosschen kant".

It was evident from the start that Rhodes would be faced with the problem of reconciling conflicting points of view. Merriman was of the opinion that "some less Elizabethan worthy" would ultimately be left to solve the difficulties, leaving Rhodes "the kudos for the business". Differences of opinion, however, proved to be insurmountable. Rhodes came to regard the Rev. J. H. Neethling of Stellenbosch as his arch-enemy in the matter of the proposed scheme, but he had other opponents. Many Afrikaners hesitated to sacrifice the college to the interests of its older Cape Town rival and feared at the same time that acceptance of the Rhodes scheme would lead to a further dilution of the Afrikaner's heritage in the ocean of English tradition. Would the products of a new university system constructed along the lines mooted by Rhodes be interested in upholding Afrikaner national character when, after twenty years, they occupied the seats of power in the land? Was bilingualism a practical possibility, or would English become even more dominant? Were there not grave moral dangers to the youth of the Dutch-speaking section if they were to be exposed to alien ways? Perhaps, as "Onze Jan" Hofmeyr suggested, Stellenbosch, a quiet backwater, was the ideal site for a South African university. Certainly, there seemed much in the choice of Groote Schuur to disquieten Afrikaners.

The University of the Cape of Good Hope, vitally concerned in any scheme of reconstruction which would obviously affect its future, had strangely little to say about the Rhodes plan. Vice-Chancellor C. T. Smith mentioned in his address on Degree Day in 1891 that the University of Toronto had been held out as a suitable model for the Cape to follow. There, a secular college and denominational institutions were associated with a teaching university. However, Smith warned that the Canadian system had not been universally approved. He felt that it would be unwise to interfere with the Cape's existing order of things until a plan had been evolved which was satisfactory to all the local colleges.

Merriman, at this time in correspondence with H. B. Webb, the director of a company with South African interests, outlined the probable position of the Cape University in the Rhodes scheme. If the university were to embrace a teaching function, expansion would follow and funds would be necessary to supplement government subsidies. Webb's offer of financial assistance was therefore to be welcomed. However, by the end of 1891, Rhodes had placed his plan in cold storage and the Webb donation remained in the hands of trustees. It was not until many years later, when university reform had been accomplished, that scholarships were instituted in the name of this benefactor.

A teaching university, which the scheme of 1891 seemed to make possible, remained an ideal to be cherished. Rhodes himself felt that something could yet be accomplished, although it might have to await his death. The Jameson Raid, however, destroyed hopes of conciliation and Rhodes gave up his plan in favour of the scholarships designed to satisfy wider needs than those of South Africa alone. Only the university college at Grahamstown which bears his name and which received assistance from De Beers and the Rhodes Trust, recalls on South African soil the former Cape Premier's university ideal. The Rhodes University College of 1904 was, however, a pygmy beside the collegiate giants of the western Cape and far from achieving independent status as a teaching university.

Cecil Rhodes had offered the riches of endowment to Cape educationists, only to withdraw them again. His proposal had shown men what was needed in a material sense to transform the university scene. The Cape had its enthusiasts for a teaching university, among them the Superintendent General of Education, Muir, and the Rev. J. J. Kotzé of Sea Point, who suggested a "Victoria Cape of Good Hope University", with a teaching, as well as an examining function, in honour of the Queen's Diamond Jubilee. The newspaper, *Ons Land,* into which the *Zuid-Afrikaan* was merged in 1894, was equally anxious to invest the Cape University with a quickening spirit, for it was but a poor thing, an institution "zonder professoren, zonder studenten, die nergens bestaat, doch overal examens afneemt". In the absence of money, however, reconstruction was out of the question and plans for a teaching university remained idle dreams.

Moreover, the reaction to the Rhodes scheme had demonstrated that the generosity of a public-spirited benefactor was not enough to provide South Africa with a worthy higher educational system. The suspicions which had been aroused in 1891 showed how difficult it had become to persuade Boer and Briton to agree. The split between the two sections was to become wider as the decade advanced. After the Jameson Raid, Afrikaners were even more keenly aware of the threat to their existence from British imperialism and the political differences between Britain and the Boer republics found their echo in the Cape Colony, with its two linguistic streams. From 1897 onwards, the Dutch Reformed *(Nederduitse Gereformeerde)* Church kept a watchful eye through its Vigilance Committee upon any possible developments in the university field which might be inimical to the interests of its adherents.

Reform, no easy task at any time in so heterogeneous a society as that of the Cape, was particularly difficult to effect in those tense days between Jameson's ill-advised exploit and the outbreak of war in 1899. During the long months which followed the firing of the first shots, until the signing of peace in 1902, practical moves to reconstruct the university system were out of the question, although the need was not forgotten.

The war itself did not leave the University of the Cape of Good Hope untouched and its activities were to some extent curtailed. Examinations were being attempted at various levels in both the Free State and the South African Republic before hostilities began. Brill's students at Grey College in Bloemfontein were already studying for the Intermediate B.A. examination at that time; English-medium schools, particularly in Johannesburg, entered pupils for the university's examinations; many, too, living in the northern republics, worked privately for the tests of the examining institution in Cape Town. These contacts between students and the university were necessarily broken for a period, as were those involving candidates living in the districts of the Cape and Natal affected by the war. By 1901, however, when the struggle between the two peoples had changed its nature, many of the old examination centres had been re-established and commissioners were again appointed for the conduct of examinations in such places as Johannesburg, Potchefstroom and Pretoria.

Among the examination arrangements which suffered as a result of the military situation were those in music. Gladys E. Watts, the university's first scholarship winner in this field, was unable to communicate with the Cape University for some time.

She was, to use an expression which occurs more than once in the letters of the Registrar, William Thomson, "shut up" in the Orange Free State. The music examiners also gave the university no small trouble. As they were sent out from England by the Associated Board of the Royal Schools, they naturally knew little of prevailing conditions and were understandably anxious for re-assurance. Eaton Faning was informed in 1901 that "the examinations will be held (De Wet permitting) at Bloemfontein, Johannesburg, Pietermaritzburg, Durban, and at all the old and at some new Centres in this Colony". Thomson also made it clear to him that the cost of living was a far graver danger than the bubonic plague which was then prevalent! It was, at all events, some encouragement to know that the English examiners would be visiting a "now historic centre".

The work of two of the colleges which prepared students for the examinations of the Cape University was seriously interrupted. The seminary of the Reformed *(Gereformeerde)* Church in Burgersdorp was closed for a period and was restricted in its operations by the military. Its theological professor, J. Lion Cachet, was arrested on a treason charge, but the case was subsequently dropped. At Kimberley, the School of Mines was forced to close during the siege of that town and was unable to open again until the second half of 1900. One of the university's examiners in mining, George F. Labram, the American engineer who designed the siege gun, "Long Cecil", was killed by a Boer shell at the beginning of that year; another American, Louis I. Seymour, who had also examined in mining for the University of the Cape of Good Hope, lost his life a few months later while serving with the British forces in the Orange Free State.

The war caused problems over the examination papers. In those days, Messrs Macmillan and Bowes of Cambridge were the university's printers and there were fears that the priority given to military stores would prevent the English firm from supplying the Cape institution's requirements on time. "Under no circumstances", wrote the Registrar in August, 1900, "should the boxes be sent by any but mail steamers as, owing to the demand for space at the Docks, it is not unusual for the other steamers to remain in the roadstead for two or three weeks". The siege of Kimberley also delayed the transmission of the draft papers to England for printing, since one of the examiners was "shut up" there.

The great struggle brought about a change in the date of the university examinations. These had always been held in mid-year, but in 1900, after representations from the western Cape colleges, additional examinations were held at the end of the year to compensate students for study time lost as a result of the conflict. The date of this second series of tests became that of the annual examinations of future years.

The war caused bitterness enough in South Africa, but the University of the Cape of Good Hope, which provided syllabuses for students of all political persuasions, remained throughout an impartial bystander. Its examinations were taken in concentration camps and Thomson recalled in later years a visit he had paid to one of them. As he walked through the camp, he noticed a Cape Matriculation certificate affixed to a tent-pole as a public testimony to the qualifications of a young school-teacher there. At the Green Point camp, C. Kewley, a Cambridge graduate and member of the Cape University Convocation, prepared students for the school examinations of the university.

Those interned on distant St Helena had reason to remember the University of the Cape of Good Hope with gratitude. Even before the war, an enquiry had come from the island for examination facilities. On that occasion, the writer had been referred to the University of London. In 1901, however, the university Council agreed to hold examinations for prisoners-of-war there, provided no undue delay was caused. Plans to hold similar examinations for those in captivity on the island of Bermuda were made in 1902, but the coming of peace brought these projects to an end. When the fighting was over and the task of reconstruction had begun, the Cape University was able to assure one prospective candidate that a conviction for high treason would not debar him from entering for an examination. He

92

would still be required, however, to submit the usual certificate of good conduct!

The Anglo-Boer War was a turning-point in the history of South Africa and in the evolution of the University of the Cape of Good Hope. The examining university would at last become an institution representative of all the colonies and before Union in 1910, a small breach would be made in the apparently impregnable wall of English language exclusiveness which had hitherto surrounded it. The gains, however, could not hide its deficiencies and it was already clear by 1902 that it was suspect in the eyes of most educationists. For although it examined many, it taught none. Its English progenitor, the University of London, had succeeded at the end of the century in transforming itself into a teaching, as well as an examining institution. The change had not taken place without a struggle and the defenders of the old order in the imperial capital had not been entirely routed. Nevertheless, it was a notable triumph for the forces of reform. Their victory did not go unperceived in South Africa.

4 New approaches

The years from 1902 until 1910 not only saw the South African colonies move towards political unity, but also the achievement of a greater degree of educational uniformity under the control of the University of the Cape of Good Hope. In the very period, however, when the Cape University attained its goal by becoming the sole degree-conferring body for a sub-continent, a campaign for a teaching university was set in motion which would, after a long and hard struggle, destroy its monopoly and transform its nature.

Connected both with the extension of the Cape University's field of operations and with the ideal of a teaching university was the demand on the Witwatersrand for technological education adequate to the requirements of an industrial region of world importance. A little had been accomplished by the Cape government before the Anglo-Boer War in the foundation of the School of Mines in Kimberley; when the conflict ended, this institution gave way to a Transvaal Technical Institute in Johannesburg, established in August, 1903 and opened the following year. Already in January, 1903, the visiting founder of England's new University of Birmingham, Joseph Chamberlain, had mentioned to an enthusiastic Johannesburg audience the need for a technological university on the Rand. Two years later, the Cambridge classicist, Sir Richard Jebb, who had come to South Africa with other members of the British Association for the Advancement of Science, spoke in the same place of the aims of a modern university. Such an institution, he said, should not only disseminate culture, not only satisfy a demand for technical skills, but also inculcate scientific habits of study. There is no doubt that many in his audience thought chiefly of the physical sciences in this context, for these reigned supŕeme in an industrial age. Examining universities were not much to the liking of those who regarded the new Transvaal Technical Institute as the germ of the future teaching university to which the British Colonial Secretary had alluded.

Not that the University of the Cape of Good Hope entirely neglected the demands of science. It had already provided mining diplomas for those who took courses at the Cape colleges and the Kimberley institution. These certificates had been requested by the South African College and before long, the School of Mines on the diamond fields was pressing for degrees in mining engineering in terms of the Amendment Act of 1896. These were somewhat tardily approved by Council in 1899. Research had also been stimulated by the award of fellowships to deserving students, of whom the scientist and future member of the university Council, Charles F. Juritz, was the first. The fellowships had not entirely succeeded in their object and were replaced, as a result of changes introduced by Council in 1906, by a D.Sc. degree in pure science, preceded by an M.Sc. in two departments. Juritz was awarded the new doctorate in 1907; in 1914, it was obtained by a woman student, Ethel Mary Doidge, who became a plant pathologist with the Department of Agriculture. Dr Doidge played a part in the early history of the University of South Africa. Science degrees in agriculture were also provided, but the proposal put forward by George Cory of Rhodes University College that a B.Sc. in pure science be instituted to effect a clear separation between the subjects in that field and those in arts was not accepted.

The need for medical training at the Cape continued to be pressed and in the early years of this century, Edward Barnard Fuller began the long campaign which earned him the title of "Father of the Medical Faculty" of the future University of Cape Town. Teaching and research in the sciences and technology, however, were essentially matters for the colleges; the university merely provided the examinations. Moreover, the University of the Cape of Good Hope was geographically distant from the industrial heart of South Africa and remote in spirit from those who governed the affairs of the Transvaal Technical Institute, renamed in 1906 the Transvaal University College.

H.S. Hele-Shaw, first holder of the Chair of Engineering at Liverpool University College in England, was an early promoter of technical and university education in Johannesburg. Just as the English institution with which he had been associated had developed into a promising civic university, so, too, he felt, should the Rand's major college, of which he was Principal. The University of the Cape of Good Hope might, he stated when he addressed its Congregation on Degree Day in 1904, be allowed to become a controlling board for South African higher education. The day was rapidly approaching, however, when it would be forced to change the character of its association with the teaching colleges.

Not that the Johannesburg institution was yet a real competitor. It had no degree-conferring powers and neither the Transvaal government nor the Cape University would recognize its Matriculation pass. It trained students for some of the Cape University's examinations, but those who succeeded in its own tests had to be content with diplomas and certificates. In the field of mining education, it long engaged in a running fight with the university over courses and regulations. Not until the University of South Africa was created could students convert their mining diplomas into degrees.

There was, however, talk of co-operation between the colonies of the Transvaal, Orange River and Natal which might have led to a federal northern university. This was sufficient to alarm the university Council in Cape Town, which had itself already called for discussions on an inter-colonial basis to regulate the higher education of the sub-continent. Lord Milner, as High Commissioner and Governor of the Transvaal and Orange River Colonies, showed some interest in the Cape University's proposals.

Towards the end of 1905, Sir John Buchanan, lately Vice-Chancellor of the university, took the matter up with Theodore Reunert, the mining engineer and founder member of the Council of Education in Johannesburg, established ten years earlier for the benefit of Uitlanders there.

The Cape University did not want to see the creation of a northern rival and its fears were largely dispelled by the influential support it received in the Transvaal. Neither Milner's successor, Lord Selborne, nor Lieutenant-Governor Sir Richard Solomon felt that the standard of education, beyond the Vaal River at least, was high enough to warrant ideas of another university "for a considerable time to come". At a Cape University dinner held in the Grand Hotel, Pretoria in August, 1906, the Vice-Chancellor, C. Abercrombie Smith, and the Pro Vice-Chancellor, Buchanan, were greatly heartened by the enthusiasm and affection for the examining university expressed by several of the guests. The Transvaal judge, J. W. Wessels, soon to join the Cape University Council, rose in defence of his Alma Mater; so, too, did his legal colleague, Rose Innes, and Lieutenant-Governor Solomon. Reference by Wessels to local "tinpot universities", however, irritated the Johannesburg college, then beginning to extend its influence on the Rand by means of evening classes held in Germiston, Krugersdorp and other towns.

The Transvaal University College had some reason to feel aggrieved. Already enjoying Council of Education support and planning Plein Square extensions which would provide it with a worthier home, even more exciting prospects were held out to it. The mining magnate, Alfred Beit, who had given his Frankenwald estate near Johannesburg to the government for educational purposes in 1904, left R400 000 when he died two years later to erect an institution on the site which he described in his will as the "University of Johannesburg". The bequest was to be used for this purpose within ten years of his death. Here at last was endowment on the grand scale and the Transvaal University College seemed to be the only possible recipient.

The University of the Cape of Good Hope was, however, beginning to become what C. Abercrombie Smith felt it should really be called, the "University of South Africa". Before the two northern colonies had attained responsible government, decisions had been taken in favour of contributing to the university funds under the Amendment Act of 1896 and thus of gaining representation on the governing Council. To the sixth Council therefore came two members from Bloemfontein and three to represent Transvaal interests. The members for the Orange River Colony were Brill of Grey College in the capital and Hugh Gunn, the Director of Education. Gunn was succeeded in the seventh Council of 1909 by the future Union Prime Minister, J. B. M. Hertzog, then Minister of Education for the colony. Hertzog resigned in 1911 and his place was taken by the noted cultural leader and churchman, the Rev. John Daniel Kestell.

The Transvaal sent its Director of Education in 1906, J. E. Adamson, who, like Kestell, was later to play a more important role in the affairs of the Cape University's successor. The other Transvaal members at that date were W. Kidger Tucker of the Council of Education and another future Prime Minister of the Union of South Africa, Jan C. Smuts. It would be a brief link for Smuts with what his mentor, J. I. Marais, had once described as a "strange heterogeneous body of mutually repellent particles". The comment was made in reply to the brilliant young Stellenbosch student's complaints about the reduction in the value of his Ebden Scholarship when the Cape of Good Hope Bank closed its doors. Smuts resigned his seat in Council when he became Minister of Education for the Transvaal in Louis Botha's government.

The University of the Cape of Good Hope had at last become the recognized examining body for the whole of South Africa, an educational pre-eminence it was to maintain until the end of its days. To celebrate its wider influence, a luncheon was given in November, 1906 to which the delegates from outside the Cape Colony were invited. Many of the strongest supporters of the university were present, among them Sir Henry de Villiers, W. P. Schreiner and F. C. Kolbe. The occasion gave another guest,

J. X. Merriman, an opportunity to dilate upon a popular theme of his. Europeans must, he said, further civilization in Africa and the Cape University was a valuable agent in this great work. Already it had greatly stimulated educational advance in South Africa; now was the time to "spread light . . . to the rest of this dark continent".

Not all, however, by the end of 1906, were convinced that the examining university in Cape Town was, in fact, the best agent to achieve this aim. Other approaches to the problem of South African higher education were mentioned at the Federal Conference on Education convened in London by the League of Empire in 1907. The Cape University was not officially represented, but several leading educationists from South Africa, including three members of the university Council, attended. These were Gunn from Bloemfontein, Thomas Muir, the Cape Superintendent General of Education, and Canon W.O. Jenkins of the Diocesan College. Muir expressed the general pleasure at the reconstruction of the University of London when he spoke at the conference and hoped that the Cape would also have a teaching university before long. The Rev. A. C. Headlam, Principal of King's College in the imperial capital, endorsed Muir's sentiments with regard to London and gave his opinion that South Africa should have two universities – one in Cape Town and the other in Johannesburg, each with affiliated colleges.

The idea of a Transvaal university had been stimulated by Alfred Beit's bequest. Jan Smuts, however, did not show himself greatly in favour of Johannesburg as a higher educational centre when he became responsible for colonial education in 1907. A growing estrangement between the Transvaal University College and the Council of Education on the one hand and the government in Pretoria on the other early made itself felt. Ideas of a Frankenwald university were dismissed, two Johannesburg high schools were permitted to compete with the college by instituting Intermediate B.A. classes and the government at length decided that it would be better to concentrate arts and pure science work in Pretoria. This would leave the Johannesburg foundation as a mining school. The Frankenwald site could then be used, perhaps, as an agricultural college in a tripartite scheme.

The division between Johannesburg and Pretoria was not popular in the mining metropolis, but Smuts was determined to implement the plan. Accordingly, the Transvaal University College was split into two sections under a joint administrative body. The Pretoria branch began work with a professorial staff of four in Kya Rosa, a house rented for the purpose in Skinner Street. H. T. Reinink of the old Gymnasium and John Purves came over from the Johannesburg college; their colleagues were D. F. du Toit Malherbe and Alfred Croom Paterson. Reinink's main task was to teach Dutch and other modern languages, the Scotsmen, Purves and Paterson, were responsible for English and classical studies respectively and Malherbe, who had been recommended by Hahn of the South African College in Cape Town, took a wide range of scientific subjects, although chemistry was his special field. It is small wonder that in those days, professorial chairs were often referred to as settees! Paterson and Malherbe played a large part in the early deliberations of the Council and Senate of the University of South Africa. The former, who became Principal of the Transvaal University College in Pretoria, later emigrated to New Zealand where he also made a valuable contribution to university life.

It was made clear to Smuts that the proposed tripartite scheme would not meet with the approval of the trustees of the Beit bequest; the Colonial Secretary was, however, insistent that Transvaal higher education should be reorganized in his own way. Moreover, after discussions with Alfred Beit's brother, Otto, and with Sir Julius Wernher, he was coming to realize by 1909 that South Africa needed a national teaching university. A Johannesburg university formed no part of his plans. Accordingly, legislation was passed in 1910, on the eve of Union, which further reduced the status of the college there. The uneasy federation was dissolved, Pretoria became the seat of the Transvaal University College and the Johannesburg institution was renamed the South African School of Mines and Technology. A separate agricultural college was also proposed. Johannesburg's college was, as G. H. L. le May has said, "back where it started, confined to the local and the particular". The dream of a great civic university had faded for the time being.

Nothing came of the proposed independent agricultural college. There was much talk in the last years of Transvaal colonial autonomy about the need for scientific research in the interests of good farming. William Macdonald, editor of the *Transvaal Agricultural Journal,* hoped to see either a national college of agriculture with degree-conferring powers, or a federal university with a strong agricultural faculty, drawing students "from Simons Bay to Zumba and beyond". A graduate in this field of both Cornell University and the University of Minnesota, Macdonald was a great admirer of the progress made in agricultural science in the United States under the beneficial influence of generous endowment. The funds set aside for the establishment of the Transvaal college proposed by Act 2 of 1910 went at length to the university college in Pretoria. In time, it would introduce agricultural studies in the city and courses in veterinary science at Onderstepoort.

No rival to the Cape University was therefore established in the Transvaal before Union; as for the other colonies, there were few who thought in terms of independent universities, except at Cape Town and Stellenbosch. However, with higher education falling to the national government after 1910, both the Orange River Colony and Natal set up – with quite indecent haste, in the opinion of some at the Cape – university colleges of their own. Maritzburg College in Natal was not elevated to higher rank, although it provided the Natal University College, created by Act 18 of 1909, with its first accommodation. The school also loaned it several teachers until the professorial staff was augmented later in the year. For Natal's new institution began life with only two professors: Alexander Petrie, the classicist from Aberdeen, and R. B. Denison, the Professor of Chemistry and Physics, who came from Yorkshire. Both gave many years of devoted service to the college and, in time, to the University of

South Africa. Meanwhile, in Durban, a technical institution had been founded, largely through the efforts of Dr S. G. Campbell, father of the poet, Roy Campbell. The Durban Technical Institute was intended to be a university college eventually and although it never quite attained this eminence, it was the father of both the Natal Technical College of today and the Durban branch of the present University of Natal.

The Orange River Colony already had the nucleus of a full university institution in Bloemfontein. Before laying down his life's work, Johannes Brill succeeded in separating the higher division from that of the school and in raising the standard of education offered to that of the Master of Arts degree level. Act 5 of 1910 crowned his efforts by placing the existence of Grey University College on a legal footing in the month before Union. Among the first professors were Adriaan Francken, W. S. Johnson, George Potts and J. H. Woolston. An Orange Free State member of the university Council from 1913, Woolston was to succumb to war wounds five years later. As at all the small colleges, members of staff were responsible for more than one department of study. Francken, who had earlier taught history, Dutch, English, French and German, was still after 1910 in charge of the first two subjects. Johnson not only lectured in English, but also in logic, Potts in 1910 was in charge of both botany and zoology and Woolston was, until 1911, Professor of Pure and Applied Mathematics.

These colleges in the Orange Free State, Natal and the Transvaal were small indeed at the time of Union. At the end of 1910, the college at Pietermaritzburg had 57 students, nearly half of whom were engaged upon legal studies. Grey University College was somewhat larger, with 73 students, twenty fewer than at the Transvaal University College in Pretoria. The School of Mines had 113 students, almost all of whom were working for mining, engineering and legal qualifications. Most of the Cape colleges were equally small in numbers. The third largest was Rhodes University College in Grahamstown, with 125 students. The Huguenot College had only 53 and the Diocesan College, in its last year as an institution of university rank, a mere 24. It was the two rival foundations in Cape Town and Stellenbosch which dominated the collegiate scene. Both the South African College and the Victoria College had enrolments which at that time approached the three hundred mark and the student population was well distributed throughout the various fields of study. Both had grown increasingly restless under the examining system; both stood poised upon the brink of a campaign which would transform the university life of South Africa.

Thoughts of change were present from the first years of the present century. In 1901, Morrison and others at Stellenbosch had felt that some kind of university reorganization was needed and some two years later, Merriman and the then editor of *Ons Land,* F. S. Malan, agreed that the Victoria College was ready for independence. The first positive steps, however, were taken by the South African College in November, 1904, when Thomas Loveday, Fremantle's successor as Professor of Philosophy, successfully moved in Senate the setting up of a committee to look into the question of university reorganization. Loveday was an obvious choice as a member of it and he was joined by six colleagues: the classicists, C. E. Lewis and William Ritchie, the Secretary of Senate, Lawrence Crawford, the energetic Carruthers Beattie, P. D. Hahn of the Department of Chemistry and the zoologist, Arthur Dendy.

The committee sought the opinions of leading educationists the world over on the merits or disadvantages of the association of colleges with a single university, having regard to the uneven stage of development and the geographical separation of South Africa's various higher educational institutions. It was hardly to be expected that the final report would be favourable to any form of federation or to the continued existence of an examining university. The climate of opinion in academic circles was everywhere against both, except in very special circumstances. London was no longer just an examining board; the examining university of Halifax, Nova Scotia had long since vanished without trace; the University of Toronto had ceased to be merely an examining machine; the University of Manitoba was in the process of becoming a teaching institution. Even where the purely examining university survived – in India, Ireland and New Zealand, as well as at the Cape – it was an experiment in higher education largely discredited. As for that closer form of association between colleges in federation, Britain had recently seen the collapse of one such institution – the Victoria University of Manchester – as a result of a desire for independence among its constituents, and particularly at the Liverpool college. The federal University of Wales might have some application to South African conditions, but would be unlikely to appeal to those who saw the South African College as a future university in its own right.

As the University of the Cape of Good Hope was itself seeking collegiate opinion on the future pattern of South African higher education, the South African College decided to publish its Senate committee report. It would be, as Mr Justice Thomas L. Graham put it, a *ballon d'essai* to gauge the degree of support for a unitary university in Cape Town. The views expressed by overseas experts and incorporated in the report were, in the main, highly favourable to South African College pretensions. They were well summed up in a private letter to Beattie from the distinguished British scientist, Lord Kelvin, who wrote in December, 1905 : "I agree with you heartily that your College is ripe for a Charter. I think it ought to be made into an Independent Teaching University and I heartily wish all success to efforts for this good object". The South African College had no hesitation therefore in advancing its claim to full university status and Crawford was only sorry that Johannesburg's Transvaal Technical Institute was not planning similar action which would doubtless have strengthened the claims of the Cape Town institution.

The University of the Cape of Good Hope asked the colleges to report on three main alternatives : maintenance of the existing system, collegiate affiliation with the university or separate charters to individual institutions or to groups of colleges. The South African College viewpoint was made sufficiently clear in its Senate committee report. In general, the other colleges, particularly the smaller ones, preferred amalgamation with the existing university, in part, as Rhodes University College explained, to maintain standards. The Diocesan College was already concerned about the possibility of losing its higher work. Canon R. Brooke would later accuse the South African College, its Stellenbosch neighbour and Rhodes University College of trying to eliminate the Anglican institution through their representatives on the university Council.

The Huguenot College, which was to become a full university college in 1907, with a representative of the Cape University on its governing Council, was seriously concerned to encourage more girls to enrol for its courses. It was therefore in favour of closer association with the examining university if only to obviate the constant competition between the colleges for places. There was much jealousy between the rival institutions and the activities of the college tout did nothing to improve relations. Another solution to its problems occurred to the Wellington foundation at this period. It could, perhaps, amalgamate with its neighbour at Stellenbosch. However, it was not anxious to lose its autonomy and the idea was successfully resisted.

At the Victoria College, there were differences of opinion upon the best course to adopt. Some on the governing body demanded independence, but Senate much preferred the system of affiliation, by means of which the colleges would be brought into closer and more clearly defined relations with the examining university. The differences were finally resolved and a loose federal arrangement was proposed, with separate examination papers for the colleges.

These divergencies in the views of the various colleges were emphasized in a lengthy Convocation debate which took place in April, 1906. The motion which was finally carried was put forward by Morrison of Stellenbosch and Martin of the Diocesan College. It requested that the Council of the University of the Cape of Good Hope "prepare a scheme of reorganization, which, while securing to the various Colleges all wholesome freedom for

105

their courses of work, will maintain the principle of a single central academic authority". This was a rebuff to the South African College and a solution which was widely canvassed at that time. What was important, as Martin pointed out, was that the university system should keep Dutch and English, north and south, together in a country seeking unity. The whole question of organization was in fact being discussed against the background of desires for consultation between the colonial governments on the higher educational issue. With this in mind, W.A. Russell, who had first-hand knowledge of the educational needs of the Orange River Colony, secured an addition to Morrison's motion that Council "take steps to arrange for . . . discussion . . . with representatives of the various South African States".

The University of the Cape of Good Hope had been made aware that the South African College proposal did not enjoy universal support and that many considered its demand for independence premature. Council was prepared to make changes, but it did not consider that the university's usefulness was at an end. Certainly, the colleges should have a greater say in university government and it had, in that connection, already made a small start by allowing assessor members to join Council committees as a sort of embryo Senate. However, at meetings in March and April, 1906, the representatives of the South African College on Council, particularly Beattie and Ritchie, continued to stress the advantages of unitary universities. At the suggestion of H.C. Notcutt and T. Walker of the Victoria College, the university Council decided to appoint a committee to discuss reform again.

The committee consisted of the Vice-Chancellor, C. Abercrombie Smith, his deputy, Sir John Buchanan, F. C. Kolbe, Advocate M. W. Searle, Ritchie and Beattie of the South African College, Morrison and Viljoen of Stellenbosch and the Rev. W.O. Jenkins of the Diocesan College. It was to prepare two schemes for further consideration. The first was for federation or affiliation; the second, for single college universities. The schemes were in due course presented to the colleges and colonial education departments for comment, before they were discussed by the governing body in February, 1907.

Reactions were predictable. The South African College was against federation; the other colleges were in favour, although the Transvaal University College in Johannesburg preferred to await the findings of an inter-colonial conference on education. The Cape University Council wanted a federal solution; so, too, did Convocation, although it, like the Johannesburg college, felt that the views of the other colonies should be taken into consideration. The university Council seems to have been greatly enamoured of its federal proposal and rather reluctant to commit it to the mercies of educationists sitting in inter-colonial conference. However, it came to accept the need and adjourned further discussion of its scheme *sine die*.

The inter-colonial conference, long delayed, at length took place in Cape Town under the chairmanship of Sir William Bisset Berry, then a member of the university Council. The Cape University's nominees, C. Abercrombie Smith, Ritchie, Morrison and Macfadyen, were not given official instructions, but were permitted to reflect the views of "different interests of education". All the members chosen, with the exception of H. J. Hofmeyr of the Witwatersrand School Board and Rhodesia's Attorney General, C. H. Tredgold, were members of the university Council. The Cape government appointed Berry, Schreiner and Muir; from the Orange River Colony came Brill and Gunn; Natal sent C. J. Mudie and Dr James Hyslop; the Transvaal's nominees were, in addition to Hofmeyr, Adamson and Wessels. Ritchie found no seconder for the idea of unitary universities and the conference report of 1908 proposed a federal university, with all colonies represented on the governing body and with a professorial Senate. The conference, however, made one fatal mistake. It decreed that English should be the language of the proposed federal university. The reaction from Dutch speakers throughout South Africa was immediate and violently hostile. *Ons Land* was indignant, Hertzog in Bloemfontein called the *Taalbond* South Africa's second university and there was some

WILLIAM RITCHIE was born on 12 October, 1854 at Peterhead, Aberdeenshire, Scotland, where he received his early education. An outstanding classical scholar at the University of Aberdeen and at Oriel College, Oxford, he also studied at Göttingen.

He began his teaching career as a private coach at Oxford and in 1879 was appointed to the staff of the Grey Institute, Port Elizabeth. In 1882, he accepted a professorship at the South African College, where he remained for 47 years and helped to lay the foundations of the University of Cape Town of today.

Ritchie was a classicist of distinction and published several translations from Plautus and Terence. His detailed *History of the South African College* in two volumes appeared in 1918. His scholarship and contributions to higher education in South Africa did not go unrecognized. In addition to the honorary LL.D. degree conferred upon him by the University of Aberdeen, he received doctorates in literature *honoris causa* from the University of South Africa in 1925 and the University of Cape Town four years later.

A member of the Council of the University of the Cape of Good Hope from 1888 until 1918, he was Vice-Chancellor between 1913 and 1916.

His death occurred at Entebbe in Uganda on 7 September, 1931.

Professor William Ritchie, M.A. (Aber. and Oxon.), LL.D. (h.c.),
D.Litt. (h.c.)(S.A.), D.Litt. (h.c.) (Cape Town)
Member of Council 1888–1918
Pro Vice-Chancellor 1911–1913
Vice-Chancellor 1913–1916
President of Convocation 1904–1914

hostility in the Transvaal legislature to the continuance of an annual grant to the Cape University. The Pretoria *Volkstem* published a declaration by over forty prominent Transvaal citizens, among them the Rev. H.S. Bosman, Professor J. Lion Cachet of Potchefstroom, N. M. Hoogenhout, D. F. du Toit Malherbe and G. S. Preller. It stated that no new university should be created "welke niet aan de Hollandse en Engelse talen een gelijk status zal toekennen".

The conference achieved nothing positive, except that it intensified the campaign for the acceptance of Dutch, forcing the university to give ground on the language issue, and made even more evident the general dissatisfaction with an examining institution. Not surprisingly, the Convocation election for members of the seventh Council in 1909 was the most hotly contested in the history of the University of the Cape of Good Hope. Candidates were put forward on the ticket of the Dutch-speaking teachers' association, the *Onderwijzers Unie,* and another list was presented by the colleges, with support from the rival professional organization, the South African Teachers' Association. The college ticket was markedly successful and the composition of the new Council was not greatly different from that of the old. Its members were to guide the fortunes of the Cape University through momentous years in the history of South Africa and of higher education there.

The new Council did at least begin by making concessions with regard to the use of both official languages in the new Union of South Africa which came into being in 1910. From the following year, candidates could write the Junior Certificate examination in Dutch as well as in English and from 1912, this rule applied also to the Senior Certificate and Matriculation examinations. Hostility to the "English" examining university would, however, be hard to overcome, for, although South Africa had been united politically, sectional differences between English speakers and Afrikaners remained strong. This aspect of South African community life would play a large part in the great debate on higher education which, in 1910, was about to open.

110

The major problem which overshadowed the future of the University of the Cape of Good Hope in 1910 was, however, its restricted function as an examining board and the growing demands to replace it, or to supplement it, by creating a teaching university. If the campaign in this direction had, in the years before 1910, made little progress, the reason is not far to seek. Teaching universities cost money and endowment on a grand scale is needed. Funds were limited in colonial days. The Rhodes gift had been withdrawn and diverted to another purpose and the Transvaal government had seen fit to delay action over Alfred Beit's "University of Johannesburg". Nevertheless, moves were being made behind the scenes in the months before Union and soon a gift was to be offered which would drastically change the higher educational scene and bring into being a "General University of South Africa". The transformation, however, was to take six years of time-consuming discussions, of proposals and of counter-proposals. When the final solution was arrived at, the old University of the Cape of Good Hope would emerge in a different form under a new name and in a new home.

5 *The transformation of the Cape university*

From 1910, higher education became a concern of the national government. Louis Botha chose François Stephanus Malan to be the Union of South Africa's first Minister of Education and he brought to his task a knowledge of problems in this field gained when he had filled a similar position in the Merriman administration at the Cape. Malan was to be ably assisted in the difficult years which lay ahead by the Under-Secretary for Education, George Morgan Hofmeyr, the former Registrar of the Victoria College.

The University of the Cape of Good Hope did what it could in the early years of Union to make itself a more distinctly national body. Having accepted Dutch up to Matriculation level, Council, in 1914 and 1915, responded to requests by permitting the use of that language for degree examination purposes. The second Afrikaans language campaign was already well under way then, but despite the efforts of such leaders in the movement as J. J. Smith and "Tobie" Muller, the university was not prepared to entertain the introduction of a new medium.

The Cape University adopted a more South African outlook in another direction by holding some of its meetings in centres other than Cape Town. Council and its committees not only assembled in the Mother City after 1911, but also in Pretoria, Pietermaritzburg and Bloemfontein. Nevertheless, the Cape institution continued to be assailed from all sides in its capacity as South Africa's examining board for both school children and college students.

Moreover, despite its belated efforts in recognizing the Dutch language, it remained a predominantly English institution. Its official business was conducted almost exclusively in English and it was not until 1916, when it had almost ceased to be, that it at last issued certificates to successful candidates in Dutch. The language of the Netherlands may no longer have been on a par with foreign tongues or with "Kafir" – a designation for Xhosa and Zulu which was dropped in 1913 – but it was still not the equal of English. This was little to the liking of Afrikaners who felt that the success of political unity was in large measure bound up with the fair implementation of language equality guaranteed in the Act of Union. The obstacle to true unity – sectional differences between the two white groups in which language played a vital part – was to loom large in the university debate about to open. It is not surprising, therefore, that F. S. Malan found that, in matters concerning higher education, he was dealing "in questions . . . which affected the heart as well as the head". The Minister of Education was himself able to break through the Cape University's English defences when he addressed the Congregation of February, 1912 in Dutch. It was the first time this had ever been done and Malan remarked in his diary: "Ik maakte geen verschoning". Unfortunately, as was then the custom on Degree Day, undergraduate ebullience resulted in so much noise that the guest speaker was almost inaudible!

In spite of small concessions over language, the University of the Cape of Good Hope was a British imperial institution and as such, took part in the first Congress of the Universities of the Empire, held in London in 1912. Alexander Mackenzie of the Victoria College attended as the university's official representative. The *Star* of Johannesburg, voicing the current dissatisfaction with examining universities, felt that it was a pity that a few South African Cabinet Ministers had not been present in order to find out what a university really was! The Cape Town institution was an insignificant and badly worn cog in an educational movement which a delegate, writing in the journal, *United Empire,* pompously described as "the regular and rhythmic pro-

113

On the death of Mr Justice C.T. Smith, Convocation elected H. R. H. THE DUKE OF CORNWALL AND YORK to succeed him as sixth Chancellor.

The second son of the then Prince of Wales (later King Edward VII), Prince George was born at Marlborough House, London on 3 June, 1865. He joined the Royal Navy as a cadet in 1877, saw service on the North American and West Indian station and rose to command the gunboat, H.M.S. *Thrush*. In 1892, he relinquished his commission and was created Duke of York.

In 1901, he and his wife visited Australia, South Africa and Canada. He was installed as Chancellor at the graduation ceremony in Cape Town on 21 August, retaining office until he resigned in 1912. Among the many honorary degrees conferred upon him during his world tour was the LL.D. of the University of the Cape of Good Hope. He also held the office of Chancellor of the University of Wales from 1902 until 1921.

The Duke was created Prince of Wales in November, 1901 and became King George V on the death of his father on 6 May, 1910. He died on 20 January, 1936 at Sandringham House in Norfolk and was buried in St George's Chapel, Windsor Castle.

H.R.H. The Duke of Cornwall and York
(later Prince of Wales and His Majesty King George V)
Chancellor 1901–1912

gress of an imperial advance". One result of the conference was the establishment of the Universities Bureau with which the Cape University was associated from the outset. Two former South African College professors, R. F. A. Hoernlé and Thomas Loveday, served successively upon the organizing committee.

The university also maintained another imperial link in its choice of Chancellor. His Majesty the King-Emperor George V had been elected in 1901 by Convocation when he was still the Duke of Cornwall and York. As an enduring sign of the connection between Royal House and colonial university, the coat of arms granted in 1903 to the University of the Cape of Good Hope at the request of the new Chancellor, then the Prince of Wales, bore the rose irradiated of York between twin annulets of fealty. The King found it necessary to relinquish the chancellorship in 1912, but Convocation chose another member of the Royal Family, the Duke of Connaught and Strathearn, to take his place.

The first World War brought the University of the Cape of Good Hope into even closer contact with the clash of ideals which Union had failed to end in South Africa. Hostilities themselves caused problems enough. There were difficulties over the supply of examination papers, still printed in England; the music examiners of 1914 were unavoidably detained when the mailboats were held up; German submarines made travel to Europe dangerous for scholarship holders. Official functions, too, had to be postponed, the last Council election was delayed and the meetings of that body and its committees in centres other than Cape Town were abandoned.

As in the Anglo-Boer War, the University of the Cape of Good Hope tried to carry out its examining obligations with impartiality. Concessions were offered to members of the armed forces and the university authorities ultimately admitted such students to degrees without examination under certain stipulated conditions. There are occasional references to the need for caution in the circumstances of the time, although the suggestion that British parentage be first ascertained before awarding

116

scholarships or that the Vice-Chancellor should pay special attention to the character of the B.A. German papers seem examples of unnecessary vigilance. However, the Cape University helped both war prisoners and internees, while the son of an enemy alien was not debarred from obtaining an exhibition award. It was also decided that candidates would not be prevented from writing examinations because they had taken part in the ill-starred rebellion of 1914. The university was not prepared, however, to present a degree *ad eundem gradum* to the Rev. W.P. Steenkamp, convicted of sedition.

The case of S. P. E. Boshoff, who would subsequently enjoy a long and honourable career in the cause of South African education and in the service of the Cape University's successor, was the subject of a close and lengthy investigation by the university authorities. Boshoff had been awarded a Queen Victoria Scholarship in modern languages and, when war broke out, was studying at the Municipal University in Amsterdam. He returned to South Africa in November, 1914 and went to his home in Senekal where, in his own words, he "got mixed up in an unexpected way with the rebellion". Boshoff was captured at the Vaal River at the time when General Christiaan Beyers was drowned, was then interned at Kimberley and Bloemfontein and finally released with other rank-and-file participants. The Cape University had been prepared to accept his absence from his studies after a talk he had had with the Registrar, William Thomson, when he arrived in Cape Town. However, when the full story came out, the scholarship award was cancelled. M. W. Searle suggested that he forfeit only the instalment due to him for the period of his involvement in the rebellion, but this was overruled.

It was against the background of British imperialism, Afrikaner nationalism and a world war which, so far as it concerned South Africa, showed how far the new nation had to travel before it could claim to be really united, that the struggle to reform the Cape University took place. There was no doubt that by 1910, the old institution had outgrown its usefulness and if, in the first

Witness ourself &c &c &c

Edward the Seventh by the Grace of God of the United Kingdom of Great Britain and Ireland and of the British Dominions beyond the Seas, King, Defender of the Faith, Emperor of India, To Our Right Trusty and Right Entirely beloved Cousin and Councillor Henry Duke of Norfolk Earl Marshal and Our Hereditary Marshal of England, Knight of Our Most Noble Order of the Garter and Knight Grand Cross of Our Royal Victorian Order, Greeting **Whereas** Our Most Dear Son and Councillor His Royal Highness George Frederick Ernest Albert Prince of Wales, Knight of Our Most Noble Order of the Garter, Knight of Our Most Ancient and Most Noble Order of the Thistle, Knight of Our Most Illustrious Order of Saint Patrick, Knight Grand Cross of Our Most Distinguished Order of Saint Michael and Saint George, Knight Grand Cross of Our Royal Victoria

Licence— The University of the Cape of Good Hope, to bear certain Armorial Ensigns.

The following description of the university's coat of arms appears in the ROYAL LICENCE of 7 October, 1903, given at Balmoral by command of His Majesty King Edward VII:

"An Anchor with cable fessewise, surmounted by an open Book inscribed with the words 'Spes in arduis', in base a Wall embattled, thereon an Annulet, on a Chief a Rose irradiated, being a representation of the Rose of York, used by King Edward the Fourth, between two Annulets; The Motto, 'Spes in arduis' as on the Book in the Arms, the whole as in the drawing hereunto annexed, the same being first duly exemplified and recorded in Our College of Arms, otherwise this Our Royal Licence and Permission to be void and of none effect.

Our will and pleasure therefore is that you Henry, Duke of Norfolk to whom the cognizance of matters of this nature doth properly belong do require and command that this Our Concession and Especial Mark of Our Royal Favour be registered in Our College of Arms, to the end that Our Officers of Arms and all others upon occasion may take full notice and have knowledge thereof; And for so doing this shall be your Warrant.

Given at Our Court at Balmoral this seventh day of October, 1903, in the Third year of Our Reign.

By His Majesty's command.

A. AKERS DOUGLAS.

Recorded in the College of Arms, London, pursuant to a Warrant from the Earl Marshal of England."

First Page of Royal Licence for Armorial Bearings, 1903

flush of a new political alignment, university reform was not a major issue, it was by no means a forgotten one. John Edgar, the first incumbent of the Prince of Wales Chair of History at the South African College, advocated a teaching university at this period; Thomas Muir, the Superintendent General of Education at the Cape, remained a keen supporter of that ideal; the problem was also debated at the colleges and in the university Council. In the eyes of many at the Cape, something new was wanted and there was little enthusiasm for the idea that running repairs might be carried out on the existing machinery. The financier, Sir Lewis Michell, let it be known in October, 1910 that the site for a new teaching institution was still available at Groote Schuur; all that was needed to start the reform ball rolling was the money.

That, as the Governor-General, Viscount Gladstone, hinted when parliament assembled on 4 November, would soon be forthcoming. Jan Smuts had seen to this by following up discussions with Otto Beit and Sir Julius Wernher in 1909. He had written to them in the following year, asking them whether they would be prepared to add to the Frankenwald bequest in order to found a national teaching university. Both were enthusiastic. Wernher offered another R400 000 and he and Beit undertook to bring the sum up to one million rands. Soon, De Beers were to add a further R50 000 to the available funds.

The donors spoke of "equal opportunities for all", implying thereby no emphasis upon multiracialism; F. S. Malan was also thinking along similar lines as he travelled south for the opening of parliament. There was, however, a difference, for he, unlike Otto Beit and Wernher, equated "equal opportunities" with "equal language rights". However, the possibility of serious conflict was not apparent when the public announcement of the Wernher-Beit bequest was made by Malan on 5 November, 1910 at the Camps Bay luncheon which followed the laying of the memorial stone of the Cape University's new hall by the Duke of Connaught. Malan hoped to see an institution arise at Groote Schuur which would incorporate all the colleges. Such a university, he said, in words reminiscent of Cecil Rhodes, would "weld the races of the country into one".

Almost immediately, there was a sharp reaction from the Afrikaner section. What would the position of the Victoria College be? In what form would it be incorporated in the proposed Groote Schuur institution? The college position would have to be carefully considered and *festina lente* was the warning cry, reinforced by a deputation to F. S. Malan which included J. I. Marais, Adriaan Moorrees, J. G. van der Horst and a future Nationalist Minister of Education, D. F. Malan. A Vigilance Committee was formed to safeguard Stellenbosch interests.

The University of the Cape of Good Hope also discussed the future at some length, seeking the views of the various colleges before coming to any definite conclusion. Its final report recommended the establishment of a national teaching university, but not, as some had been suggesting, a purely post-graduate one. It further pointed out that a teaching university with a full range of undergraduate and post-graduate work, "would be incompatible with the continued existence of . . . Colleges . . . in its neighbourhood". Council considered that, as only the South African College and the Victoria College would be likely to merge in any Groote Schuur university, the other colleges should be allowed to affiliate with it. Nothing, in fact, was to be done which would harm any of the more distant colleges. Finally, as the Cape University did not wish to see itself destroyed in any new scheme, Schreiner's proposal that the teaching university should be developed from the existing examining university was also adopted.

The colleges agreed that the time had come for a national teaching university, but there was no unanimity beyond that point. The School of Mines hoped to become the technological faculty of the new university; Wessels, now Sir John and chairman of the Council of the Transvaal University College in Pretoria, put up a strong case for a post-graduate university. This, he felt, would be preferred by Afrikaners since it would cater for

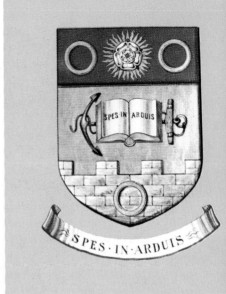

Emblem before 1903

*Coat of arms as shown
in the Royal Licence*

The university's COAT OF ARMS is described in the Royal Licence of 1904 (see p. 119).

The Rose of York was incorporated in the official armorial bearings to honour the Prince of Wales who, as Duke of Cornwall and York, had been installed as Chancellor in 1901. The battlements symbolize Good Hope Castle and the three annulets were included to represent Van Riebeeck. The open book bearing the words *Spes in Arduis* is the central feature in both the earlier emblem of the university and the coat of arms granted by King Edward VII.

The motto *Spes in Arduis* ("hope through difficulties") is attributed to the Cape judge and writer, Egidius Benedictus Watermeyer, first President of the Board of Public Examiners in Literature and Science.

*Coat of arms as represented by
the College of Arms*

THE
UNIVERSITY
OF THE
CAPE OF GOOD HOPE

The foundation-stone of the first section of the U N I V E R S I T Y B U I L D I N G in Queen Victoria Street, Cape Town was laid by the Governor, Sir Walter Hely-Hutchinson, on 24 February, 1906. The ceremony was a memorable social occasion.

The appearance of the completed structure was outlined in the programme of proceedings:

> "The central feature of the University Building will be the Grand Aula or Ceremonial Hall, and round this will be grouped on three faces the suites of Administration rooms. The general treatment of the elevation is in the style of the Italian Renaissance. The Hall is in plan an adaptation of that of the ancient Greek Theatre, a form eminently suitable for an auditorium . . . Ample provision has been made for the embellishment of the Hall by means of paintings, etc., in the panels of the walls and ceiling".

It was further stated that South African materials had been chosen for the construction: "the base in Paarl Granite and the superstructure in Flatpan Stone from the Orange River Colony".

When the hall was formally opened in 1913, the future of the University of the Cape of Good Hope was already in the balance. Its sucessor in Pretoria was at length compelled to dispose of the property in 1932, at a figure considerably below the municipal valuation of approximately £55 000 (R110 000). The building today houses the Cape Archives.

The University Building, Cape Town, 1907

125

H. R. H. THE DUKE OF CONNAUGHT AND STRATHEARN was chosen by Convocation in 1912 to succeed His Majesty King George V as Chancellor.

Prince Arthur William Patrick Albert was born at Buckingham Palace, London on 1 May, 1850. The third son and seventh child of Queen Victoria, he was invested as Duke of Connaught and Strathearn in 1874.

After training at Woolwich, he began his military career in 1868, rising to the rank of Field-Marshal in 1902. He fought at Tel-el-Kebir in 1882, served in India from 1886 to 1890 and was later Commander-in-Chief in Ireland and in the Mediterranean area. From 1911 until 1916, he was Governor-General of Canada.

The Duke of Connaught came to South Africa in 1910 to open the first Union parliament. On that occasion, he laid the foundation-stone of the new university hall and received the honorary degree of Doctor of Laws. His son, Prince Arthur of Connaught, was Governor-General of South Africa from 1920 to 1923.

The Duke died at Bagshot Park, Surrey on 16 January, 1942 and was buried in the royal mausoleum at Frogmore in Berkshire, near Windsor Castle.

Field-Marshal H.R.H. The Duke of Connaught
and Strathearn, K.G., K.T., K.P., P.C.
Chancellor 1912–1942

126

more mature students who would better be able to withstand the dangers of a cosmopolitan atmosphere away from home! The post-graduate university or research institute had initially some attraction for the smaller colleges, as it would preserve their separate identities. All of them, however, the Pretoria college excepted, came at length to have reservations about such an institution. If the proposed Groote Schuur university were to be composed of the South African and Victoria Colleges in amalgamation, then a federal solution might be the best answer for the other colleges.

The South African College would have nothing to do with federation; the new university would have to be a single, national teaching institution, purely residential, except for the handful of private students who might wish to make use of its examinations. The Victoria College, however, fearful of losing its special character as the higher educational centre for the Afrikaner section, was only willing to associate with the Cape Town college in the proposed venture if both kept their separate identities within the framework of the new university.

F. S. Malan had, therefore, to satisfy many different viewpoints and, in the nature of things, it is not surprising that he took his time in framing a bill. Viscount Gladstone, speaking on Degree Day in February, 1911, gave those who favoured a federal solution to the university problem some encouragement. Malan himself, visiting Europe later in that year in connection with the imperial education conference held in London, took the opportunity of seeing how two federal systems in the British Isles worked and how far they met the problems of distance and twin cultures. The University of Wales, established in 1893, had achieved some success, but it was, even as early as 1911, subject to stresses. The day of the unitary civic university had dawned in neighbouring England and some at the Cardiff college looked enviously at the flourishing independent universities in Manchester, Liverpool and Leeds which had emerged from the former federal Victoria University. However, Principal E. H. Griffiths of Cardiff, then Vice-Chancellor of the University of Wales, spoke to Malan of the value of a federal system as a cohesive force in the Principality.

In Ireland, Malan met President B. C.A. Windle of University College, Cork, a foundation which, until 1908, had been associated with the examining Royal University. The new National University of Ireland which had then come into being was a federal institution with three widely scattered constituents, one of which – that at Galway – would at length become a noted centre for graduate studies in a number of fields through the medium of the Irish language. Already, the principle of compulsory Irish for Matriculation had been accepted by the federal university. Here, perhaps, was a model which the bicultural Union of South Africa might follow with profit. The Minister of Education must have noticed, too, that a fourth college in Belfast had been granted independent status. It stood apart from the others in many ways and was by far the most developed. Were there not analogies to be seen in the South African context – in Cape Town, in Stellenbosch or, perhaps, in Johannesburg?

It was said of Viscount Gladstone's distinguished father that whenever his government was riding for a fall, it chose the subject of university reform in the British Isles as a horse! Higher education in South Africa was not, perhaps, quite so intractable a topic as that, but there is no doubt that Malan's first bill satisfied nobody. In the first place, it upset the University of the Cape of Good Hope by decreeing the dissolution of that institution. Then, it insisted on a post-graduate university, when for most people such a foundation would only be a costly luxury, designed mainly to ensure the continued existence of the colleges. Furthermore, the bill took no account of the possibility of a merger of the Victoria and South African Colleges and proposed a federal relationship between the colleges and the proposed university. Finally, Malan insisted on referring to the need for linguistic equality. In so doing, it would almost seem as though he were bent upon setting the donors against him.

The bill was shelved and with it disappeared another, designed to make further financial provision for higher education. This legislation had been based upon the findings of a commission appointed under the chairmanship of the university Registrar. The Thomson Commission of 1911 had gathered much useful evidence in the course of a tour of the colleges. Not the least startling fact which emerged from its findings was that, while the annual *per capita* cost to government of educating a Victoria College student was approximately R66 and was nowhere higher in the Cape Province than R114 at Rhodes University College, the *per capita* cost at the four colleges in the other provinces ranged from R198 at Pretoria to R284 at the School of Mines in Johannesburg!

The disadvantages of a purely post-graduate university were stressed by J. E. Deurden, the zoologist at the Grahamstown college, whose knowledge of Johns Hopkins University in Baltimore made him well qualified to speak of that institution's early attempt to concentrate upon the training of research students. The disadvantages of any sort of university other than the unitary type were skilfully brought before the public in a series of lively articles in the *Cape Times* which appeared between March and June, 1912. South Africa, it was demonstrated, should look to the civic universities of England, and particularly to that at Liverpool, for there could be seen the proof that research and great teaching could thrive in an institution serving a populous commercial centre.

The donors were not dissatisfied with the language aspect alone. In January, 1912, their legal adviser, Bourchier F. Hawksley, enumerated other objections. He stated that a post-graduate institution was undesirable, that government control was likely to be too stringent and that Malan had been too conciliatory to college interests. Malan was both disappointed and frustrated and spoke of introducing legislation "met of zonder overeenkomst met Beit en Wernher". The proffered financial aid was, however, a tempting bait, although the task of winning the approval of the trustees was made more difficult after the death of Wernher in May, 1912. For the mining magnate directed that his

130

contribution could only be made if the constitution of the future university were approved by two influential South African figures, Lionel Phillips and Leander Starr Jameson.

Negotiations continued with the trustees and in January, 1913, Malan published a second bill which enjoyed the very unenthusiastic support of Otto Beit, Phillips and Jameson. This proposed the Intermediate B.A. examination as an entrance qualification, the perpetuation of the Cape University in the proposed new institution, the creation of local faculties at colleges which remained separate and the merging into the new institution of those colleges which wished to do so. On the language issue, Malan compromised by promising no more than that bilingualism would be fostered where possible.

By this time, Stellenbosch opposition to incorporation within the new university had grown stronger; moreover, the crisis which resulted in the split between Botha and Hertzog and the formation of a National Party brought the future of the Victoria College even more plainly into the picture as a political issue. Adriaan Moorrees, D. F. Malan and J. G. van der Horst, in the name of the Vigilance Committee, rose to the defence of the college when the bill was published. They pointed out that the Groote Schuur scheme had no roots in South African history and that the Victoria College stood for a cherished ideal in the eyes of many Afrikaners. That section, as the former Free State President, M. T. Steyn had said, would never sell its children for half a million pounds. Some in the Dutch Reformed *(Neder-duitse Gereformeerde)* Church, among them the Revs B. P. J. Marchand, H. P. van der Merwe and D. J. Pienaar, were not opposed to Groote Schuur; the great majority, however, sided with the Ermelo minister, the Rev. Paul Nel, and the Rev. Muller of the seminary in looking with suspicion upon the whole scheme. The trouble, as Muller pointed out in a letter to *Ons Land* in February, 1913, was that Malan, as a result of the gift which made all things possible, had his hands tied in his efforts to establish a university which would find favour with both white sections.

131

With all this, English-speaking South Africa was out of sympathy. Some were disillusioned and wished that the bequest could be allocated to promote study abroad. The bill, in fact, aroused so much protest that it was referred to a select committee of the House of Assembly which recommended a full-scale enquiry by an impartial commission. This was duly appointed and Sir Perceval Maitland Laurence was chosen as Chairman. He was joined by two South Africans, Melius de Villiers, formerly Chief Justice of the Orange Free State, and the Rev. H. S. Bosman of the Dutch Reformed *(Nederduitse Gereformeerde)* Church in Pretoria. The fourth member was John Perry, Professor of Mechanics at the Royal College of Science in London. Wilfred G. R. Murray, the Cape University's Assistant Registrar, acted as Secretary. Laurence found this "a queer team to drive", but in 1914, it at length produced a report, with some reservations from Perry.

The Laurence Commission advocated two federations, a northern and a southern, the latter having its seat at Groote Schuur. The School of Mines was to be the technological faculty for both groups. The college at Grahamstown would have to decide which federation suited it best. The bequest was to be divided. The lion's share, R700 000, would go to Groote Schuur, with R50 000 each to the colleges at Stellenbosch and Grahamstown. In recognition of Alfred Beit's original gift to the Transvaal, R100 000 each were allocated to the proposed northern university and to the School of Mines and R50 000 to the Johannesburg Council of Education. There was some talk that the creation of a northern university might bring Southern Rhodesia closer to the Union; that territory did at least begin in 1915 to contribute to the funds of the Cape University under the 1875 Extension Act.

The report did not please many. Some, among them John Perry, felt that to deprive one institution of the whole bequest would prevent the founding of the type of university which the trustees had in mind. The unitary university enthusiasts looked with no favour upon federation. Even the Commissioners saw it only as a transitional phase, for as they admitted: "Federal

132

government is essentially weak government". Nevertheless, although the report would never be acted upon in its entirety, the federal idea remained. This form of association was, in any case, coming to appeal more and more to the smaller colleges, some of which feared both the power of the western Cape institutions and the threat which Groote Schuur might pose to their own positions.

H. E. S. Fremantle, too, saw a solution in temporary federation while the smaller colleges grew towards independence. Just as the Minister of Education had done in 1911, Fremantle, by now in Hertzog's political camp, paid a visit to Britain in 1913, meeting Principal Griffiths of Cardiff and other university men. He also saw Jameson, Otto Beit and the South African High Commissioner in London, Sir Richard Solomon. Beit was evidently particularly worried at this time, fearing that Afrikaners would insist upon compulsory bilingualism. This was a very real anxiety then and later in the English language institutions, for if the teaching staffs were to be bilingual, good men from abroad would probably not apply for posts.

W. G. R. Murray observed later that the Cape University Registrar, Thomson, and the future Principal of the Cape Town college, Carruthers Beattie, were the main opponents in the reform struggle. Thomson enjoyed considerable prestige, although Murray felt that Beattie had the advantage, as he was a good mixer and was the friend of such influential people as the Cape Town businessman and college benefactor, J. W. Jagger, and the editor of the *Cape Times*, Thomas Maitland Park. The contest did not lie entirely between them, however, and Thomson's role in the discussions is perhaps exaggerated. Beattie, on the other hand, was certainly the leading figure on the South African College staff in the campaign for a teaching university.

Maitland Park was not the only newspaperman to lend support to the college; G. A. L. Green of the *Argus* was also active and later served as a representative of the executors of Alfred Beit and Sir Julius Wernher on the provisional committee which at length brought an independent university into being in the

133

Mother City. On the Stellenbosch side, the Victoria College gained additional support after 1915, when the National Party's newspaper in Cape Town, the *Burger,* began publication under the editorship of D. F. Malan.

Little had been heard of the University of the Cape of Good Hope during those days of proposals and counter-proposals for university reform. The college members of its Council, understandably enough, would have been only too pleased to see the end of the examining institution and there is no doubt that the university no longer carried quite the same weight in discussions on the future of higher education in South Africa.

The Laurence Commission solved nothing and, with the coming of the first World War and armed rebellion, men's thoughts were, for a time, directed into other channels. However, it was in the first full year of the world struggle that a key was found to unlock the door barring progress towards a solution to the university question. When J. H. Marais of Coetzenburg died in May, 1915, he left R200 000 to the Victoria College. The Rev. C. F. J. Muller, who died in the same year, had hoped to see at Stellenbosch the creation of an "echte Hollandsch-Afrikaansche Universiteit" and this now became a practical possibility. F. S. Malan had played his part in securing the gift for the college; it was to enable him to pass the legislation which he would come to regard, rightly, as his major achievement as Minister of Education.

In the same year, the South African College decided to approach the trustees with proposals which would make it the sole heir to the Wernher-Beit bequest. Agreement was finally reached at a London meeting attended by Beit, Jameson, Phillips, Hawksley and Maitland Park, now a member of the South African College Council and then on holiday in Britain. In the parliamentary elections of 1915, the South African Party retained power, with Unionist support, and Malan was able to plan his legislation, reasonably secure in the knowledge that the Nationalists would not oppose reform measures which would give the Victoria College independence. This proved to be the case, although Fremantle felt that the institution there had been robbed in order to benefit the South African College, now to be incorporated in a new University of Cape Town.

For the smaller institutions, Malan proposed a federal university which would inherit the traditions, the assets, the Royal Charter and the armorial bearings of the University of the Cape of Good Hope. It was decided, to the regret of some, to move its administrative headquarters from Cape Town. The main contenders for the federal seat were Bloemfontein, Johannesburg and Pretoria. A majority of college representatives favoured the mining metropolis, but this view was overruled and Pretoria was eventually chosen. Various names were suggested for the new institution. The Cape University Council in committee suggested the inclusion of the word "Federal" in the title; the South African College Senate proposed either the "Royal" or "King George's University"; even the idea of a "Malan University" was somewhat maliciously canvassed! The final choice – the "University of South Africa" – was considered in some quarters to be too dignified a title for a mere collection of colleges which would ultimately seek independence. It certainly did not please the supporters of the teaching universities in the western Cape that what they considered an inferior competitor should bear a national name.

The colleges which would come under the wing of the new university were generally well satisfied with the federal arrangement. For tiny Huguenot it was the only possible answer, although none of them was yet large enough to contemplate independence. The Natal University College regretted the failure of the national university ideal and there was some talk at Bloemfontein of amalgamation with the Transvaal University College, a possible prelude to greater centralization. The Pretoria college was seen by some as the major constituent, occupying a position in relation to the federal university similar to that which the South African College had held for so long in the Cape University system.

There was, inevitably, little enthusiasm on the Rand for the university proposals. Johannesburg considered that it had been unfairly treated, particularly as the South African College in Cape Town had alone inherited the Wernher-Beit bequest, together with a magnificent site at Groote Schuur for future expansion. The School of Mines, the Council of Education and other interested parties tried hard to block the proposed legislation in a last-ditch attempt to salvage something from the wrecked hopes of a great civic university in the north. Several Rand members of the House of Assembly did their best to further the city's claims in parliament; George S. Corstorphine, the Principal of the School of Mines, William Dalrymple of the Council of Education and Mayor J. W. O'Hara of Johannesburg worked tirelessly to enlist public support for a Witwatersrand university. All efforts, however, proved unavailing and, apart from interest on the original bequest from Alfred Beit, Johannesburg received nothing from the moneys donated for university development. The South African School of Mines and Technology had to prove itself before it was able to become a real university college and not merely a technological institute. It became clear that future greatness would depend upon local effort and although the Johannesburg institution co-operated loyally with the federal university, it inaugurated, with the aid of a Witwatersrand University Committee, a campaign for full university status. The School of Mines had the support of the City Council, which provided it with the campus at Milner Park.

It is Act 12 of 1916 – the federal part of the legislative trilogy – which is of the greatest importance in the continuing history of the University of the Cape of Good Hope under its new title. The Cape institution debated all three bills in February, 1916 and made a number of suggestions. One of these, proposed by Fremantle, was that the constituent colleges of the federal university should have the right to promote legislation which would lead to their secession. The School of Mines in Johannesburg was expressly named as a college which, if it so requested, could be separated from the University of South Africa by proclamation in the *Government Gazette.*

136

The religious neutrality which was a feature of the Cape University was maintained in the Incorporation Acts of all three of its successors. The so-called "conscience clause", however, would come to be regarded in some Afrikaner circles as restrictive and unchristian. Some of the controversial features of the old examining institution fell away in the constitution and regulations of the federal university. The mixed degree and the Intermediate B.A. examination disappeared, the practice of awarding degrees *ad eundem gradum* was discontinued and internal college examiners were permitted.

Although examinations in music and for the Junior Certificate school examination remained functions of the federal university, other non-graduate work was handed over to new bodies, whose affairs the University of South Africa merely administered. A Joint Matriculation Board was created to deal with the university entrance examination for all South African universities, while a Joint Committee for Professional Examinations took over the work in these fields which had previously been the responsibility of the Cape University. Scholarships and other awards were allocated to all three universities on an equitable basis, having regard to any special provisions made by the donors. Holders of certificates or diplomas issued by the old university, the School of Mines or the former South African Republic could be recognized as graduates of the University of South Africa if their qualifications were considered of sufficient standing. Cape University Convocation members were, naturally, permitted to join the university Convocation of their choice.

Private students, although few at that period, were not forgotten, for the admission of external candidates to degree examinations was no longer to be permissive, but a legal obligation of the federal university. Some of these worked alone, but others attended schools or unaffiliated colleges. It had long been the custom for certain secondary schools to enter promising candidates for the university's higher examinations, although with the coming of the federal university, this practice would soon come to an end. Students attending the Arts Department of the Re-

ACT NO. 12 OF 1916 decreed that the University of the Cape of Good Hope was to be incorporated in a federal University of South Africa. The change was to be effected on 2 April, 1918.

Although there was no break in the continuity of the university, despite its new title, its constitution was radically amended. Control was vested in a Council and Senate, upon which six constituent colleges were represented. The central administrative body was responsible for such functions as the organization of examinations, the tabulation of results and the issue of certificates.

When this Act was passed, two other Acts transformed the Victoria College into the University of Stellenbosch and incorporated the South African College in a University of Cape Town.

Act No. 12 of 1916

Act No. 12 of 1916.

BE IT ENACTED by the King's Most Excellent Majesty, the Senate and the House of Assembly of the Union of South Africa as follows:—

INCORPORATION AND SEAT OF THE UNIVERSITY.

University of the Cape of Good Hope to become and be incorporated in a federal university on appointed day.

1. (1) Upon a date to be fixed by the Governor-General by proclamation in the *Gazette* (hereinafter referred to as "the appointed day"), the University of the Cape of Good Hope (which is incorporated and governed under the laws specified in the First Schedule to this Act and is hereinafter referred to as "the old university") shall become and be incorporated in a federal university.

(2) Such university (hereinafter referred to as "the University") shall exist for such purposes, with such constitution, and with such rights, powers, privileges and duties as are described in this Act, and shall, subject to the provisions of this Act and of any other law, be recognised as the successor of the University of the Cape of Good Hope.

Name and administrative seat of the University.

2. The name of the University shall be "the University of South Africa," and its administrative seat shall be at Pretoria.

Constituent colleges of the University.

3. (1) The institutions specified in the Second Schedule to this Act shall, subject to the provisions hereinafter contained, be constituent colleges of the University, and the relationship which each such college shall bear to the University shall be as provided by this Act and by the statutes hereinafter defined.

(2) Notwithstanding anything in this Act contained, the provisions of any law whereby any such institution is incorporated or governed shall remain in force and the provisions of every such law and any rules or regulations made thereunder shall, subject to the provisions of sub-section (3), continue to be construed as if this Act had not been passed.

(3) Nothing in this Act or in any other law contained shall be construed as preventing the council of a constituent college from establishing such faculties or departments as it may deem fit: Provided that it shall not, without the consent of the Governor General, apply towards the maintenance of a faculty or department not established at the commencement of this Act any money granted to the college from public funds.

(4) The council of any constituent college shall have power to promote legislation providing for the incorporation of such college as a university.

CONSTITUTION AND GOVERNMENT OF THE UNIVERSITY.

Constitution of the University.

4. The University shall consist of—

(*a*) a chancellor;
(*b*) a vice-chancellor;
(*c*) a council;
(*d*) a senate;
(*e*) convocation;

formed *(Gereformeerde)* Church seminary at Potchefstroom, however, would be regarded as external candidates for the examinations of the University of South Africa unless the authorities there sought the incorporation of a college and applied to have it admitted as a constituent of the federal institution. The best avenue to choose for the future prosperity of higher education in Potchefstroom was already the subject of earnest discussion there in the closing years of the University of the Cape of Good Hope.

The links which would bind the constituent colleges to the federal mother were more substantial than anything which had marked the relationship of colleges with the examining university. They were now to be an integral part of the federation, with professors and heads of department forming a legally constituted Senate and with one representative of each of their own Senates and Councils taking a scat on the governing Council of the University of South Africa. The federal university retained the right enjoyed by its predecessor of having a representative on the governing body of the Huguenot College and also continued to appoint nominees to the Council of the recently established South African Native College. This foundation was not a constituent of the federal institution and would not, for some years, undertake work of university level.

The three University Acts became law on 27 April, 1916, receiving in due course the customary approval of the British parliament. A Statutes Commission was appointed to give effect to the legislation so that the new universities could begin operations on the appointed day, 2 April, 1918. The members of the commission – Melius de Villiers, assisted by Thomson for the university, Beattie and G.G. Cillié for the major Cape colleges, Viljoen for the smaller ones and with Wilfred Murray as Secretary – faced no easy task. As Murray later told the Under-Secretary, George Hofmeyr, "I wonder whether anyone dreamed what an Augean stable you were turning us loose on". The statutes were, however, framed in time and given legal effect by Amendment Act 9 of 1918, while financial relations between

140

government and the universities and university colleges were regulated by Act 20 of the previous year.

Malan had triumphed over all obstacles and the bequest had been won at last, even if its final destination was not to everyone's liking. On Degree Day in 1917, a grateful Cape University conferrred upon the Minister of Education an honorary doctorate in laws as some reward for his achievement. Although, as Vice-Chancellor Searle said at the last graduation ceremony in Cape Town in the following year, the university would live on, the end of an era had been reached. The Cape Town building, for which Sir John Buchanan had striven so hard, was leased to the South African College which, even before its incorporation into the University of Cape Town, was beginning to burst at the seams. There, towards the end of March, 1918, a visitor found history being taught "in een zijzaaltje" and "in de grote zaal beneden, met plek voor omtrent 300 mensen vond ik in een hoekje een professor met 4 of 5 mannetjes bezig". The Cape University's headquarters – long the haunt of examiners and committee-men – had at last become a place of instruction.

The University of the Cape of Good Hope had outlived its usefulness, but its contribution to the progress of higher education in South Africa had been considerable. It had provided an impartial forum to judge the intellectual abilities of thousands of young men and women at the Cape and beyond its borders and its courses of study and examinations had done much to stimulate national collegiate growth. The new teaching universities at Cape Town and Stellenbosch had an assured future. Could the same be said of the federal University of South Africa? For how long would its constituents be content to remain within the fold? There were many who had little faith in a federal organization as a permanent solution to the university problem. It did not, as *Ons Land* pointed out, create the ideal type of university. Would the University of South Africa therefore be no more than a temporary experiment in the further development of South African higher education? The future would decide.

THE LAST COUNCIL MEETING of the University of the Cape of Good Hope was held on 15 March, 1918. Already, at a meeting in February, a vote of thanks had been passed to those who had long served the university: Professor P.D. Hahn, who had been elected by Convocation to the first Council in 1876; the Rev. Professor J.I. Marais, a member since 1883; the Rev. Dr F.C. Kolbe and J.R. Whitton, who had joined in 1885; Dr William Thomson, the Registrar, who had been chosen as a Council member in the same year as Professor Marais; and Sir John Buchanan and Professor William Ritchie, members since 1888.

Some at this final gathering looked forward eagerly to the coming of a greater university; there was sadness, too, however, for whatever the shortcomings of the examining institution, it had achieved much in the brief history of South African higher education.

On the following day, the last graduation ceremony of the University of the Cape of Good Hope was held and the Vice-Chancellor, Mr Justice Searle, delivered the address. His theme was, appropriately: "Exit the old; enter the new".

Last Council of the University of the Cape of Good Hope, 1918

Rear (l. to r.): Dr G.S. Corstorphine; Dr A.I. Perold; Rev. A.P. Bender; D.J. Ackermann; C. Murray; Dr G.G. Cillié; Dr W.A. Macfadyen; Rev. N.J. Brümmer; Dr S. Schonland; Dr C.F. Juritz; Dr W. Thomson (Registrar); Rev. Dr W. Flint.

Centre (l. to r.): J.R. Whitton; J.E. Adamson; W. Ritchie; J.T. Morrison; Mr Justice M.W. Searle; Rev. Dr F.C. Kolbe; Sir John Buchanan; Dr J.C. Beattie; Rev. Dr J.I. Marais; Sir John Kotzé.

Front (l. to r.): Rev. J.M. Russell; Rev. D.G. Malan; W.G.R. Murray (Asst Registrar); Rev. Dr L. Sormany; Sir W. Bisset Berry; Dr P.D. Hahn; Dr W.J. Viljoen; Rev. A. Moorrees; Sir John Wessels; Dr A. Ogg; Dr S.G. Campbell; A.H. Mackenzie; Dr L. Crawford; Dr J.W. Bews.

MALCOLM WILLIAM SEARLE, who came to the Cape as a small child with his parents, was born on 7 December, 1855 in Blackheath, England. He was educated at the Diocesan College and obtained the B.A. (Cape) degree in 1875, winning a University Scholarship.

He continued his studies at Cambridge, passing the second-class mathematical tripos in 1880 and the second-class law tripos in the following year. He was called to the English bar in January, 1882 and returned to the Cape shortly afterwards to begin his professional career.

Searle took silk in 1893 and for the next seven years was legal adviser to the High Commissioner. Appointed a Junior Puisne Judge of the Cape Provincial Division in 1910, he became Judge President in June, 1922. He received a knighthood in the New Year's Honours List of 1923.

A member of the university Council from 1897 until 1918 and Vice-Chancellor for the last two years of that period, he was also active in the affairs of the Diocesan College.

Sir Malcolm Searle was killed in a train disaster at Salt River, Cape Town on 9 June, 1926.

The Hon. Sir Malcolm William Searle,
Kt, B.A. (Cape and Cantab.), LL.B., K.C.
Member of Council 1897–1918
Pro Vice-Chancellor 1915–1916
Vice-Chancellor 1916–1918

144

6 The federal university

The University of South Africa quietly took over from its predecessor on the Tuesday after the Easter holiday in 1918. What celebration there was to mark the arrival of the appointed day was confined to the constituent colleges. There was little enough cause for rejoicing at that time. The first World War was well into its fourth year and peace seemed a distant prospect as the German spring offensive ground slowly to a halt on the western front in Europe.

The university's new administrative headquarters were somewhat less impressive than those of the old institution in Cape Town. Offices in Somerset House, Vermeulen Street, Pretoria had been rented from the businessman and public benefactor, Charles W. Maggs, and at least provided adequate accommodation for Registrar Thomson and his assistants – Charles Cameron Grant, Harold M. Harradine and Margaret R. Gordon. These four had come over from the Cape University and had migrated to the Transvaal to serve its successor. However, the first Vice-Chancellor, W. J. Viljoen, and his deputy J. E. Adamson, regarded the rented offices merely as a temporary expedient and expected to see the university speedily housed in a more suitable building, with a hall large enough to hold the annual graduation ceremonies. The University of South Africa was nevertheless destined to remain at Somerset House for more than a quarter of a century.

Although the university began life in a relatively insignificant home, its governing Council was, from the start, widely representative of national higher educational interests. Indeed, it reflected more than a national outlook, as Southern Rhodesia elected to take part in its deliberations when the first Council was constituted. Much later, in 1944, the mandated territory of South West Africa followed suit. The governing body was smaller than that which had administered the affairs of the Cape University in its last years. In addition to the nominees of the college Senates and Councils, eight members were appointed by the Governor-General and four were chosen by Convocation. The professorial element on Council was strong, for not only did the constituents send members of the teaching staffs to its meetings, but Convocation, still employing the competitive ticket system, usualy gave preference to college professors as the representatives of its interests. Among the many who took their seats as college or Convocation nominees in the period to 1946 were R.B. Denison and the Orcadian botanist, J. W. Bews, from Natal, A. Stanley Kidd of Rhodes University College and D. F. Malherbe of Bloemfontein, South Africa's first Professor of Afrikaans.

It became the practice to appoint the heads of the provincial education departments in an *ex-officio* capacity on the Governor-General's list. This brought to the service of the University of South Africa a number of men with considerable administrative experience. They included Viljoen of the Free State and the Cape, Adamson and N. M. Hoogenhout of the Transvaal, Hugh Bryan and F. D. Hugo of Natal, S. H. Pellissier from Bloemfontein and the Cape Superintendent General of Education, W. de Vos Malan. In 1932, S. P. E. Boshoff began his association with the governing body as Director of Education in Pretoria, a post which he held until 1934.

Southern Rhodesia and South West Africa were also represented by the heads of their education departments. The Yorkshireman, L. M. Foggin, appointed in 1918, was for many years the Rhodesian member; W. Orban was South West Africa's first nominee. This extra-territorial representation lasted until 1954.

Many members of Council were long associated with the university. Two college Council delegates – the Catholic churchman from Natal, the Rev. Leo Sormany, and the Huguenot institu-

147

In 1918, the new University of South Africa moved into rented offices in SOMERSET HOUSE, Vermeulen Street, Pretoria. It was a pleasant enough building, although less impressive than the premises in Cape Town and lacking a hall suitable for graduation ceremonies.

More offices were rented in Somerset House as the work of the administration grew. Rapid expansion after 1946 compelled the university to seek other accommodation, however, and the building was vacated in 1949.

Somerset House, which housed the first offices of the University of South Africa

omerset House

*Main
entrance*

tion's representative, the Rev. William Flint – were among those who had earlier served the examining university in Cape Town. Two other college Council members – W. P. Bond of Grahamstown and the Rev. H. J. R. du Plessis of Potchefstroom – sat for many years in the federal Council; so, too, did the English-born future Supreme Court judge, Percival Carleton Gane, chosen on separate occasions by the Rhodes University College Council and by Convocation. Ferdinand Postma of Potchefstroom, a tower of strength throughout the federal period, became a member of Council in 1919.

William Thomson, who retired as Registrar in 1922 and subsequently became Principal of the University of the Witwatersrand, was chosen as a member of Council by the Governor-General in 1924. As Sir William, he was to serve until his death in 1947, thus maintaining an almost unbroken association with the University of the Cape of Good Hope and the University of South Africa for more than sixty years. A. J. R. van Rhijn of the Bloemfontein *Volksblad*, parliamentarian and future Union High Commissioner in London, was another member who gave long service to the Council; so, too, did his fellow-Afrikaner, the cultural leader, P. C. Schoonees. Both were appointed by the Governor-General, who also selected A. A. Roberts, later the Union's diplomatic representative in Canada. He, like M. C. Botha earlier, sat on Council while at the same time holding the office of Secretary for Education. This link with a government department was, however, exceptional. Botha, Roberts and Van Rhijn were all elected Vice-Chancellor, Van Rhijn being chosen for two successive terms in 1948 and 1950.

Two men who became the first Principals of independent universities were appointed to the Council of the University of South Africa in the federal period which ended in 1951. These were H. van der Merwe Scholtz of the Bloemfontein college and E.G. Malherbe of Natal. Scholtz joined Council in 1944 and Malherbe in the following year. Both were to retain a connection with a reconstructed University of South Africa. The architect of the legislation of 1916, F. S. Malan, was also a Council member for

150

some years. He sat briefly in 1932, when he acted as Director of Education for the Transvaal, and again from 1936 until 1940 as the representative of the Council of the Wellington college. He was chosen as Vice-Chancellor in 1936 in succession to F. D. Hugo.

The Chancellor of the University of the Cape of Good Hope, the Duke of Connaught and Strathearn, consented to serve the federal university. Following his death in 1942, the first South African Chancellor, Nicolaas Johannes de Wet, was appointed. Three Vice-Chancellors, in addition to Van Rhijn, served successive two-year terms of office. These were W. J. Viljoen, his successor in 1922, J. E. Adamson, and Ferdinand Postma, who was Vice-Chancellor from 1940 until 1944. The Vice-Chancellor from 1930 until 1932, N. M. Hoogenhout, died in office.

From 1918, women began for the first time to take a part in the government of the university. Ethel M. Doidge of the Department of Agriculture was chosen as a member of the first Council by the Governor-General and in 1940, the Huguenot Council selected as its representative Marjorie A. Malan, the wife of the sitting Cape Superintendent General of Education. The Wellington institution was well served by its lady professors. Among those who became members of the Council of the federal university were the Americans, Bertha Stoneman and Florence M. Snell, and the Afrikaans-speaking Principal, Anna J. D. de Villiers.

The Registrar was also Secretary of the Joint Matriculation Board, the Joint Committee for Professional Examinations, and, later, of the Carnegie Corporation Visitors' Grants Committee and the Voortrekker Centenary Memorial Fund. He was also Secretary of Convocation. That body gradually became, so far as its annual meetings were concerned, a mere appendage of the professorial Senate and an ineffective advisory group. It continued to meet each year until 1930, choosing an annual President and occasionally voicing its opinions upon matters of interest to the university. Its first President was B. A. Tindall, destined for high legal office; subsequent holders of the title included Sir George Cory and H. T. Reinink, both of whom served for two

WILLEM JACOBUS VILJOEN was born on 5 October, 1869 at Richmond in the Cape, where he received his early education. He then went to Cape Town and Stellenbosch, matriculated in 1887 and obtained the B.A. degree at the Victoria College three years later. Further study abroad followed. He attended the Universities of Amsterdam and Leiden and gained a doctorate in philosophy at the University of Strasburg. He was admitted to the degree of M.A. (Cape) in 1903.

In 1894, he was appointed to the staff of the Victoria College as Professor of History and Modern Languages. There, for many years, he played a leading part in academic life.

Viljoen was chosen as Director of Education for the Orange Free State in 1910. An advocate of simplified written Dutch, rather than of Afrikaans, he encountered opposition from those who saw in the introduction of the younger language a means to hasten bilingualism.

In 1918, he became the first Afrikaner to hold the post of Superintendent General of Education at the Cape.

Viljoen wrote a number of books, among them a translation into Afrikaans of *Jock of the Bushveld*. In 1923, he received an honorary doctorate in civil law from the University of Oxford.

A member of Council from 1897 until his death, he was elected Vice-Chancellor of the new university in 1918, retaining this office until 1922.

Willem Jacobus Viljoen died at Sea Point, Cape Town on 19 July, 1929.

Professor Willem Jacobus Viljoen, M.A., Phil.D., D.C.L. (h.c.)
Member of Council 1897–1929
Pro and Deputy Vice-Chancellor 1916–1918; 1922–1926
Vice-Chancellor 1918–1922
(Photo: University of Stellenbosch)

successive years. After the election of S. H. Pellissier as President in 1930, a quorum was only once found for the annual meeting, when in 1936, Professor Emeritus Adriaan Francken of the Bloemfontein college was chosen to fill the vacant presidency for the coming year.

Convocation did, however, continue to elect members of Council by postal vote and could also be called upon to choose the university's Chancellor in similar fashion. In 1942, one of the most bitterly contested elections took place for the four seats on the fifth Council. During the second World War, as in the first, South Africa was a divided land and it was generally felt that the major contending tickets in this Convocation election were politically inspired. One, alleged to have the support of either the militant *Ossewa-Brandwag* organization or the exclusive Afrikaner *Broederbond,* included two sitting members of Council: Professor W. F. C. Arndt of Bloemfontein and the former Prime Minister's son, Dr Albert Hertzog. The other candidates on this ticket were Dr Nicolaas Diederichs, for some years on the staff of the Free State college, and Professor J. C. van Rooy of Potchefstroom. It was opposed by another ticket which would seem to have enjoyed United Party support. This consisted of a Transvaal candidate, T. P. C. Boezaart, Alexander Kerr of Fort Hare in the Cape and two former Rhodes Scholars: Leif Egeland of Natal and I. S. Fourie of the Orange Free State. Fourie had recently represented the Bloemfontein college as a member of the university Council. Arndt was subsequently chosen by the Senate of his college, but the ticket on which his name appeared as a Convocation candidate was decisively beaten by the opposing one. Egeland and Kerr received an equal number of votes to head the poll; they were closely followed by Fourie and Boezaart.

The passions aroused by this contest gave rise to fears that a similar struggle would mark the election, then pending, of a new Chancellor. Already, a special war measure of 1941 had done away with the Convocation meeting of that year in the interests of economy. Two years later, the statutes were amended to allow the Vice-Chancellor to act as President of Convocation and in

154

the same year, legislation was passed which gave Council the right to choose the Chancellor. In this way, Convocation's power was curbed and a possible crisis averted. Convocation retained the privilege of choosing Council members, however, although few made use of their postal votes. This, in a university whose governing body was entirely European, might cause difficulties in the future, for already in 1942, non-European members were coming forward as candidates for Council seats.

The establishment of a university Senate of college professors and heads of department represented a break with the old Cape University. Under Senate's direction, a faculty system came into being to co-ordinate the work of the colleges. The first Chairman of Senate was George Corstorphine of the School of Mines; among those who succeeded him were Paterson of the Transvaal University College, Bews of Natal, Postma of Potchefstroom, T. F. Dreyer of the Free State college and J. Smeath Thomas of Rhodes University College.

The Faculty of Veterinary Science, whose first Dean was Sir Arnold Theiler, and that of Agriculture, under J. M. Hector and J. C. Ross, were concerned with studies at the Pretoria college only. The Faculty of Medicine, founded in 1920 with E. P. Stibbe as Dean, was restricted to courses at the School of Mines, subsequently renamed University College, Johannesburg. The Faculty of Education did not come into existence until 1927, when Sir John Adamson, then Master of Rhodes, became Dean. One of his successors was the outstanding educationist, J. Chris. Coetzee of Potchefstroom. An active Faculty of Engineering existed, with one short gap, until 1949. The School of Mines provided the first Dean in John Orr, but for many years the only constituent giving instruction in this field was the Natal University College. Its professors, H. Clark and J. H. Neal, long alternated as Dean. A Faculty of Social Science was created in 1944 under J. de W. Keyter of Bloemfontein.

The present Faculties of Arts, Commerce and Administration, Law and Science date from the beginning of the University of South Africa's history. Reinink of the Transvaal University Col-

NICOLAAS MARAIS HOOGENHOUT was born on 9 January, 1876 at Wellington (Cape). He was the eldest son of C.P. Hoogenhout, one of the leaders of the first Afrikaans language movement and it was in his father's school at Groenberg that the boy received his primary education. He matriculated in 1894 at the high school in Wellington and attended the Victoria College, where he obtained the B.A. degree in 1897 and the M.A. two years later.

After teaching for some months at Gill College, he studied modern languages at the University of Strasburg, gaining a doctorate in philosophy in 1902.

On his return to South Africa, he lectured at the Victoria College and taught at Wellington. In 1904, he was appointed Headmaster of the Eendracht School in Pretoria. He became Vice-Principal of the Pretoria Normal College in 1908 and Principal in 1922. Dr Hoogenhout was also Professor of Education at the Transvaal University College from 1922 until 1928 and Principal there from 1925 to 1927. In June, 1928, he was appointed Director of Education for the Transvaal, a post which he held until his death.

He was a member of several educational and cultural organizations and published a number of books and articles.

Chairman of the Council of the Transvaal University College, later the University of Pretoria, from 1929 until 1932, he also served on the Council of the University of South Africa from 1925 to 1927 and again from 1928 until 1932. Chosen as Vice-Chancellor in 1930, he did not live to complete his term of office.

Nicolaas Marais Hoogenhout died in Pretoria on 9 February, 1932.

Dr Nicolaas Marais Hoogenhout, M.A., D.Phil.
Member of Council 1925–1927; 1928–1932
Vice-Chancellor 1930–1932
(Photo: University of Pretoria)

lege was the first Dean of the Faculty of Arts; others included Postma, Scholtz and the Potchefstroom historian, A. J. H. van der Walt. In the Faculty of Commerce, whose first Dean was J. Findlay of the School of Mines, J. E. Holloway and E. H. Brookes of the Transvaal University College played an important part in the early days. In 1927, Orlando Oldham of Natal became Dean, holding the office until 1937 and again from 1942 until 1944. The Faculty of Law was first presided over by W. Pittman of the Transvaal University College. F. B. Burchell of Natal and C. P. Brink of Bloemfontein gave long service as Deans at a later stage. Alexander Ogg of the School of Mines was the first Dean of the Faculty of Science in 1918; other incumbents included Bews of Natal, W. F. Barker of Rhodes and W. H. Logeman of the Bloemfontein college.

Two committees of Council were responsible for the school and music examinations of the federal university. Both these secondary functions caused problems enough. A movement away from university control of school examinations manifested itself at an early date. By 1933, only government or provincial schools in Natal, Swaziland and South West Africa still presented candidates for the university's Junior Certificate examination; the other provinces had by then instituted tests of their own. Many private schools, however, found the examination useful, among them those of the Catholic Church. There was a growing demand for the representation of groups of schools by assessor members on the Council committee and the university finally acceded to it, with certain qualifications, in 1934. In that year, R. F. Currey, Rector of Michaelhouse and representative of the "Conference" schools, and F. C. McManus of the Christian Brothers' College, Kimberley, the nominee of the Catholic group, were chosen as assessor members.

Music examinations caused many difficulties. The University of South Africa found itself in an uncomfortable position, seeking to satisfy not only the Associated Board in London, but also the musical profession and the South African public. The Music Committee of Council did not reflect the collective voice of the

158

profession. The lawyer and historian, Manfred Nathan, has spoken of the part he played in its deliberations between 1924 and 1930. "I was on the music committee", he wrote in his autobiography. "The others seem to have assumed, quite erroneously, that I was an authority . . . They might as well have put me on the finance committee"! When in 1923, Percival R. Kirby and Theophil Wendt attempted to assess the work of candidates with a severity unknown before, there was consternation in the musical world. It was the appointment of such local examiners in musical theory which marked the beginning of a split with the Associated Board. The English examiners had been under fire for their inability to cope when they visited Afrikaans-speaking areas; the Associated Board, however, would not have examiners chosen on any but musical and professional grounds. There was, too, a certain prejudice in some quarters in favour of the imported article. In the thirties, the university nevertheless began to use South Africans for practical examinations as well as for the theoretical papers. Relations with the Associated Board began to deteriorate and there was, even before the second World War, talk of a complete break with the English body. This at length took place in 1945.

There is no doubt that the work undertaken by the University of South Africa in these subsidiary areas was of great financial benefit to it. A later Registrar, Langham Murray, was to say on one occasion at least that it was the fees received from candidates for the university's various examinations which kept the institution going in times of crisis. And money problems long plagued the authorities. The government grant was generous enough in the first years. The university received over R8 000 a year between 1919 and 1923 and nearly R17 000 in 1925. in 1930, the sum allocated was approximately R6 000, but from that year, the contribution began to fall steadily through the period of world depression until in 1933, the state subsidy was a mere R500. This was little more than the University of South Africa obtained from the government of Southern Rhodesia and only a sixth of the amount the Cape government had given the examining university

159

JOHN ERNEST ADAMSON was born on 11 January, 1867 in Wakefield, Yorkshire, England. After attending a local school, he trained as a teacher at St Mark's College in London, completing his course in 1890. He began his career as a lecturer at the South Wales Training College in Carmarthen and, by studying privately, obtained the M.A. degree in philosophy of the University of London in 1901. Twenty years later, he gained a London doctorate.

In 1902, he became head of the Pretoria Normal College and three years later, was appointed Director of Education for the Transvaal, a post he held until 1924.

An outstanding educationist, he wrote much on the philosophy of his subject. His invaluable services earned him the C.M.G. in 1923 and a knighthood in the following year.

On his retirement in 1924, he became the first Master of Rhodes University College, where he continued to lecture in his field of study until 1930. For many years afterwards, he retained his interest in educational matters.

A member of Council, with one brief interlude, from 1906 until 1930, he succeeded W.J. Viljoen as Vice-Chancellor in 1922, serving in this capacity until 1926.

Sir John Adamson died at Muizenberg in the Cape on 26 April, 1950.

Sir John Ernest Adamson, Kt, M.A., D.Litt., C.M.G.
Member of Council 1906–1909; 1909–1930
Dean of the Faculty of Education 1927–1929
Deputy Vice-Chancellor 1918–1920; 1921–1922
Vice-Chancellor 1922–1926

160

in 1873 ! Not surprisingly, an anxious delegation, consisting of Vice-Chancellor Pellissier, Charles C. Grant, Thomson's successor as Registrar, and the Chairman of Council's Finance Committee, A. A. Roberts, waited upon Jan Hofmeyr, the newly appointed Minister of Education! The situation improved a little with the implementation of the Adamson departmental committee recommendations. In 1934 and for some time thereafter, the University of South Africa received R2 000 a year, although there was another drop in 1937 to R1 000. In the last years of the second World War, however, the situation became less precarious, until by 1946, the university was in receipt of a government grant of over R7 000.

Some relief came, when the depression was at its height, through the sale of the university building in Queen Victoria Street, Cape Town. The appendage, Poplar Lodge, was in use as the headquarters of a local university representative and the main building for occasional conferences, but by the mid-twenties, when the University of Cape Town proposed to relinquish its lease, the property seemed destined to become a financial liability. In proposing any sale, the feelings of the original donors had to be considered and in Sir John Buchanan and H.W. Baumgarten they had redoubtable spokesmen. Moreover, in disposing of the property, the University of South Africa had to keep in mind a stipulation that it must be used solely for educational purposes. After much discussion, legislation was passed which enabled the university to sell the buildings concerned for R90 000. A commemorative Hiddingh-Currie Scholarship was instituted to satisfy the donors' representatives and from 1932, the property was taken over to house the Cape provincial archives. When all commitments had been met, the university received just over R70 000, a sum very considerably below the municipal valuation.

It was in its federal role that the University of South Africa was intended to play a significant part in the development of higher education. It began life as the mother of six small constituent colleges, too small at that stage, despite H. E. S. Fremantle's pleas for collegiate independence, to stand upon their own

162

feet. At the end of 1918, the Pretoria college was the biggest, with over 250 students, but the neighbouring School of Mines in Johannesburg was rapidly overhauling it, having then 179 students. Rhodes and Grey University Colleges had not reached an enrolment of 150, the Natal college had a mere 86 and the Huguenot institution only 56, of whom 8 were men. Federation sat lightly upon the colleges, for the administration of the federal institution had no control over internal collegiate affairs or even upon the appointment of staff.

The Johannesburg college moved rapidly towards independence under the guidance of Jan Hofmeyr, who became Principal after the death of Corstorphine in 1919. By 1921, it boasted nearly 900 students and was a university college serving a wide area of southern Africa. Although there were misgivings in University of South Africa circles that the loss of so healthy a constituent might jeopardize the stability of the federal structure, the University of the Witwatersrand was created by Act 15 of 1921 and severed its ties with the federal university in the following March. There were signs that other colleges would like to take the same course. However, it was only in Pretoria that practical effect was given to dreams of independence. There, after the rejection by the Transvaal University College in 1924 of a proposed amalgamation with the new university on the Rand, a campaign was launched which led to the passing of Act 13 of 1930, establishing the University of Pretoria on Kruger Day, 10 October. The federal university, shorn of yet another constituent, was in despondent mood. It regarded itself, as a recently elected Council member, Professor E. H. Brookes, put it, as "a gradually dissolving and obviously transitory body", destined to "break up into its component parts at a distant, but not indefinitely distant, date". Nor did it keep its despair to itself, for on Graduation Day in March, 1930 – some months before the Transvaal University College gained its independence – Vice-Chancellor Hugh Bryan confessed that the University of South Africa could no longer "pretend a passionate devotion to (its) continually dwindling federation".

163

CHARLES CAMERON GRANT was born on 15 July, 1873 at Glenlivet, Banffshire, Scotland. From Keith High School, he attended the University of Aberdeen, where he obtained the M.A. degree.

He came to South Africa to teach immediately after the Anglo-Boer War and in 1903, became head of the school at Winburg in the Orange River Colony. In view of the bitterness then existing between English speakers and Afrikaners, it says much for Grant that his transfer in 1904 to Bloemfontein evoked vehement local protest.

On the outbreak of the first World War, he was in charge of the office of the Department of Education in Bloemfontein. He joined the army and saw service in South West and East Africa, attaining the rank of Captain.

He was appointed Assistant Registrar in January, 1918 and succeeded Thomson as Registrar in 1923. It was the end of an era, for henceforth the Registrar no longer exercised the same influence over university policy as had been the case under Cameron and Thomson. There were other changes, too. Grant's rule was more benevolent than that of his predecessor, who had been something of a martinet in matters of dress, behaviour and smoking in the office!

Charles Cameron Grant retired in 1934 and died in Cape Town on 19 August, 1949.

Charles Cameron Grant, M.A., M.B.E.
Registrar 1923–1934

The six CONSTITUENT COLLEGES originally incorporated in the University of South Africa were:

Grey University College, Bloemfontein
> (from 1935, the University College of the Orange Free State);

Huguenot College, Wellington
> (from 1920, Huguenot University College);

Natal University College, Pietermaritzburg
> (from 1931, also in Durban);

Rhodes University College, Grahamstown;

South African School of Mines and Technology, Johannesburg
> (from 1920, University College, Johannesburg);

Transvaal University College, Pretoria.

Potchefstroom University College joined the federation in 1921. Previously known as Potchefstroom University College for Christian Higher Education, it resumed this title in 1933.

Apart from Huguenot University College, which undertook a new function in 1951, these colleges all became independent universities.

Coats of Arms of the University and those of its Colleges which became independent Universities, with Dates of Independence

1916

SPES BONA

1916

Pectora roborant cultus recti

1916

SCIENTIA ET LABORE

1922

AD DESTINATUM PERSEQUOR

1930

SPES IN ARDUIS

STELLA AURORAE

1949

DEO SAPIENTIAE LUX

1950

VIS·VIRTUS·VERITAS

1951

IN U HG

1951

There had, however, been compensation for the loss of the Johannesburg college, when the Reformed *(Gereformeerde)* Church authorities at Potchefstroom sought admission as a constituent for a new college which had been created out of the Arts Department of the theological seminary. There was some hesitation in university circles about admitting a small and possibly weak newcomer; on the Potchefstroom side, there was disappointment that the secular nature of the federal university necessitated the removal of the words "for Christian Higher Education" from the title of the new institution. However, doubts on both sides were overcome and Act 25 of 1921 brought Potchefstroom University College into the federation. Twelve years later, the "verminkte vaandel", as Ferdinand Postma described it, was repaired and the title of the college again bore witness to the religious ideal which animated its leaders.

For a number of years there was always the possibility that other institutions might become constituents. There was initially considerable uncertainty about the scope of higher education in the Union. A definition was at length embodied in the Financial Relations Fourth Extension Act of 1922 which covered a wide field, placing even schools for the teaching of domestic science under the Department of Union Education. The Higher Education Act of the following year made specific regulations for the control of all schools, colleges and institutes which fell within the sphere of action of the Union government. Training colleges for teachers might one day seek higher status; of more immediate importance was the effect of the new outlook upon the technical colleges and the South African Native College.

The technical colleges, and particularly that at Durban, would greatly benefit if the gateway to university education were widened. The Natal foundation was not only providing full-time courses in engineering and commerce, but was also giving lectures in fine arts and tutorial classes in other university subjects. The result of the latest developments in the organization of higher education was to allow the Durban institution, now renamed the Natal Technical College, to establish Departments of Commerce,

168

Engineering and Fine Arts of full university standard, in collaboration with the Natal University College in Pietermaritzburg. Other technical colleges, united from 1926 in a national association, saw visions of similar future greatness.

The South African Native College at Fort Hare, near Alice also stood on the threshold of significant advance at this period. In 1923, Zachariah K. Matthews, the future Botswana Ambassador to the United States, became the first student there to obtain a B.A. degree. Fort Hare was ready to join the ranks of the university colleges, however slender its resources and few its successes. Its students worked externally for University of South Africa degrees, although the federal institution had a connection with the college in the appointment of two members to its governing Council. One noted supporter of non-European education, Professor G. F. Dingemans of Rhodes, was to assist the college as a member of its Council for over a quarter of a century. The Higher Education Act of 1923 recognized the South African Native College as an institution of university college standing and, with courses largely determined by the syllabuses of the federal university, Fort Hare would inevitably be drawn closer to the federation.

In 1937, the University of South Africa made certain concessions to the college which gave lecturers there status as internal examiners and allowed the institution to draft its own syllabuses. The South African Native College did not, however, become a federal constituent and although Principal Kerr gained a university Council seat in the "political" election of 1942, this did not imply official recognition of a special relationship with the federal body.

Although there was no reason to doubt the standing of the South African Native College as a higher educational institution, there were serious misgivings in many quarters about the claims of technical colleges to be so regarded. When, in 1927, a commission was appointed under J. G. van der Horst to investigate the university position in the country, the University of South Africa showed itself clearly hostile to the extension of

169

The first meeting of the university SENATE was held at Somerset House, Pretoria on 20 April, 1918, a week after the inaugural meeting of the new Council. Subsequent meetings were held at collegiate centres. The Chairman of Senate also took the chair at meetings of the Senate Executive Committee.

Chairmen of Senate, 1918–1928

Dr G.S. Corstorphine
(School of Mines), 1918

Prof. A.C. Paterson (Transvaal
University College), 1918–1922

Prof. J.W. Bews
atal University College),
1922–1924; 1934–1936

Prof. P.J. du Toit
(Transvaal University College),
1924–1926

Prof. F. Postma (Potchef-
stroom University College),
1926–1928; 1936–1938

university college status to technical institutions. The report of the Van der Horst Commission in 1928 proposed an end to further encroachment and also to the link between the Natal Technical College and the Natal University College. No official line of demarcation was ever drawn between university work and other forms of advanced training, but it was made plain that government would no longer consider technical colleges as embryo technological universities. The federal university therefore gained no new constituents and students at all other institutions were treated as external candidates for its examinations.

The colleges of the University of South Africa were geographically remote from each other and, in local eyes, more important than the distant examining machine in Pretoria to which they were attached. In this role – so much like that of the old Cape University – the federal university was not without its critics. Results were sometimes delayed and the prestige of the university suffered in consequence. It was not always the fault of the administration in Somerset House, Pretoria. In 1929, for example, an examiner left for his honeymoon at an inconvenient moment, giving instructions that no scripts were to be submitted to him for marking while he was away!

The University of South Africa was not, as its predecessor had been for so many years, confined to the chosen administrative seat. Meetings of Council and Senate took place at intervals at all the collegiate centres except Wellington. These were not, however, frequent visits and in the early twenties, an imaginative scheme was put forward by J. E. Holloway of the Transvaal University College, which would bring the colleges together at a central place as residential teaching institutions. Their assets were to be vested in the federal university, which would appoint the teaching staff. It was proposed that Council should be so constituted that it would reflect all the local interests which had hitherto played an important part in the history of the constituents. This dream of a South African Oxford or Cambridge never became a reality, however, although it remained a talking point for a couple of years. Regional pride was strongly against the plan and there were some who saw in it nothing more than a way of enhancing the prestige of the Pretoria college, for it was generally felt that the capital city would be chosen as the central site.

Graduation Day long provided a meeting point for the students and staffs of the constituent colleges, although from time to time, local ceremonies were held. The first function took place in 1919 at the Raadzaal on Church Square, Pretoria. It was followed by an "At Home" in the somewhat incongruous surroundings of the zoological gardens in the city! Honorary degrees were conferred upon those stalwarts of the old university, Kolbe, Marais and Whitton, and a large number of mining diplomas were converted into B.Sc. degrees. More than a hundred degrees by examination were awarded on the results of the university's first examinations, delayed the previous year by the influenza epidemic which swept the world at the close of the first World War. One LL.B. capped on this occasion was the future State President of the Republic of South Africa, Charles Robberts Swart; several who would subsequently give much time to the affairs of the federal university also received degrees, among them the distinguished educationist, E. H. Brookes, a future Registrar, Petrus A. Taljaard, and the literary figure, P. C. Schoonees. The Graduation Day function was soon transferred to the Grand Theatre in Pretoria and the students of the local college undertook to organize the lively procession through the streets of the city with which the proceedings opened. The Varsity Ball became one of the social highlights of the season.

In August, 1929, an additional ceremony was held at the Transvaal University College to honour certain visiting members of the British Association for the Advancement of Science, one of whom was the future United Kingdom Minister of Health, Major Walter Elliot. The time for retrenchment was, however, at hand and Graduation Day, like the research fellowship created at the beginning of the federal university's life, soon came to an end. After 1930, moreover, the new University of Pretoria began to hold its own ceremonies and the local *Pretoria News* felt that

173

THE FIRST GRADUATION CEREMONY of the University of South Africa was held in the Pretoria Raadzaal on the first anniversary of the university's inception, 2 April, 1919.

The names of 138 graduates appear in the programme, together with those of 99 former holders of mining diplomas who were now entitled to the degree of B.Sc. in engineering. Honorary doctorates were also conferred upon three members of the Council of the old university: F.C. Kolbe, J.I. Marais and J.R. Whitton.

Many who had made, or were later to make valuable contributions to public life were awarded degrees in 1919. Among them were E.X. Brain of the South African Railways, A.A. Coaton, General Manager of De Beers, the historians, I.D. Bosman and A.E. du Toit, the future State President, C.R. Swart, two leading judges, J.E. de Villiers and A.C. Malan, the cabinet minister, S.P. le Roux and four men who distinguished themselves in the world of letters: P.C. Schoonees, J.R.L. van Bruggen, R.M. Titlestad and Gerrit Dekker.

Programme of the first Graduation Ceremony of the
University of South Africa, 1919

Universiteit van Zuid-Africa.

PROMOTIEPLECHTIGHEID,
2 April 1919.

KANSELIER :

Veldmaarschalk Z.K.H. De HERTOG VAN CONNAUGHT en STRATHEARN, P.C., K.G., K.T., K.P.

VICE-KANSELIER :

Dr. W. J. VILJOEN, M.A., Phil. D.

PLAATSVERVANGEND VICE-KANSELIER :

JOHN E. ADAMSON, M.A.

Voorzitter van de Senaat -   -   -   -   Professor A. C. PATERSON, M.A.

DEKENS VAN DE FAKULTEITEN :

Letteren - - - -	Professor R. A. LEHFELDT, B.A., D.Sc.
Wis-en Natuurkunde - -	Professor A. OGG, M.A., B.Sc., Ph.D.
Rechtsgeleerdheid - -	Advokaat W. PITTMAN, B.A.
Technologie - - -	Professor J. ORR, B.Sc., M. Inst. C.E.
Landbouwkunde - -	Professor J. M. HECTOR, B.Sc.
Handelswetenschappen -	Professor J. FINDLAY, C.A., F.S.A.A.

Registrateur -   -   -   -   Dr. W. THOMSON, M.A., B.Sc., LL.D.

Buckley & Van Duyn, Printers, etc., Pretoria.

the federal Graduation Day would certainly be robbed of much of its appeal with the loss of the largest constituent. A ceremony was held by the University of South Africa at the Grand Theatre in 1931, when Vice-Chancellor Hoogenhout kept his speech within the limits acceptable in a "day (which) regards long addresses with as little favour as long skirts and long sermons". The following year's function, held this time in the Plaza cinema, was the last corporate one for many a year.

These Pretoria gatherings did not always earn the uncritical acclaim of the general public. The editor of the *Pretoria News,* Vere Stent, once poured scorn on South Africa's university world, in which Deans of Faculty enjoyed good pay, light work and the not very onerous responsibility of introducing plain girls and bovine young men into academic society! However, this was a particularly jaundiced view and for many, the annual presentation of degrees by the federal university made it, for a few hours, something more than an examination factory. Once these functions began to be associated with the separate colleges, the division between the active teaching parts and the administrative headquarters became more marked. One corporate ceremony was arranged in 1946, but as the Director of Demobilisation refused to provide travel vouchers for the sixteen students concerned, only one put in a personal appearance!

Honorary degrees continued to be conferred throughout the life of the federal university. Between 1920 and 1934, several men who had served on the Council of the Cape University were thus rewarded for their contributions to national life. Doctorates in laws were bestowed upon Sir John Buchanan in 1925 and upon Sir John Wessels nine years later; doctorates in literature were awarded to the Rev. Adriaan Moorrees in 1920 and to William Ritchie in 1925. The Rev. J. D. Kestell was capped at Bloemfontein as a Doctor of Divinity in 1933. His connection with the Cape University was not of long duration, but he gave many years of useful service to its successor and became its third Vice-Chancellor in 1926. A later Vice-Chancellor, M. C. Botha, received an honorary doctorate in literature in 1936.

176

Doctorates were also awarded between 1933 and 1945 to four other members of the Council of the federal university: R. B. Denison of Natal (D.Sc.), G. F. Dingemans of Rhodes (D.Litt.), Jacob D. du Toit of Potchefstroom, better known as the poet "Totius" (D.Litt.), and Alexander Kerr of the South African Native College (LL.D.). Among Senate members, Gerrit Besselaar of Natal (D.Litt.), Orlando Oldham of the same college (M.Com.) and Adriaan Francken of Bloemfontein (D.Litt.) obtained honorary degrees; so, too, did Sir Arnold Theiler of Onderstepoort, who had earlier received a similar distinction from the examining university. He became a Doctor of Veterinary Science of the University of South Africa in 1925. In keeping with tradition, these degrees *honoris causa* were not conferred while the recipients were attached to the university.

In 1920, a doctorate in laws was bestowed upon Prince Arthur of Connaught, the Governor-General and son of the Chancellor of the university at that time. Similar recognition was also accorded N. J. de Wet in 1943, when he succeeded the Duke of Connaught as titular head of the university. Other recipients of honorary degrees included the American educationist, Anna E. Bliss of Huguenot (D.Litt.), the geologist, Alexander Logie du Toit (D.Sc.), the politician and judge, Sir Thomas Graham (LL.D.) and the archivists and historians C. Graham Botha (M.A.) and Andries Dreyer (D.Phil.). The African teacher and founder of the Ohlange Institute, John Langalibalele Dube, was awarded a doctorate in philosophy in 1936. This was the first time that a non-European had been selected for such an honour in South Africa. It was, however, unfortunate that problems of race should have arisen in choosing the place where the degree was to be conferred. Dube wished to receive it in Natal, but the ceremony had to be held at the South African Native College in the Cape.

One subject which concerned both the federal administration and the colleges was the question of language. Here, the University of South Africa was committed to a policy of equality and, almost from the beginning of its career, was prepared to accept

177

JOHN DANIEL KESTELL was born on 15 December, 1854 in Pietermaritzburg, where he received his early education. In his youth, he accompanied his father to the diamond fields as a digger, before enrolling at the Stellenbosch Public School in 1873. After he had matriculated, he attended the local theological seminary and completed his training for the church at the University of Utrecht in the Netherlands.

He began his career as a minister in the Dutch Reformed *(Nederduitse Gereformeerde)* Church at Dutoitspan in 1881, moved to Kimberley in the following year and to Harrismith in 1894.

Kestell served as an army chaplain during the Anglo-Boer War and was one of the secretaries at the peace negotiations. He then travelled with the Boer generals, De Wet, De la Rey and Botha, to Europe and on his return, became minister at Ficksburg. In 1919, he was appointed editor of the *Kerkbode* and in the following year was chosen as Principal of Grey University College, where he remained until 1927.

His great work as a church leader and Bible translator earned him wide recognition. He also inspired the *Reddingsdaad* and *Helpmekaar* movements. Three honorary doctorates were conferred upon him: the D.D. of the University of South Africa in 1933, the D.Litt. of the University of Pretoria in 1934 and in the same year, the LL.D. of the University of Cape Town. In addition, Kestell was Chancellor of the University of Stellenbosch from 1939 until his death. His books include a biography of Christiaan de Wet.

Vice-Chancellor of the University of South Africa from 1926 to 1928, he served that university and its predecessor as a Council member for three periods between 1911 and 1930.

He died in Bloemfontein on 9 February, 1941 and was buried at the foot of the *Vrouemonument*.

The Rev. John Daniel Kestell, D.D. (h.c.),
D.Litt. (h.c.), LL.D. (h.c.)
Member of Council 1911–1913; 1918–1919; 1920–1930
Dean of the Faculty of Arts 1923–1924
Vice-Chancellor 1926–1928
(Photo: Government Archives)

Afrikaans as an alternative to Dutch. The university was also more truly representative of the two language groups in the country than it had ever been under its former designation, or, indeed, than it was to become at a later stage in its history. Although English, both as a medium of instruction and at meetings of the various administrative bodies, enjoyed a marked superiority in the earliest years, Afrikaans came to be used more and more frequently. Moreover, the principle that minutes and agendas should be published in both official languages had been accepted as early as 1921. Two members did much to foster the use of Afrikaans in university circles : Ferdinand Postma of Potchefstroom and S. P. Barnard of the Bloemfontein college.

The Registrar, William Thomson, was regarded in some circles as a determined opponent of Dutch and Afrikaans. He was given a few words of advice by the Pretoria *Volkstem* soon after the opening of the university's offices in Somerset House : " 'n Teënstander van gelijke regte . . . is 'n anakronisme . . . Die Noordelike Universiteit word 'n beslis tweetalige Universiteit, of gladniks; en ons wou die Registrateur van die begin af goed laat verstaan, dat ons hier g'n nonsens op daardie stuk gaan verdraag nie" !

Thomson, however, was the subject of further attacks. When, for example, Theophilus Scheepers of the Middelburg (Transvaal) High School received his M.A. diploma in English, he wrote a bitter letter of complaint to the university in October, 1919, asking whether Dutch was felt to be "te onbeschaafd voor 't fijne gevoel van de Universiteitsraad" ! Again, in 1921, the Registrar came under fire, when a correspondent in the *Volkstem* asked whether Thomson was "zulk 'n gebrekkig opgevoed man, dat hij alleen Engels kent". The writer offered to send his "huisbooi" to help the Registrar, for he was " 'n flukse ou kaffer" who could speak three languages fluently ! The matter was brought to the attention of Prime Minister Smuts in a less provocative manner by A. D. R. Bisschop, one of a Pretoria family much to the fore in the current fight for language rights. Bisschop pointed out that the neglect of Dutch in official notices, such as the one from the university which had occasioned the *Volkstem* letter, caused great offence in South Africa. It was, he said, "plagerijen zoals deze, welke ons verbitteren, en welke bijdragen tot een slechte verhouding tusschen de rassen in deze Unie". With evident relief, Patrick Duncan, the Minister of Education of the day, welcomed the satisfactory disposal of the issue in an exchange of letters between the Registrar and G. S. Preller, historian and assistant editor of the newspaper in question. Preller's role in the language struggle was a considerable one.

With Thomson's retirement, the language problem in administration appears to have been solved. It was, however, to remain a live issue in the teaching sphere. Potchefstroom had, from the beginning, been an institution for Afrikaners, but the colleges in such Afrikaans-speaking areas as Pretoria, Wellington and Bloemfontein continued to reflect the dominance of English which had for so long characterized South African higher education. The Transvaal University College had always tried to maintain a bilingual approach and was proud to proclaim in 1923 that it was "less provincial or sectional in character" than any other college in the country. It needed, in any case, the financial support of Pretoria's many English speakers and fought hard in the twenties to maintain its policy against increasing pressure from Afrikaans speakers for the wider use of their language in lecture rooms. Similar tensions were in evidence at Grey University College in Bloemfontein, where Senate in 1929 opposed the permanent appointment of D. F. Malherbe as Principal because he championed the cause of an Afrikaans-medium university college. Many on Senate felt that the institution should try at all costs to appeal to both sections of the European community.

When the new University of Pretoria came into being in 1930, it was confidently asserted that, so far as language was concerned, the foundation would continue to reflect the desires of both sections. Two years later, however, the phased elimination of English as the general medium of instruction began. This gave encouragement to those who wished to see the same thing happen at Grey University College in Bloemfontein. One step

Universiteit van Suid-Afrika.

Voortrekker Eeufees - Jaar

1838 GRAAD VAN BACCALAUREUS ARTIUM. 1938

SPES IN ARDUIS

Hiermee verklaar ons dat

Special degree certificates with an appropriate design were issued by the university in 1938 to commemorate the VOORTREKKER CENTENARY.

A Voortrekker Centenary Memorial Fund was also established to provide awards for writers on the Great Trek period, or on the general development of South Africa to 1875. Initially, an annual prize of £60 (R120) was offered for an essay on a set subject.

The fund is still in existence and offers bursaries for masters' and doctoral examinations (R120 and R500 respectively). Dissertations and theses may now deal with South African themes to 1900.

Degree Certificate: Voortrekker Centenary, 1938

taken there in 1935 – a change of title to the University College of the Orange Free State – served to strengthen the bonds linking the institution with a predominantly Afrikaans-speaking province. By 1942, H. van der Merwe Scholtz was advocating that the future policy at Bloemfontein should be to create an Afrikaans-medium college, but that a high degree of bilingualism should be encouraged. At this period, too, the selection of Anna de Villiers as Principal of the Huguenot University College heralded a greater emphasis upon Afrikaans, although there was some opposition to this in the college Senate.

The appointment of bilingual teaching staffs at universities and university colleges had been regarded by the Minister of Education in 1930, D. F. Malan, as the best way of ensuring fair treatment; his attempt at that time to speed the pace of this change through government control over appointments was regarded with suspicion in some circles, however. English speakers in particular feared that the supply of able lecturers and professors would dry up if bilingualism were insisted upon. As in the last days of the Cape University, they protested that South Africa would be denied the services of highly qualified men and women from the British Isles and elsewhere if newcomers were to be compelled to learn Afrikaans.

The opening of a teaching university in Pretoria raised the question of the best place for the federal administrative headquarters. When the future of the Cape Town building had been under discussion, Baumgarten had suggested that the University of South Africa should return there, This, however, would have placed the federal university on the periphery of its group of constituent colleges. A change of seat was, however, envisaged and a clause was inserted in the University of Pretoria Act to give effect to it. A move to Bloemfontein was canvassed by many, but there was no unanimity on the subject within the university. Although the question was debated at intervals over a long period, Council came to no firm conclusion. Grant's successor as Registrar, Langham Murray, was not in favour of leaving the capital and, as a counter to Bloemfontein's offer of a site, sought

184

without success to wring a similar concession from the City Council of Pretoria. The municipal authorities did, however, provide an annual contribution of R300 to the university's funds from 1940. The move to Bloemfontein was successfully resisted.

The University of South Africa, although not a shining light in the higher educational firmament, played its part in intellectual movements at home and abroad. It was represented at the quinquennial congresses of the imperial universities and on the Universities Bureau in Britain; its delegates attended such world conferences as that on higher education held in Paris in 1937. It was also touched by the activities of certain organizations which flourished in the inter-war years, when the League of Nations seemed to guarantee friendship and understanding among peoples. The University of South Africa gave its support to the conferences of the New Education Fellowship organized in South Africa by E. G. Malherbe; it played its part, too, in fostering good international relations through the work of the South African Universities Lectureship Committee and the Carnegie Corporation Visitors' Grants Committee. The South African Institute of Race Relations also had a university representative on its governing body. Frank Buchman's Oxford Group made its impact upon student life in those years. On more than one occasion a conscience was stirred by the realization of moral guilt and the federal university received a penitent, if belated apology for cheating in examinations!

As a federation of constituent colleges, however, the future looked bleak after the loss of the Pretoria institution. Although the Huguenot University College remained small, the other four grew steadily in size and influence. In 1930, both the Natal and Rhodes University Colleges had enrolments of over 400, while Grey University College had more than 300 and that at Potchefstroom nearly 250. Natal, the largest, took the first steps towards independence and much of the credit is due to the pioneering work undertaken by J. W. Bews, who became Principal at this time. He had first contemplated a federal university for Natal, including colleges for African and Indian students and with

185

HUGH BRYAN was born on 21 August, 1871 at Lyddington, Rutland, England. He was educated at Oundle School and Queen's College, Cambridge, graduating in classics.

He taught for a number of years in England and was at Dover College in 1902, when he decided to emigrate to Natal. He was on the staff of Maritzburg College until 1904, when he joined the inspectorate. Chief Inspector in 1917, he was appointed Superintendent of Education for Natal in 1923, a post he held until 1930.

Between 1934 and 1937, he acted as Registrar at the Natal University College and, after the outbreak of the second World War, returned to teaching at Hilton College. A good sportsman, he was also prominent in the Rotary movement.

A member of Council from 1923 until 1930, he served as Vice-Chancellor for the last two years of this period.

Hugh Bryan died on 9 July, 1955 at his son's house in Kloof, near Durban. His funeral took place at Pietermaritzburg, which had long been his home.

Hugh Bryan, M.A.
Member of Council 1923–1930
Vice-Chancellor 1928–1930

facilities for Europeans in both Durban and Pietermaritzburg. Although the first part of his dream was never realized, the second came to pass. The link with the Natal Technical College was broken in 1931 and the recently completed Howard Memorial College in Durban was taken over by the present university, together with the technical institution's university departments there. The School of Art continued to serve both colleges until 1935.

The coming of the second World War in 1939 prevented any further collegiate defections for some years. Although, once again, there were serious differences of opinion on the role the nation should play in the conflict, the University of South Africa maintained the tradition of neutrality it had inherited from its predecessor. The armed forces of the Union gained study concessions and those in internment and prisoner-of-war camps in South Africa had reason to be grateful for opportunities provided to further their education. The wide distribution of the country's military forces also greatly extended the university's work.

Apart from the disputed Convocation election of 1942, there were few incidents which brought the university into the political arena in those troubled years. There was, however, some student unrest at Potchefstroom and Senate anxiety at the Huguenot University College in Wellington about the possible effect of pro-German propaganda there. The complaint of a parent whose child had failed a music examination took on a new and topical note : "Ons as ouers moet erken dat die dogter miskien gefouteer het om Duits te sing wat moontlik onwenslik was in hierdie tyd van groot bitterheid" ! One last echo of wartime animosities was heard in the first days of peace, when an examination paper in political science included questions on national socialism which would, perhaps, have been better omitted. The matter caused ill-feeling and questions were asked about it in parliament.

The war also caused administrative problems, made no easier by financial starvation. Annual Senate meetings were abandoned and the Senate Executive Committee enjoyed greatly enhanced powers. It was found that the statutory provisions for university administration were inadequate for efficient government and

188

Council and Senate discussed the problem at some length in committee. Reconstruction, however, had to await the coming of peace. Then, too, the financial position of the nation's universities was investigated by a committee of enquiry under the chairmanship of P. J. du Toit, the Director of Veterinary Services.

However, by 1945, the special problems of the University of South Africa went far beyond the financial. The colleges had grown enormously and, with the exception of little Huguenot, which had 120 students in that year, were ready to assume full independence. The enrolments for 1946 made this abundantly clear, for returning servicemen greatly increased the numbers studying at the big four. At Natal, there were almost 2 000 students, a figure not far short of the enrolment at the University of Stellenbosch. Both Rhodes University College and the University College of the Orange Free State had more than 1 000 students, while about 800 were enrolled at Potchefstroom. The South African Native College, too, with some 300 students in 1945, had made rapid strides. It was not yet ready for university status, but it was now pressing for admission to the federal fold. Some were prepared to accept it as a constituent without question; others were as strongly opposed to such a move, for the race problem would certainly arise over the admission of its representatives on Senate and Council.

Early in 1946, the Natal University College gave notice of its intention to seek independent status. This development led to the appointment of a commission under the chairmanship of E. H. Brookes to report on the future of the University of South Africa. Brookes and his fellow Commissioners – K. Bremer, P. J. du Toit and Eliza B. Hawkins, with J. E. S. van Zyl as Secretary – announced their findings in May, 1947. They recommended independence for all the constituents, with the exception of the Huguenot University College. They considered that the Wellington institution should discuss the possibility of affiliation with the University of Stellenbosch. However, if that proved impossible, they were prepared to give it a period of grace, during which it would have to prove itself. For the South African Native College,

S E N A T E lost many valuable members when the Transvaal University College became the independent University of Pretoria in 1930.

Fears were expressed that the loss of this constituent college would inevitably lead to the dissolution of the federal university. This did, in fact, occur at a later stage. In the intervening years, however, the remaining colleges continued to work harmoniously in the academic life of the University of South Africa.

Chairmen of Senate, 1928–1944
(For the period 1934–1938,
see Chairmen of Senate, 1918–1928)

Prof. A.E. du Toit
(Transvaal University College),
1928–1930

Prof. T.F. Dreyer
(Grey University College/
University College of the
Orange Free State),
1930–1932; 1938–1940
(Photo: U.O.F.S.)

Prof. G.F. Dingemans
odes University College),
1932–1934
oto: Rhodes University)

Prof. J. Smeath Thomas
(Rhodes University College),
1940–1942

Prof. J. McKinnell
(Natal University College),
1942–1944

affiliation with Rhodes in Grahamstown was suggested, since there, the report stated, "no hostility on racial grounds" existed.

These recommendations were implemented, step by step. The college at Fort Hare joined its Grahamstown neighbour, an arrangement which lasted for almost a decade. The Huguenot University College neither succeeded in affiliating with Stellenbosch, nor in recapturing past glories. It ceased to exist in its old form from the end of 1950, being transformed into a training college for the social workers of the Dutch Reformed *(Nederduitse Gereformeerde)* Church which had originally sponsored its inauguration. One by one, the other colleges left the federation. Act 4 of 1948 established a University of Natal which began operations in March of the following year; Act 21 of 1949 created the University of the Orange Free State from March, 1950; Rhodes University came into being on 10 March, 1951, in terms of Act 15 of 1949; a week later, Act 19 of 1950 was implemented, when Potchefstroom University for Christian Higher Education gained its independence.

The federal university thus ceased to be; the University of South Africa, however, lived on. That it was able to do so stems from the fact that it was compelled to provide examinations not only for its college students, but also for private, or external candidates. This side of its work was of minor importance in 1918; by 1945, however, there was immense pressure from unattached students of all races to obtain qualifications without attendance at a university or college. In 1918 and for many years thereafter, the external student was regarded with little favour and many hoped to see his eventual disappearance from the university scene. By 1945, his needs could no longer be ignored. The satisfaction of this demand laid the foundations for the University of South Africa of today.

7 *The growing problem of external study*

The University of South Africa was legally bound, under section 18 of Act 12 of 1916, "to make provision for examining every . . . student . . . not a student at a constituent college". It has been suggested that the relevant section was included as an after-thought to conciliate the few who, in the last days of the University of the Cape of Good Hope, called attention to the plight of non-collegiate students. Whatever the reason, the legislation of 1916, in the words of a later Registrar, Langham Murray, turned "a right of the old University . . . into a compulsion", so far as the new one was concerned. Section 18 was to open wide the door to an ever-increasing number of private students. In 1919, they numbered 208; by 1944, more than 3 000 external candidates sought the degrees and diplomas of the university. The inter-vening years also saw a notable increase in enrolments at the colleges and independent universities of South Africa, but the proportion of external students to the national total rose from 8,6% in 1919 to 21,5% in the last full year of the second World War.

The federal university did not teach private students; it merely examined them. Not all such candidates for its examinations, however, were entirely deprived of instruction, for even before the disappearance of the University of the Cape of Good Hope, tutorial classes and correspondence colleges had been founded in South Africa to cater for their needs. Among the latter, the University Correspondence College of Cambridge, England ex-tended its activities to the colonies before Union, providing the

SAMUEL HENRI PELLISSIER was born on 10 November, 1887 in the old mission house at Bethulie in the Orange Free State. Taught by his father until he was 11 years of age, his subsequent schooling was interrupted by the Anglo-Boer War.

He matriculated in 1905 and after a period as a school-teacher, attended Grey College, where he obtained the B.A. degree in 1909 and a teaching certificate in the following year. Further study in the Netherlands ensued. On his return, he became Vice-Principal of schools at Lindley and Boshof, before accepting a principalship at Ficksburg in 1917.

From 1927 until 1947, he was Director of Education for the Orange Free State and from 1948 to 1959, Chairman of the Board of Control of the South African Broadcasting Corporation. Samuel Henri Pellissier's services were recognized in 1944, when an honorary doctorate in education was conferred upon him by the University of Stellenbosch. In the cultural field, he was the founder of the *Volksang* and *Volkspele* movement and took a prominent part in national festivals. He also published in 1956 a biography of his French missionary grandfather, Jean Pierre Pellissier.

A member of the university Council, with one brief intermission, from 1927 until 1954, he was chosen as Vice-Chancellor for the period 1932 to 1934.

Dr Samuel Henri Pellissier, B.A., D.Ed. (h.c.)
Member of Council 1927–1948; 1948–1954
Vice-Chancellor 1932–1934
President of Convocation 1930–1931

courses of study which helped such students as Gerrit Besselaar, long Professor of Modern Languages at Natal, to obtain academic qualifications. Undertakings of this kind were to proliferate in the twenties and thirties. Some, like the *Helpmekaar* of the *Transvaalse Onderwysersvereniging*, founded in 1927, developed out of the pioneering efforts of teachers or teaching associations; one – the *Volkskorrespondensie Kollege* of the next decade – sought the collaboration of a recognized university college – the federal constituent in Bloemfontein.

Two commercial institutions which did much to help the external student were David Young's Rapid Results College of Durban, established in 1928, and P. W. Zorn's University Correspondence Courses of Pretoria, directed in the late thirties by S. P. E. Boshoff and S. J. Hofmeyr. This firm, in association with the *Helpmekaar* college, became the Transafrica Correspondence College of Johannesburg, initially under the control of Boshoff and H. G. Luttig. By 1945, there were over twenty such businesses in existence. Some, perhaps, were not of high standing, but the best of them had the interests of the private student at heart.

Some external students were, in fact, attending recognized teaching institutions. The difficult position of candidates for university examinations who studied at the Potchefstroom college led to the inclusion of that institution in the federal fold; students studied for degree examinations at training colleges for teachers such as those at Paarl in the Cape and Heidelberg in the Transvaal; the technical institution in Durban also provided graduate courses before these were placed under the jurisdiction of the Natal University College. Attempts were made on more than one occasion to bring certain students into association with the university on a group basis. The Catholic Dominican Sisters of King William's Town approached the university for recognition of this kind in 1937, but the move aroused religious animosities. The militantly Protestant Grand Lodge of the Loyal Orange Institution of South Africa rejoiced because the Catholic application was turned down; others wrongly interpreted the rejection

196

as an example of anti-Catholic bigotry. A similar request for group recognition came at a later date from the Seventh-day Adventist Church, whose students study at Helderberg College in the Cape. This, too, was initially opposed by the University of South Africa.

The great majority of students, however, were not affiliated with any teaching institution, other than the correspondence colleges. They were often confused with another group which was making an impact on the university scene in the twenties – the extra-mural students. The Transvaal University College was a pioneer in this type of extension work and an extra-mural division had been formed there soon after the close of the first World War. Paterson and Macfadyen had helped to establish it and its further development owed much to the efforts of Holloway and Brookes in the fields of commerce, law and administration. The type of facility provided by the college and the opportunities for advancement which the federal university's examinations afforded those who studied privately were both part of what Brookes described in 1930 as "a rising tide" which was making itself felt in education "the world over".

The chance to earn a degree as an external student was welcomed by those who lived in neighbouring territories with no local university institutions and by non-Europeans in the Union for whom collegiate facilities were lacking. The South African Native College could not cope with the increasing demand for places, even though it took a certain number of non-Africans; at other university foundations the problem of race integration arose. In Durban, where Mabel Palmer began classes for Indian students in 1936, the road to further advancement for this section seemed to be barred by the hostility of some members of the Natal University College Council to the mixing of races on the campus. Articulate Indian opinion, on the other hand, wanted no part in the provision of a separate college for Indian students. In fact, no further expansion of such facilities for non-Europeans in South Africa took place until the efforts of the Dutch Reformed Churches resulted in the creation of the Pretoria *Kolege*

LANGHAM DALE MURRAY was born on 4 November, 1892 at Sea Point, Cape Town and was named after his great-uncle, the university's first Vice-Chancellor. After matriculating at the Boys' High School, Stellenbosch, he took a B.A., with honours in classics, at the Victoria College in 1911.

His subsequent studies as a Rhodes Scholar at Trinity College, Oxford were interrupted by the first World War, in which he saw active service. He was taken prisoner in 1918 and was awarded the D.C.M. He returned to Oxford, completed his degree and in 1919, joined the staff of the University of South Africa. He became Registrar in 1934, retiring early in 1953.

A man of great courtesy and conservative by nature, he is remembered, like Sir William Thomson, for an astonishing memory for names and figures. His years as Registrar were not easy ones. The second World War and the introduction of the Division of External Studies in particular caused immense complications in university administration.

Langham Murray moved to Salisbury shortly after his retirement and was for a time Secretary-Treasurer and later Registrar of the University College of Rhodesia and Nyasaland, today the University of Rhodesia. In 1956, he became an examinations officer in the Southern Rhodesian Ministry of African Education, retiring from service with the Rhodesian government in February, 1973. He was awarded an honorary doctorate in administration by the University of South Africa in its centenary year.

Dr Langham Dale Murray, M.A., D.Admin. (h.c.), D.C.M.
Registrar 1934–1953

ya Bana ba Afrika in 1946. Much was expected of this venture, but it never rose to great heights.

A further reason for the growth of the system of external study lies in South African conditions during the depression years. Then, the examinations of the University of South Africa offered an opportunity for improvement to many whose parents could not afford to send them to a teaching university or university college. Finally, the examinations for external students were often welcomed by older men and women who, for one reason or another, had found it necessary to discontinue their studies after leaving school. Many of them were in full-time employment and had no other way of obtaining graduate qualifications.

The phenomenal and unexpected increase in the number of external students for the various examinations of the university between the two World Wars undoubtedly helped the administration financially. Nevertheless, from an academic standpoint, there was much to be said against external study and there were many, particularly in the federal Senate, who looked with great disfavour upon the prevailing system. That it should be abolished as quickly as possible was a general sentiment in South African university circles throughout the twenties and thirties.

However, if that were to happen, the field would be left open to an outside institution and students would simply turn to the external examinations of the University of London. One of the correspondence firms – Union College of Johannesburg – pointed this out in 1929, suggesting at the same time that the English university's degree requirements were not so restrictive as those of the University of South Africa. The Van der Horst Commission had made it clear in 1928 that it expected to see a speedy end to external degree work and it was one of the arguments advanced by the federal university at that time that it could at least combat the influence of the University of London in South Africa for as long as the system was tolerated. For by 1928, the University of South Africa, which had earlier tried to defend the external degree, had come to accept that it must ultimately go. What it was not prepared to accept, however, was that other universities in the country should in the meantime be allowed to provide degree examinations for private students. And in the early thirties, the new University of Pretoria was anxious to take a bite from the external cake.

A draft bill was, in fact, prepared in 1932 to enable any university to examine external candidates, although such students would be compelled to take part of their courses internally. This would have affected all external candidates for the University of South Africa's degree examinations, except those at the South African Native College who were specially exempted from the provisions of the bill. There was an immediate outcry from individuals, teachers' organizations and spokesmen for the non-Europeans, and the bill was shelved when Hertzog and Smuts unexpectedly joined forces in the political compromise of March, 1933.

One of the most serious accusations levelled against the external student was that the standard of attainment which he brought to the examination table was markedly lower than that achieved by the collegiate student. Many circumstances contributed to this, but the blame was largely laid at the door of the correspondence firms. In 1932, when the University of South Africa suggested that their activities should be controlled, it was said that some of these institutions deliberately misled students, engaged ill-qualified staff, overcharged and provided inadequate assistance. Moreover, the federal university came to resent the use by one of them of the word "university" in its title. This problem would arise again in 1944 in a different context, when the Catholic authorities decided to establish a collegiate foundation at Roma in Basutoland, forerunner of the present university for the former High Commission territories, today Lesotho, Botswana and Swaziland. The term "university" should, in the eyes of the federal body, be restricted to independent degree-conferring institutions or to the federal constituent colleges.

Irritation over the poor quality of students trained by the correspondence colleges long tended to reinforce the idea that the system of external study should be brought to an end. There

MARTHINUS CHRISTOFFEL BOTHA was born on 26 August, 1886 in the district of George (Cape). He had a hard struggle to complete his education, for he came from a poor family and was compelled to work in a number of fields, including teaching, after he left primary school. He obtained the B.A. degree at the Victoria College in 1914 and after a further period as a schoolmaster, was appointed to a post at the University of Cape Town in 1918 as a lecturer in Dutch and Afrikaans. He pioneered the teaching of Afrikaans at that university and advanced to a professorship in 1921, when he had received his M.A. degree.

In 1929, he was appointed Superintendent General of Education for the Cape Province and five years later, became Secretary for Education in the Department of Union Education. Chairman of the Board of Control of the South African Broadcasting Corporation from 1936 until 1942, he was Principal of the University of Pretoria from 1941 until his retirement in 1947. A champion of Afrikaans, it was largely as a result of his efforts that the University of Pretoria was able to establish a Faculty of Medicine in which that language is used as a medium of instruction.

Professor Botha was awarded an honorary doctorate in literature by the University of South Africa in 1936 and an honorary LL.D. by the University of Cape Town in 1950.

He served the University of South Africa as a member of Council almost continuously from 1929 until 1936 and again from 1954 to 1959. He held the office of Vice-Chancellor between 1934 and 1936.

Professor Botha's death occurred in Cape Town on 3 January, 1959.

Professor Marthinus Christoffel Botha, M.A.,
D.Litt. (h.c.), LL.D. (h.c.)
Member of Council 1929–1934; 1934–1936; 1954–1959
Vice-Chancellor 1934; 1934–1936
(Photo: University of Pretoria)

203

were few suggestions that the University of South Africa itself should become a teaching university for the benefit of this class of students. Nevertheless, such a revolutionary proposal had occurred to some. As early as January, 1926, Arthur Ritchie Lord, Professor of Philosophy at Rhodes University College, had put the idea forward. His memorandum, which deserves to be remembered as the precursor of later developments, envisaged a tutorial system, with university lecturers available for guidance and interviews. It met, however, with little encouragement and his alternative, that the colleges undertake this kind of work, failed to interest the constituents.

By 1936, J. W. Bews of Natal was alarmed to note that, for the first time, the federal university had a larger enrolment of non-collegiate students than internal ones. A Senate committee was appointed to look into the problem and a number of suggestions were made, including one which had enjoyed the support of D. F. Malan as Minister of Education some years before. This was that a joint board should administer external examinations. Correspondence courses and vacation schools run by the university or by the colleges were suggested, but it was pointed out "that competition with existing Correspondence Colleges will not provide a 'walk-over' ". Lord's ideas of ten years earlier were at last gaining some degree of acceptance and Mabel Palmer in Natal submitted a detailed scheme embracing a correspondence college as part of the university, with itinerant tutors and recognition of approved commercial undertakings. How strong hostility still was to the idea of external study, however, may be gauged from the reaction of the Potchefstroom constituent, which advocated the addition of the words "external student" to degree certificates so earned.

The federal Senate at length produced a report which went no further in the direction of tuition than the possibility of starting vacation schools at the colleges. It also recommended the extension of the degree course for external students from three to four years, an idea which had been suggested several years before by E. H. G. Arndt of the Department of Economics at the Transvaal

University College. E. H. Brookes, however, accused the committee members in a minority report of displaying excessive caution and disagreed with the "underlying assumption of the majority . . . that the University should take no responsibility for the teaching of External Students".

The course for private students in the popular field of commerce and administration had already been lengthened; by 1938, this was extended to all departments of study. The administrative head of the University Correspondence Courses firm, S. J. Hofmeyr, complained immediately and submitted that the regulation was *ultra vires*. The university was forced to take action since a case was to be brought before the courts to test the legality of the measure. Steve Hofmeyr's contention also led to a conflict between the federal university and the Department of Union Education over the presentation of regulations for prior approval. The offending rule was suspended, while both the University of South Africa and the Department of Union Education sought legal opinion on Hofmeyr's argument. There was no unanimity here and the university authorities requested either legislative action to enable them to differentiate between internal and external candidates, or at least the opportunity to discuss the problem with the Minister of Education.

Meanwhile, the Minister, Jan Hofmeyr, had resigned for a brief spell over the native representation question and had been replaced by Henry A. Fagan. It was the new Minister who, with the Secretary for Education, G. von W. Eybers, met a joint delegation of Council and Senate on 25 November, 1938. The member of Council and future Vice-Chancellor, A. A. Roberts, was the chief spokesman for the external students, in the absence of Brookes. While he felt that there was a tendency for some correspondence colleges to become mere degree mills, he considered that the university Senate members were generally far too hostile to this method of study. This was strongly denied, but Professor Dreyer of Bloemfontein was not prepared to see the rights of internal students prejudiced in any way. Professor J. McKinnell of Natal mentioned the proposal which had been

FRANÇOIS DANIËL HUGO was born on 27 February, 1883 on the farm Grootstraat in the Touws River district of the Cape. At the age of 12, he enrolled at the Spes Bona School, De Doorns and subsequently attended the South African College, where he obtained the B.A. degree in 1906. He also qualified as a teacher at the Normal College in Cape Town.

He joined the inspectorate of the Natal Department of Education, was made a full Inspector in 1912 and was transferred for health reasons to the head office in Pietermaritzburg four years later. He was appointed Acting Chief Inspector in 1923, a post which was made permanent in 1931. In that year, he became Superintendent (later Director) of Education for Natal and retained this position until 1941, when he entered the service of the national government as Secretary for Union Education. He retired in July, 1944.

François Daniël Hugo was long active in the life of the Afrikaans-speaking community in Pietermaritzburg and as the first Afrikaner to take charge of the Natal Department of Education, did much to encourage the study of his home language in a largely English-speaking province.

He served on the university Council in his official capacity from 1931 until 1941 and was chosen as Vice-Chancellor for two years in 1936.

He died on 4 September, 1959 at Strand, near Cape Town.

François Daniël Hugo, B.A.
Member of Council 1931–1941
Vice-Chancellor 1936–1938

made to institute oral examinations as a supplementary test of the external student's ability. The Vice-Chancellor, F. S. Malan, alluded to the peculiar difficulties of the South African Native College in its relations with the federal university and F. D. Hugo spoke of the interest then being shown by Indians in Natal on the subject of higher education.

The discussion led to the framing of a bill which included the extension of the external course to four years. Widespread indignation followed, on a scale which suggests that it was not entirely spontaneous. Certainly, the commercial firms, doubtless fearing a loss of income, were implicated. The Minister, the Department of Union Education, individual members of parliament, the federal university and the press were bombarded with angry letters. The new measure, as a Wynberg (Cape) correspondent in the *Argus* pointed out, showed the external student little consideration. The authorities, he went on, with a delightful disregard for metaphor, were simply "putting spokes in our wheels thus rendering the way for us more difficult to pave". Another in the *Diamond Fields Advertiser* rose to the defence of the correspondence firms which he described as "the poor man's home university". Steve Hofmeyr of the University Correspondence Courses submitted to the Chairman of the Public Service Commission a statement which enumerated various disabilities under which the external student worked. He also pointed out that three-quarters of his students were teachers and civil servants who needed special consideration.

Protests were as strong from the Afrikaans-speaking section as from the English. The *Transvaler's* editorial of 22 February, 1939 spoke of the issue as one which concerned "die versterking van die Afrikanerdom", while the Bloemfontein *Volksblad* painted a touching picture of the tired external student sacrificing his leisure while others enjoyed social relaxation. The *Vaderland* struck a lighter note: " ,Wat is 'n eksterne student, Jaap?' vra Vroutjie my gisteraand. ,Eksterne student, skatlief? Dis 'n man wat hom in sy vrye tyd met studie besig hou – ek bedoel studie vir 'n graad, nie van sy finansiële moeilikhede soos ek nie.' . . .

208

,En wat mag interne studente presies beteken, . . . ?' ,Tog baie
duidelik, . . . Interne student is 'n man wat die hele dag sy vrye
tyd maak en dit aan sy pa oorlaat om in sy vrye tyd oor die
finansiële moeilikhede te bekommer.' " !

The general indignation even led to the establishment in
Johannesburg of an external students' association which presented a petition to the Minister of Education, protesting against
what it described as "a form of class legislation". The barrage
of words achieved the desired result and the external student was
able to show that he had some political influence. The bill, which
contained other clauses such as that which provided for additional
examination centres, was amended and Act 21 of 1939 made no
mention of the four year course. It appeared in the annual
Calendar until 1951 as a suspended measure, but the University
of South Africa remained for some time critical of external
standards and increasingly dissatisfied with the work of some of
the correspondence firms which provided the instruction.

It was in part this lack of confidence in the work of the commercial undertakings and in part the coming of war in 1939
which led to a change of attitude within a university which had
done little enough in the past to assist the private student. The
Registrar's Secretary, Kreine Alexander, submitted a report on
the University of London's external system early in 1939, but at
that date Senate did not consider that the limited assistance
afforded students by the English body was applicable to South
African conditions. However, book loan facilities were improved
with the co-operation of the State Library in Pretoria and a
watchful eye was kept upon the whole situation. Problems soon
arose in connection with wartime study, involving such an extension of external examination as the holding of practical tests
in science in distant Cairo.

From 1942, there was a sharp rise in external enrolments for
examination purposes, after an initial drop in the first years of
the war. The University of South Africa might soon have to face
a deluge of applications when serving members of the armed
forces returned to civilian life and saw the advantage of "learn-

FRANÇOIS STEPHANUS MALAN was born on 12 March, 1871 at Bovlei, near Wellington in the Cape. After attending schools in the Paarl district, he entered the Victoria College, where he obtained the B.A. degree in 1892. He completed his studies at Christ's College, Cambridge, gaining an LL.B. in 1895.

Finding little work as an advocate on his return to the Cape, he turned to journalism and became editor of *Ons Land*. During the Anglo-Boer War, he suffered imprisonment for his outspokenness, but came to see the importance for South Africa of harmony between Boer and Briton.

In 1900, he was elected to the House of Assembly as the member for Malmesbury, a seat he retained in the Cape and Union parliaments until 1924. He held cabinet rank under Merriman, Botha and Smuts and was South Africa's first Minister of Education. His major achievement in this capacity was the university legislation of 1916. Elected a Union Senator in 1927, he was President of the Senate in 1940 and 1941.

F.S. Malan was active in the affairs of the Dutch Reformed *(Nederduitse Gereformeerde)* Church and also in cultural life. A founder member of the *Akademie* in 1909, he helped to further the cause of Dutch and Afrikaans. In 1912, he became the first speaker in the history of the examining university to give a graduation address in Dutch. His writings include a biography of Maria Koopmans-De Wet and a chapter in the eighth volume of the *Cambridge History of the British Empire* (1936).

A member of the British Privy Council in 1920, he also received honorary degrees from two universities: the LL.D. of the University of the Cape of Good Hope in 1917 and the D.Ed. of the University of Stellenbosch in 1931.

F.S. Malan served briefly on the Council of the University of South Africa in 1932 as Acting Director of Education for the Transvaal and again from 1936 until 1940 as a representative of the Huguenot University College. He was chosen as Vice-Chancellor for two years in 1938.

He died in Cape Town on 31 December, 1941.

Senator François Stephanus Malan, B.A., LL.B.
LL.D. (h.c.), D.Ed. (h.c.), P.C.
Member of Council 1932; 1936–1940
Vice-Chancellor 1938–1940
(Photo: Government Archives)

ing while earning". Now that the university seemed certain to lose several, if not all of its constituent colleges, its role as inquisitor for students not connected with those scattered teaching units assumed a greater importance. There were even enquiries from beyond the borders – from Kenya, where post-matriculation work was contemplated; from the Northern Rhodesian Copperbelt, requesting external courses in mining engineering; from Moçambique, where the organization called British Education in Lourenço Marques began to think of providing instruction based upon the university's examinations. Here was an opportunity for the federal university to extend its influence yet further and, indeed, to perpetuate its own existence.

A movement which would in time lead to the reconstruction of the University of South Africa began in 1944. At the Senate meeting held that year in Bloemfontein, the problem of external study was discussed with a view to submitting evidence to the recently constituted Committee on Adult Education under the chairmanship of G. von W. Eybers. On this occasion, a motion was put forward by the historian of the University College of the Orange Free State, C. J. Uys, in the name of the Senate of his college. It proposed that the federal university "stappe doen om die beheer oor die opleiding van studente wat begerig is om . . . eksamens ekstern af te lê in oorweging te neem met die doel om moontlik self in die behoefte vir onderrig deur middel van korrespondensielesings te voorsien". This motion was accompanied by a memorandum drawn up by Uys himself. The federal university, he insisted, had two courses open to it : to undertake correspondence work or to draw the commercial firms into the federation. The University of South Africa could no longer stand aside. A new approach was required, consistent with the needs of the present, for as Uys said : "Ons roeping is om ons eie beskawing te bestendig en aan te help, wat sy eie behoeftes en eise het, nie die beskawing wat deur die middeleeuse universiteit gedien is nie".

The University of South Africa was never enthusiastic about the incorporation within the federal framework of commercial

212

institutions of which it disapproved. They, in their turn, defended themselves before the Eybers Committee with spirit. There is no doubt that the best of them, among which may be mentioned the Rapid Results College and the Transafrica amalgamation, did in fact do good work and provided a useful service for many thousands of students. The correspondence firms were at least able to resist the recommendation of the committee that they be state-controlled; government accepted the alternative of a national association which would set and maintain standards of conduct.

The federal university was to move away from the commercial undertakings and at length enter into competition with them. Senate's Standing Committee on External Students recognized in 1944 "that the external student system has come to stay and that (it) is undesirable that the training of such students be left solely to commercial institutions". It therefore recommended the appointment of an officer to be known as the "Director of External Studies", with clearly defined repsonsibilities. Government assistance was to be sought to help finance the proposed extension of the university's functions. The constituent colleges were lukewarm in their approval of this new departure. The Potchefstroom institution went so far as to suggest that an investigation into the external student problem undertaken by the officer designated by the Senate committee would, "uit die aard van die saak", be no objective enquiry.

Individual expressions of opinion varied. One of the more ardent supporters of any scheme to bring the university into closer contact with the external student body was E. Eybers, head of the Department of Education at Bloemfontein. "It requires", he said, "only a limited vision, backed by a controlled imagination, to foresee the immense opportunities presented for satisfying an urgent need for disinterested service . . . There is similarly an almost limitless scope for assistance to the Africans who are more than ever hungering for education". On the other hand, the Registrar, Langham Murray, was unenthusiastic. "External Studies", he wrote in October, 1944, "are not university educa-

213

FERDINAND POSTMA was born on 15 July, 1879 at Aliwal North and received his early education at Middelburg (Cape) and Burgersdorp. In 1898, he wrote the Intermediate B.A. examination at the theological school of the Reformed Church in the latter town, continuing his studies at the *Vrije Universiteit* in Amsterdam. He passed the *Candidaatsexamen* in 1904, a success which entitled him to admittance as a B.A. of the University of the Cape of Good Hope.

On his return to South Africa, he was appointed professor at the theological school in Burgersdorp and moved with it in 1905 to its new home at Potchefstroom. In 1911, he became a candidate for the ministry of the Reformed Church and three years later, received a doctorate from the *Vrije Universiteit* for a thesis presented in Latin.

When the Arts Department of the theological school was converted into a university college in 1919, Ferdinand Postma was chosen as Principal. He held this post until his death, combining his duties with active teaching until 1945. He fought hard for the incorporation of the college as a constituent of the University of South Africa and when this had been achieved in 1921, campaigned for the restoration of its full title: Potchefstroom University College for Christian Higher Education.

Professor Postma was a member of several educational and cultural bodies, among them the *Suid-Afrikaanse Akademie vir Wetenskap en Kuns* and the Joint Matriculation Board. A Fellow of the Royal Society of Arts, he was a prolific writer. His publications include a biography of Paul Kruger and the first Afrikaans-Latin dictionary.

In 1949, the University of South Africa presented him with an honorary doctorate in education. He had devoted many years to the service of the federal institution. A member of Council from 1919 until 1950 and Vice-Chancellor for two terms between 1940 and 1944, he was also Chairman of the Committee of Studies in Classics and twice Dean of the Faculty of Arts and Chairman of Senate.

Ferdinand Postma died in Potchefstroom on 4 November, 1950.

Professor Ferdinand Postma, B.A., Litt.Dr.,
D.Ed. (h.c.), F.R.S.A.
Member of Council 1919–1950
Vice-Chancellor 1940–1944
Dean of the Faculty of Arts 1924–1926; 1931–1933
Chairman of Senate 1926–1928; 1936–1938

tion. The essential element in a university education is sitting at the feet of a Gamaliel; it is not merely acquiring knowledge, which is a subsidiary element in the process; it is the association for a period of the immature and enquiring mind with the trained and stored mind of a teacher, and is thus 'education' in the truest sense of the word''. It was, Murray considered, a fallacy to imagine that the passing of examinations entitled a candidate to a degree. As for the proposed Director, he doubted whether many students would seek his advice on their studies, if that were to be his main function. Moreover, the new officer would be placed in an anomalous position as an administrator with academic duties. It would almost be a return to the first years of the University of the Cape of Good Hope, when the Registrar played so intimate a role in university affairs.

Council decided to appoint a Director of External Studies on a temporary basis for one year. Several names were suggested for the post, including that of the university's most distinguished external student of earlier days, E. H. Brookes, then a Union Senator. The man finally chosen was Professor A. J. H. van der Walt of Potchefstroom University College for Christian Higher Education. His first task was to consider the whole question of external student of earlier days, E. H. Brookes, then a Union on the subject was to guide the future academic development of the University of South Africa. He concluded, after a comprehensive survey of the problem, "that the aims of the University, namely, to ensure a satisfactory training for external students, thereby safeguarding the standard of the degrees, and to serve the general interests of university education, could best be realised by the institution of a Department of External Studies to undertake the training of students in the faculties where this is practicable". As some subjects, particularly those requiring laboratory work, did not lend themselves to tuition by correspondence, he felt that it would be "expedient to limit the work of the proposed Department to the Faculties of Arts, Law and Commerce".

The conclusions reached were in agreement with those expressed by the Eybers Committee in a report published in the

216

same year. They were accepted, with minor changes, by the Council of the University of South Africa. Professor van der Walt was invited to take charge of the new section, an invitation which he accepted with the promise that he would do all within his power "om van die nuwe onderneming 'n sukses te maak, in belang van die goeie naam van die Universiteit, van die opvoeding en van die eksterne studente".

It was to be expected that, when a bill was published early in 1946 to give effect to the new approach in university education, there would be opposition from the commercial firms, for they, as Langham Murray felicitously put it, "like the silversmiths of Ephesus feared that their craft would be endangered". L. L. Boyd of the Rapid Results College submitted a memorandum to government pointing out that Professor van der Walt's strictures on the work of the correspondence colleges were not based upon direct consultation with them. He was also opposed to anything in the operation of the proposed scheme which would in any way place the University of South Africa at an advantage. Another critic was S. P. E. Boshoff of Transafrica and a Convocation member of the university Council. He wrote at some length on the question in a series of articles entitled "Rommelpot in die hanekot", which appeared in the commercial firm's journal, *Horison,* and were subsequently issued in pamphlet form. In them, Professor Boshoff showed a similar irritation with the assumption that the correspondence firms were unequal to the task of providing an efficient service and wondered whether the University of South Africa's new department would do better.

Jan Hofmeyr, as Minister of Education and Finance, had to tread lightly in the delicate matter of placing a state-aided institution in open competition with private concerns. The government was prepared to find a subsidy of R17 000 on the understanding that the University of South Africa would itself raise R20 000. This financial support would give parliament a voice in deciding future policy should a deficit occur in the working of the scheme. The Higher Education Amendment Act received the assent of the Governor-General on 8 May, 1946. It had met

ALFRED ADRIAN ROBERTS was born on 18 February, 1890 at Fauresmith in the Orange Free State. He matriculated at Selborne College, East London, graduated at the Transvaal University College in 1911 and completed his studies at Trinity Hall, Cambridge, where he passed the law tripos.

He practised in Pretoria until 1919, when he was appointed Registrar of the Transval University College, a post he held until 1929. He then resumed his legal career, becoming law adviser to the government in 1935.

Secretary for Education in the Department of Union Education from 1944 until 1949, he was subsequently chosen as South Africa's High Commissioner in Canada. During his four years in this office, he was several times a delegate to the United Nations Organization. In 1954, he led the South African delegation to the Commonwealth Conference in Lahore.

In 1960 and 1961, he was an acting judge of the Transvaal Provincial Division and at the time of his death, Commissioner for Patents. A man of diverse interests and the author of several legal works, he was also a member of a number of educational bodies. In 1959, the University of Cape Town conferred on him an honorary LL.D. degree in recognition of his services.

A member of the Council of the University of South Africa from 1930 until 1946, he was chosen as Vice-Chancellor for two years in 1944.

Alfred Adrian Roberts died in Pretoria on 7 April, 1964.

Adv. Alfred Adrian Roberts, M.A., LL.B., LL.D. (h.c.), Q.C.
Member of Council 1930–1946
Vice-Chancellor 1944–1946
President of Convocation 1928–1929
(Photo: University of Pretoria)

218

with some opposition in its passage from such determined supporters of the commercial undertakings as the Dominion Party member for Pinetown, J. S. Marwick, the British-born Labour Party member for Durban North, the Rev. C. F. Miles-Cadman of the Anglican Church, and the Transvaal Nationalists, S. J. Swanepoel of Gezina and W. D. Brink of Christiana. Jan Hofmeyr was able, however, to reassure the House of Assembly that the Division of External Studies would devise a method to ensure that its students obtained no unfair advantage over those who studied with the private concerns. Senator Brookes gave the bill his blessing in the upper House and in the House of Assembly, the New Zealand-born educationist and economist, J. R. Sullivan of the Durban (Berea) constituency, spoke for many when he expressed the hope that the new venture would "lead ultimately to the establishment of a great national university – a people's university – in South Africa".

By the time the Brookes Commission of 1947 was deliberating on the future of the University of South Africa, the institution had therefore been set upon a new path. It had not yet ceased to be a federation of colleges, but its future greatness would not lie along federal lines. It had often been the object of attack in its Cape days as a mere examining board; as a federal university, it had lived under the threat of dissolution almost from the day of its birth. It had, however, at last succeeded in justifying its existence by undertaking the tuition and guidance of those candidates for its examinations whose welfare it had largely ignored for almost three quarters of a century.

8 First steps along a new path

Professor van der Walt began his career as full-time Director of the Division of External Studies on 15 February, 1946, with one typist, Pamela R. Storey, to assist him. The University of South Africa of today, both as a teaching institution and as an administrative body, had been born.

The new section was not, however, welcomed with open arms on all sides. Even within the university, it was very much a fledgling in the nest and, for many, an unwelcome intruder. The salaries of Director and Registrar had been placed upon an equal basis to avoid any suggestion that the head of the teaching branch of the university was to be considered a more important officer than the senior administrative official. For the Registrar's office was, after all, the nerve centre which controlled not only collegiate affairs and examinations, but also the vital matter of finance. Langham Murray, ever courteous and gentlemanly as Registrar, was nevertheless zealous in guarding the rights of the existing administration. The Division of External Studies, if it ever survived its infancy, was to be no more than a constituent section of the University of South Africa, with a specialized task.

And indeed, Langham Murray was not one of those who expected it to succeed. He said so on more than one occasion and was confident that he would outlive the newcomer. He would doubtless have agreed with much that was asserted about its probable direction by the Natal University College in 1947, when an "External University" was described as "an overflow activity of

The distinguished historian and university administrator, ANDRIES JACOBUS HENDRIK JOHANNES VAN DER WALT, was born on 12 October, 1893 in the district of Steynsburg (Cape). His early education was seriously interrupted and he did not matriculate until 1916. An outstanding university student, he completed his studies at Potchefstroom University College by obtaining the M.A. degree in 1921. Seven years later, he was awarded the degree of D.Phil. by the Kaiser Wilhelm University in Berlin.

He had already lectured at Potchefstroom before he left for Germany and on his return, was appointed Professor of History there. He played an active part in the academic life of the college and of the federal university. Long a member of the Committee of Studies in History of the University of South Africa, he was Dean of the Faculty of Arts from 1943 until 1946. The author of a number of books and articles, he collaborated with J.A. Wiid and A.L. Geyer in the production of a general history of South Africa in two volumes.

In 1945, Professor van der Walt was invited to report upon the possibility of inaugurating a system of tuition for external students. His findings were accepted by the university and in the following year, a Division of External Studies was established under his guidance.

He remained Director of External Studies until 1953, when he became the first Principal of the University of South Africa, a position he held until his retirement three years later. On 14 July, 1956, the university conferred upon him an honorary doctorate in literature and philosophy. It was a fitting tribute to his academic achievements and his great work in pioneering new methods of teaching in higher education.

Professor van der Walt, who had been a member of Council since 1946, retained his connection with the governing body until 1971, when he declined further nomination. His death occurred in Pretoria on 16 August, 1972.

Professor Andries Jacobus Hendrik Johannes van der Walt,
M.A., D.Phil., D.Litt. et Phil. (h.c.)
Member of Council 1946–1971
Director of External Studies 1946–1953
Principal 1953–1956
Dean of the Faculty of Arts 1943–1946

223

the university proper", powerless to maintain standards and leading directly to the creation of "a cramming shop".

As the Director and his staff began to feel that their role in higher education was not necessarily going to be a transient one, the gap between the administrative and teaching sections grew wider. There seems, for example, to have been a good deal of unnecessary letter writing, when frank discussion of problems would perhaps have cleared the air. There was also too much overlapping of the sections and a certain amount of friction regarding promotion prospects among the senior administrative staffs of each as the Registrar approached retiring age.

And, if there was a lack of faith in the value of the Division of External Studies in Langham Murray's department, this only reflected similar scepticism elsewhere. There were some who hoped to see the University of South Africa make a success of its new undertaking; many, however, of those who sat on its Council or who safeguarded the interests of the constituent colleges in the federal Senate treated the Director's small staff with condescension. College professors and heads of departments far outnumbered the representatives of Professor van der Walt's section at Senate meetings in the early days and academic control was firmly exercised by the college members throughout the federal period. Indeed, it was to be some years before the Division of External Studies would have its own Chairman of Senate and a full range of faculty Deans.

However, it must be admitted that those who lectured under Professor van der Walt were as yet beginners in their trade. It was therefore no bad thing that the colleges held the initial balance of power. In that way, uniform high standards could be maintained in the interests of the university as a whole. This, at all events, was how the situation was regarded by W. F. Barker, the Professor of Chemistry at Rhodes University College, who served as Chairman of Senate from 1948 until 1952, in succession to H. van der Merwe Scholtz of the University College of the Orange Free State.

So far as meetings of the university Council were concerned,

224

the Division of External Studies spoke only through the Director, and then merely by courtesy of Senate. Ten of the twenty-five members represented college interests, while the heads of the provincial education departments and their colleagues from South West Africa and Southern Rhodesia also attended. In this connection, it may be noted that the teaching division faced some initial hostility, both in Cape and Transvaal educational circles, with regard to the recognition of external degrees.

There was one other body directly concerned with the university's new task – the Joint Committee of Council and Senate for External Studies. This consisted of the Chairman of Senate and two other Senate members, the Vice-Chancellor, the Chairmen of Council's Finance and Staff Committees, the Principal of the South African Native College, the Deans of the Faculties of Arts and of Commerce and Administration and the Director of the Division of External Studies. The Director was later supported by one of his colleagues.

Here, as in other spheres, the teaching arm of the university was largely manipulated by outsiders. The Director could, however, usually count on the support of the Principal of the Fort Hare college – Alexander Kerr until 1948, when he was succeeded by C. P. Dent. Although that institution enjoyed a special link with the federal university until its brief affiliation with Rhodes, its students were still considered to be external candidates for examinations. The University of South Africa and its Division of External Studies were also fortunate in having A. J. R. van Rhijn as Vice-Chancellor from 1948 until 1952. The Nationalist Member of Parliament for Bethlehem in 1948, Dr van Rhijn became Administrator of South West Africa two years later. He was at all times a strong supporter of the university's teaching venture, both in the House of Assembly and in other areas of public life.

Once the Division of External Studies had been approved, Council authorized the appointment of a number of lecturers and clerical officers. It was, however, none too easy to find staff of any kind at that end of war period. The vast expansion of the existing universities and colleges to meet the needs of returning members of the armed forces absorbed most available lecturers; moreover, there seemed little certainty that the new section would become a permanent addition to the teaching universities. Many approved posts remained vacant and most of the lecturers appointed came to the University of South Africa from other fields of education, particularly the secondary schools. Most of the men and women selected for posts in the early years and subsequently were Afrikaans-speaking. This circumstance at once reflects the greater degree of bilingualism among teachers in this group, a wider hostility towards the new method of university teaching among English-speaking graduates and above all, the availability of larger numbers of Afrikaans-speaking candidates for posts.

The first member of the teaching staff to be appointed was H. J. J. M. van der Merwe, head of the Department of *Afrikaans en Nederlands,* who had just received his doctorate from the University of Pretoria. He was then teaching in an acting capacity at the College of Education in the city, after several years as a teacher at the Central Junior High School, housed in the building in Van der Walt Street from which a young Winston Churchill had made his escape during the Anglo-Boer War.

The appointment of three more senior lecturers soon followed. These were A. S. Roux and C. B. Smit, both long in the service of the university, and K. D. Venter, who died shortly after his recent retirement. A. S. Roux, head of the Department of Psychology, came to the university with teaching experience not only in schools, but also in the correspondence college field with which the Division of External Studies was now in competition. C. B. Smit of the Department of Geography was on the staff of the Pretoria Technical College, whose Principal, J. P. Duminy, was to prove a good friend to the new university venture. K. D. Venter was the first head of the Department of Economics and joined the staff of the University of South Africa with extensive teaching experience in the Cape and the Transvaal. A great practical joker, he helped to make the task of getting the Division of External Studies on its feet a little lighter.

These were the men who gathered at Somerset House on the morning of 30 July, 1946 to meet the new Director and to plan the course ahead. They were soon joined by others. At the second formal meeting of the staff on 3 September, 1946, in an association which ultimately became the Board of Tutors, six more lecturers and senior lecturers were present. These were P. J. Coertze, J. Albert Coetzee, C. F. J. Muller, F. M. P. Oosterhof, H. L. Swanepoel and J. A. van der Walt. Two – C. F. J. Muller and J. A. van der Walt – were to make a permanent career with the university.

Dr Coertze was the first member of the teaching staff to be appointed with full-time lecturing experience at another university. He came to the Division of External Studies from Stellenbosch as Senior Lecturer in African Studies. This embraced the fields of anthropology, Bantu languages and Native administration, now separate departments. He did not, however, remain long with the new teaching section, leaving in 1949 to join the staff of the University of Pretoria as Professor of Bantu Languages. Already, in 1947, the university had appointed the man who was to succeed him. E. F. Potgieter, who left to assume the rectorship of the University College of the North in 1959, was a tower of strength in the university and worked in close harmony with the Director to promote its welfare. Long after his departure, he maintained a close interest in the affairs of the University of South Africa as a member of its Council.

Dr J. Albert Coetzee headed the Department of Politics and Public Administration, separately designated in the early *Calendars*. He has been described as the stormy petrel of the first years, with wide-ranging interests by no means confined to the teaching of his subject. His resignation in 1950 was occasioned by his aspirations as a journalist and his subsequent career took him into provincial and national politics. He was for some years the Nationalist Member of Parliament for the Kempton Park constituency in the Transvaal. His place was taken in October, 1950 by a young clerk in the university's administrative section, Willem

227

A. Kleynhans, later to obtain a professorship in the Department of Political Science and Public Administration.

C. F. J. Muller joined the staff of the Division of External Studies as Senior Lecturer in History, after a distinguished university career at Stellenbosch and Oxford. The son of the brilliant Rev. "Tobie" Muller, he brought to the new venture in Pretoria some experience of university teaching at Stellenbosch and school teaching in Cape Town. Christoffel Muller obtained his doctorate under H. B. Thom in 1947 and was to become the leading authority on the Great Trek period in South African history.

F. M. P. Oosterhof had been a Dutch exchange student at the University of Pretoria before the war and had joined his nation's armed forces, only to be imprisoned by the Japanese in the Far East. When the world conflict ended, he returned to South Africa and was appointed to the teaching staff of the university as Lecturer in French and in Classics. He was later promoted to a senior position and in 1949, was granted leave to study for his doctorate in Paris. After his return, he obtained a professorship at Stellenbosch and held this post until his death a few years later. His absence in 1949 and 1950 brought to the service of the Division of External Studies a young scholar who was later to return in a permanent capacity to the Department of Classical Languages. This was G. van N. Viljoen, who had been recommended to Oosterhof as a suitable temporary replacement by Hilgard Muller, then lecturing in Latin at the University of Pretoria and destined to become South Africa's Minister of Foreign Affairs.

The first appointment in the Department of Law was that of Dr H. L. Swanepoel, who subsequently lectured in that field at Potchefstroom. As he was unable to move permanently to Pretoria, his place was soon taken by Dawid J. de Villiers, who had already joined the administrative staff of the university's teaching section as a clerk. Advocate de Villiers, who died in Pretoria in January, 1967, was a graduate of both Stellenbosch and Oxford, with experience in the correspondence college world. He was affectionately known to his colleagues as "the Judge" and to him fell the spade-work in developing the university's present Faculty of Law.

J. A. van der Walt was the first Senior Lecturer in Sociology. He had obtained his M.A. from the University College of the Orange Free State and joined the Division of External Studies after a period as a school-teacher in Bloemfontein. He obtained his doctorate under J. de W. Keyter, and was later appointed to a professorship as head of his department.

By the date of the staff meeting of 16 October, 1946, three more pioneers had been appointed. J. H. (Demps) van der Merwe joined the staff as Senior Lecturer in Mathematics. He was awarded a Ph.D. degree by the University of Cape Town in 1956 and became a professor and head of the Department of Mathematics and Applied Mathematics. Hugo Hofmeyr, a qualified chartered accountant, was the first appointment in the Department of Accounting. His tragic death two years later left a vacancy which was filled by L. M. du Toit, who had experience in both the private sector and in government service. He was to become head of a separate Department of Auditing, created in 1960.

The third newcomer was D. H. Cilliers, who had wide experience in primary and secondary education in the Cape Province before he joined the University of South Africa to organize a Department of Education. Danie Cilliers, who was born on a mission station in what was then the Nyasaland Protectorate, completed his doctoral thesis under the guidance of the Potchefstroom educationist, J. Chr. Coetzee. After the single department had been divided into four within the Faculty of Education, D. H. Cilliers became head of the Department of Method and Administration, later the Department of Didactics and Comparative Education.

Early in 1947, the first series of appointments was completed when Edward Davis became head of the Department of English. Davis, born in London, emigrated to South Africa in 1922 and obtained an M.A. degree at the University of the Witwatersrand. He later spent two years at Oxford and immediately prior

NICOLAAS JACOBUS DE WET was born on 11 September, 1873 at Mooifontein, Aliwal North (Cape), where he first attended school. He obtained the B.A. degree at the Victoria College in 1893 and studied subsequently at Cambridge, gaining the LL.B. and winning the Chancellor's Gold Medal.

In 1896, he was admitted to the Cape bar and also to that of the South African Republic, where he practised until the outbreak of the Anglo-Boer War. He served on the staffs of Generals de la Rey and Botha during the conflict.

After the war, he resumed his practice and also entered politics, becoming a member of both the Union House of Assembly and Senate. He was Minister of Justice from 1913 until 1924, when he again returned to private legal work.

Appointed to the bench in January, 1932, he became Chief Justice on 19 July, 1939. From July, 1943 until December, 1945, he acted as Officer Administering the Government, following the death of the Governor-General, Sir Patrick Duncan.

He was chosen as Chancellor in 1943 and installed on 13 April, 1944, when an honorary LL.D. degree was conferred upon him by the university. He resigned the chancellorship in 1951.

Chief Justice N.J. de Wet died in Pretoria on 16 March, 1960.

Chief Justice the Right Hon. Nicolaas Jacobus de Wet, B.A., LL.B.,
LL.D. (h.c.), P.C.
Chancellor 1943–1951

230

to his appointment with the Division of External Studies was on the staff of the Krugersdorp High School. He left the university at the end of 1962 for Tel Aviv in Israel, but returned to South Africa to become Professor of English at the University of Port Elizabeth.

Professor A. J. H. van der Walt found particular difficulty in recruiting suitable men as Lecturers in Commerce and in Philosophy. Not until 1949, when F. E. Rädel became a full-time member of the teaching staff, was a permanent Lecturer in Commerce appointed. Dr Rädel was born in Germany and had come to Stellenbosch as an exchange student in 1939. He was interned as an enemy alien from 1940 until 1946, but was then able to return to the university to complete his doctorate. In 1948, he began work as a part-time lecturer in the Department of Economics and ultimately took charge of the Department of Business Economics.

The vacancy in the Department of Philosophy was not filled until 1951, when the internationally known scholar, Herman J. de Vleeschauwer, was selected. Dr de Vleeschauwer, who was born in Belgium in 1899, had been associated with higher education in his own country since his appointment to the University of Ghent in 1924. An honorary LL.D. of the University of Glasgow, he had been a prolific contributor to many European scientific journals.

From 1947, other men were appointed as the work of the new section increased. L. J. le Roux was briefly attached to the Department of Economics, before joining the University of Pretoria, where he obtained a professorship in a different field – that of chemistry. R. D. Tromp, long with the university, was appointed to the Department of Geography and J. L. Steyn, later Professor Steyn, began work with H. J. J. M. van der Merwe in *Afrikaans en Nederlands*. The sensitive poet from the Scottish Highlands, F. D. Sinclair, joined the Department of English. His death in 1961 was a sad loss to the university and to South African letters. Also attached to this department for a period was Mrs Phyllis Warner, a pioneer in the development of the modern theatre in this country. To the Department of Psychology came Mrs L. C. Gerdes. She was to become the second woman member of staff – after Anna F. Steyn of the Department of Sociology – to hold a professorship in the university as reconstituted in 1946. Finally, Christoffel Muller was joined in the Department of History by Theo van Wijk, who had been a government archivist in Windhoek, South West Africa. At the time of his appointment, he was lecturing at Rhodes University College, Grahamstown. He married Cilna J. Labuschagne of the Department of Sociology in the University of South Africa and, as Professor van Wijk, was to contribute outstanding services to the university, both as teacher and as administrator.

The staff in the early years was never able to cope with all its problems without the assistance of temporary helpers in the various departments. Sometimes additional aid was needed when permanent members of the teaching staff were unavoidably absent. This occurred, for example, in the Department of History, when the former Boksburg Headmaster, A. E. du Toit, was brought in to replace Dr Muller, who was sent to the United States of America in 1951 to carry out important archival research. The late Dr du Toit was long associated with the department and was a well loved figure. Francis Ward assisted in the Department of English in 1948. Father – later Monsignor – Ward was Chancellor of the Catholic Archdiocese of Pretoria at the time of his death in December, 1971.

The first year in particular imposed a very heavy burden upon the small staff of the Division of External Studies. Lectures had to be written and translated for each stage of the various courses in order to provide for the needs of those students who in 1947 elected to enrol with the university rather than with one or other of the commercial correspondence colleges. It was also decided at an early stage that the lecturers would, from the start, undertake post-graduate work wherever possible and at the same time handle all correspondence in connection with it. The compilation of lectures imposed special problems. Not only were many members of staff unfamiliar with the technique of giving instruc-

233

tion in this way, but books were also in short supply in the years immediately following the end of the second World War. This meant that the lectures had to be more comprehensive than might otherwise have been the case. In some fields, outsiders were called in to help, as with F. J. Language, later the Professor of Anthropology at the University of the Orange Free State, but then working for the Brakpan Municipality. The Director himself took a hand in compiling history lectures.

It was a period of unremitting labour and although the *Sunday Times* of Johannesburg gave some publicity to the recreational activities of one zestful lecturer who liked to skip barefoot through the dewy grass of Burgers Park in the early morning sunshine, few members of the Director's team found much time for relaxation during the working day. Office hours were long, too – and more applicable to those for civil servants than to those for university lecturers. Until 1950, when a "mornings only" rule was introduced, staff were expected to be on duty from 8 o'clock in the morning until 4 o'clock in the afternoon in summer and from half past eight until half past four in winter. An hour and a quarter was allowed for lunch.

A larger clerical and administrative staff was soon needed to cope with the increasing volume of work. From the Registrar's office came the Accountant, Barend F. J. van Rensburg, as Secretary to the Division of External Studies. He was later to become Registrar himself, but at that period, few in Langham Murray's department felt that his transfer would be a stepping-stone to further advancement. Others came with him and new appointments were made. Stephanie Solomon joined Pamela Storey and each year saw the arrival of more clerks and typists. Stephanie left the university, returning later as Mrs van Niekerk. She was to become Secretary to the Department of Mathematics and Applied Mathematics.

The early administrative staff included proof-readers, production and despatch clerks and librarians. An Organizer to the Division was decided upon and F. H. J. Quass was chosen for the post. He was soon succeeded, however, by Alewyn J. Vorster.

234

*The Proes Street, Pretoria home of the
Division of External Studies*

The formation of the DIVISION OF EXTERNAL STUDIES resulted in an increase
in the staff of the University of South Africa. Somerset House could not
accommodate all the additional members and a private house in Proes Street,
Pretoria was rented. It provided a temporary answer to a growing problem.

The Librarian was Heinz O. K. Zastrau, who eventually joined the Rand Afrikaans University in Johannesburg. Another of the early clerical assistants was Michiel G. van Niekerk, who rose to be the university's Chief Despatch Officer.

Under Langham Murray's control, and responsible, among other duties, for examination arrangements, was the Assistant Registrar, Petrus A. Taljaard. He, like Principal Clerk H. W. Harold Hewson, returned after retirement to work for the modern university. Both died recently. Louis G. van der Merwe, long to play a leading role in university administration, became Chief Clerk at this period and in 1948, Johannes J. Brits was appointed Senior Clerk. Others who would give many years' service to the University of South Africa included Albertus T. Laubscher, then a Principal Clerk, and two juniors, Willem H. le Roux and Gerhardus C. Kachelhoffer.

An efficient service could never have been provided if all newcomers in those months of rapid expansion had been accommodated in Somerset House, the university's home since 1918. There was some talk that the owners of the building would soon construct another nearby, more suitable to the University of South Africa's needs. This never materialized, but in the meantime, something had to be done quickly to solve a growing problem. Accordingly, a property was acquired at 222, Proes Street. This private house was a welcome addition to the university's accommodation. It was not an imposing building, but suitable offices were in short supply in those early days of peace; it was, however, reasonably central and accessible and had, in the back yard, a large room which seemed to have been both stable and storeroom combined. This was ideal for the production department which soon became known as the stable section! Even the library found a temporary home there. There was one drawback, however. Whenever it rained, water poured through the roof!

The house provided offices for the Director and for the Secretary and his staff. There was also room for some of the lecturers, although most of them remained at Somerset House. At length, however, the accommodation problem grew so critical that many lecturers were allowed to work at home. Several departments – of one staff member each, it should be remembered! – were compelled to share an office. At one period, the Departments of Law, Psychology, Sociology and French (with Classics) were housed together, with desks almost touching. Geography shared with History and also, for a time, with English. Inevitably, there were some disagreements between members of staff working in close proximity, but on the whole, relations were remarkably harmonious. The members of the Division of External Studies grew to know each other well and the hard work of the first months was relieved by occasional humorous incidents. J. A. van der Walt of the Department of Sociology later recalled Advocate de Villiers's discomfiture when he collected a present from his mother-in-law. She had sent him a box of tomatoes by train from Nelspruit and he was by no means pleased when he found that he had to pay railage charges which cost him more than three times the price of a similar box in the Pretoria market!

Staff meetings often took place under the large wild fig tree in the garden of the Proes Street house, sometimes to celebrate such events as the Director's birthday. The easy, friendly informality of those early months may be seen in the minutes of meetings, where congratulations upon staff anniversaries and, on one occasion, an engagement, were duly recorded by A. S. Roux of the Department of Psychology, who acted as Secretary.

Lectures, despite all difficulties, were finally completed and handed over to the production staff to be put into suitable form for despatch. The Division of External Studies had to face problems in this field, too. There was, for example, a general shortage of paper and of duplicating machines after the war. The Pretoria branch of the well-known firm of Gestetner assisted the university to overcome the deficiency; so, too, did J.A. van der Walt of the teaching staff. Translation and proof-reading tasks had to be shared and even the Director and the Secretary were pressed into service here. As a special precaution, lecturers were requested to keep duplicate copies of all the material which they compiled, as the fire hazard in old buildings was by no means a

HERMAN HEINRICH GERHARD KREFT was born on 18 June, 1888 in the mission house at Tulbagh (Cape). On matriculation in 1904, he trained as a teacher at the Normal College, Cape Town. After teaching for a year, he enrolled at the South African College, where he graduated with honours in modern languages in 1909. He returned to teaching until 1915, when he was made Inspector of Schools for the Burgersdorp-Aliwal North area.

He became Director of Education for South West Africa in 1922 and 12 years later, was transferred to the Transvaal as Technical Adviser to the provincial Department of Education. From 1937 until his retirement in 1948, he was Director of Education for the Transvaal.

He actively promoted language teaching. As a member of the Joint Matriculation Board he helped to introduce German as a third language and, with the assistance of missionary bodies, did much to foster the teaching of African languages in South West Africa. He received the honorary LL.D. degree from the University of Cape Town in 1948.

After his retirement, he devoted himself to the interests of children in need of special care.

A member of Council from 1937 until 1948, he was chosen as Vice-Chancellor for two years in 1946.

Dr Herman Heinrich Gerhard Kreft, B.A., LL.D. (h.c.)
Member of Council 1937–1948
Vice-Chancellor 1946–1948

238

matter to be neglected. The Secretary's connection with teaching was not, incidentally, confined to occasional assistance in producing lectures. At one time, his services were enlisted as acting head of the Departments of Commerce and Accounting!

The need to produce lectures of good quality was of the utmost importance, for it was through them that Professor van der Walt and his colleagues would make their chief impact upon the student body. A high standard of tutorial guidance would do much to convince candidates for university examinations that enrolment with the new teaching arm rather than with the commercial colleges was the best guarantee of success in their studies. It would be some time before the colleges withdrew from the field of undergraduate instruction and in 1947, many firms were still confident that their courses were more comprehensive than anything the University of South Africa could offer.

The Division of External Studies had one advantage in its contest with the commercial undertakings, for it operated under the name of the university; on the other hand, it laboured under a serious disability. The private firms could advertise their courses and their successes; Professor van der Walt and his colleagues could not. Any attempt to do so would have been construed by the commercial correspondence colleges – both individually and in association – as unfair competition from a state-aided institution. The Director was able to offset this restriction in some measure by writing articles for popular periodicals and specialist journals. A *Newsletter* was also published in 1947, a modest journal which was expanded the following year as *The External Student.* This publication was issued annually from 1950 under the title *Student* and later adopted yet another name, *Unisa.* It was early decided to distribute copies of the journal to such institutions as teacher training colleges and hospitals and to make them available to various government departments. For some time, too, the examination successes of students enrolled with the Division of External Studies were listed in its pages.

By the end of February, 1947, all was ready for the start of postal tuition. The first batches of lectures were prepared for

240

despatch and a small ceremony was held on Saturday morning, 1 March, to inaugurate the new service. The Vice-Chancellor of the day, H. H. G. Kreft, gave a short address before sealing the first packet. The name of the recipient has been recorded and it was thus that A. P. J. Heiberg of Boksburg, who obtained his B.A. degree in 1948, played his small part in the continuing history of the University of South Africa. A new era had dawned.

9 *Early expansion*

When Professor A. J. H. van der Walt and his colleagues began to prepare for their first students, it was impossible to estimate just how many candidates for the degree examinations of the University of South Africa would decide to make use of the tuition offered. In fact, 1 250 men and women enrolled in 1947, a total representing no more than one-third of all those registered with the university for examination purposes. The success of the new venture may be gauged from the rise in enrolments over the next four years and, more particularly, from the increasingly larger share of the total number of external students seeking graduate qualifications. In 1948, the Division of External Studies had 1 751 students, or over 40% of all those registered for examinations; by 1951, the Director and his staff were providing tuition for 2 455 students, or more than 53% of the total number. This gain was, to a very large extent, at the expense of the commercial undertakings. The Division of External Studies, it may be added, in keeping with the traditions of the university of which it formed a part, existed to help students of all races. In 1949 and 1950, more than one student in three came from the African, Coloured and Indian sections of the community.

This steady increase in student numbers brought in its train new problems for the University of South Africa. It soon became clear that 222, Proes Street could only be regarded as a temporary home for the overflow population of Somerset House. Fortunately, new office blocks were being constructed in Pretoria

242

and rooms were rented on the top floors of the Transvalia Building on the corner of Central and Pretorius Streets. Here, in what Edward Davis of the Department of English described at the time as "a truncated skryscraper", the entire lecturing staff of the Division of External Studies and a considerable part of the administrative section were housed. At last, the Director's promise of a single room for all had come true. It was, however, a brief respite from overcrowding. The university continued to expand and soon a house in Skinner Street and offices in Security Building, Pretorius Street were taken over. At last, in 1949, the University of South Africa vacated its accommodation in Somerset House. The Registrar's section moved further along Vermeulen Street to Kerry Building, which also provided a new chamber for meetings of Council.

It was time for the university to find a home of its own. Already, a committee, consisting of the Director, the Chairman of Council's Finance Committee, J.P. Duminy, and another Council member, S. P. E. Boshoff, had recommended this course and Council endorsed its findings, placing a cautions ceiling on the purchase price of the necessary land. The cheapest site availble was on the south-eastern outskirts of Pretoria's central area, but this did not meet with the Registrar's approval. Langham Murray wanted the university to remain somewhere near Church Square, the heart of the city, and even the final choice did not entirely satisfy him. This was a plot of land in Skinner Street, purchased for R12 000. The University of South Africa took the opportunity of reminding government of the loss it had sustained when it had sold the only other home it had ever possessed – the building in Queen Victoria Street, Cape Town. It asked, as some compensation for its earlier unhappy experience, for the sum of R90 000 to add to the amount received at the time of the Cape Town sale. The Treasury, with some advice about simplifying the proposed design of the new headquarters, was prepared to find the money and in time, on a site already occupied by a house leased by the university, new offices were destined to arise. It was hoped that this new building would bring to an end the need

Administrative Staff
Division of External Studies, 1948

1st Row (l. to r.): W.A. Kleynhans, B.Com., B.A.; P.A. Olivier; H.J. Nel;
P.J. Fouché; I. Lubbe; H.O.K. Zastrau, B.Sc.

2nd Row (l. to r.): D.M. Fourie; G.J. Eysell, R.D. Jacobs; A.J.H. van der
Walt, M.A., D.Phil. (Director); I.S. Willis; S.S. Oosterchrist; M.I.G.
Visser.

3rd Row (l. to r.): C.P. Botha; H. Malan; R. Erasmus; J.D. Louw, B.A.;
B.F.J. van Rensburg, B.Com., B.A. (Secretary); A.J. Vorster, B.A.;
A.M. Steyn, B.A.; C.W. Mouton, M.A.; E. Smit.

4th Row (l. to r.): N. Kruger; E. van Rensburg; A. Louw; D.W. Steenkamp;
V.M. Moran; D.E. Rogers; A.C. Steyn.

5th Row (l. to r.): E. Lowry; N. Fourie; A. Nortjé; M.G. van Niekerk;
H.W. Dragt; G. Zietsman; C.C. Coetzee, B.A.

244

Administrative Staff
Division of the Registrar, 1948

Back row (l. to r.): J.S.N. Marais; F.J.D. Stokes-Waller; C. Botha; A.J. de
V. Alberts; C.I. Fourie; H.M. Beukman; D.U. Kleynhans; J.A. Venter;
P.G.J. de Villiers; J.A. Erasmus.

Centre row (l. to r.): G.B. van Malsen; J.G. Smuts; A. Grimbeek; O.H.
Smart; A.E. Nel; C.E. van der Westhuizen; M. Balt; A. Krige; M.J.H.
van Graan; P.N. Botha, B.A.

Front row (l. to r.): G.C. Kachelhoffer, B.Admin.; W.H. le Roux, B.A.;
P.J. Retief; J.J. Brits, B.A.; P.A. Taljaard, B.A., LL.B. (Assistant Regis-
trar); Langham Murray, M.A. (Registrar); H.W.H. Hewson, B.Com.,
A.C.I.S.; L.G. van der Merwe, B.Com.; A.T. Laubscher, B.Econ.;
K. Alexander, M.A.; P.W.J. du Toit.

ALBERTUS JOHANNES ROUX VAN RHIJN was born on 7 July, 1890 at Van Rhynsdorp (Cape). He matriculated at the Wellington High School in 1907 and graduated three years later at the Victoria College. He went to Germany in 1911 to study chemistry and geology, but returned to South Africa on the outbreak of war in 1914, when he became Vice-Principal of the Calvinia High School.

He was appointed to a lectureship in chemistry at the University of Stellenbosch in 1920 and in the same year obtained his M.Sc. degree. In 1921, he returned to Germany, where he gained a Ph.D. in chemistry *magnus cum laude*. He then became head of the Calvinia High School, but in 1925, accepted the editorship of the Bloemfontein newspaper, the *Volksblad*, a post which he held for more than 20 years.

He was elected M.P. for Bethlehem in 1948 and was made Administrator of South West Africa two years later. In 1953 he became Minister of Health and Mining, and from 1954 he was responsible for the portfolios of Economic Affairs and of Mining. From 1959 until the end of 1960, he was the Union's High Commissioner in London.

A member of the university Council from 1930 until 1953, he was chosen Vice-Chancellor for the period from 1948 to 1952.

Dr van Rhijn died in Bloemfontein on 30 December, 1971.

Dr Albertus Johannes Roux van Rhijn, B.A., M.Sc., Ph.D.
Member of Council 1930–1953
Vice-Chancellor 1948–1952

for rented accommodation in the city which, by 1950, was costing the University of South Africa nearly R14 000 per annum.

One of the first problems facing the Division of External Studies was the provision of adequate library facilities for students, many of whom lived far from Pretoria and all of whom, in the immediate post-war years, were faced with the chronic shortage of suitable text books. Both a loan library and a reference library would be needed. The first, with the help of an initial grant of R15 000, was early established and in one year managed to acquire more than 10 000 books. For the benefit of students who had not enrolled for the university's courses, as well as for those working through the Division of External Studies, the annual *Calendar* drew attention to the loan facilities offered by other libraries, including the National Students' Library of the Department of Union Education in Pretoria, the State Library in the capital, the Johannesburg Public Library and one at a greater distance – Denny's Student Library in the Strand, London.

Arrangements were also made with the Department of Union Education to build up the holdings of its library on Church Square so that external students could use it for reference purposes. However, the scheme did not prove satisfactory and before long the reference section was brought under the control of the Division of External Studies itself. It was the beginning of the library as we know it today and, as the Librarian, H. O. K. Zastrau, pointed out in 1951, the new comprehensive library system gave every student the assurance that all his needs were cared for by a single authority.

Annual grants for the purchase of books were not large in the early years. From the R2 400 received for the 1948–1949 period, the grant was increased in the early fifties to something over R6 000. This sum represented about 9% of the money made available by the university for the development of the Division of External Studies each year. The amount provided never met expenditure, but the annual deficit was made good through the generosity of well-wishers. The library received gifts of books as

248

well as cash from many sources. One of the largest and the first of its kind was a donation of 840 volumes from the French government. These were presented to the university in 1950 by the French Ambassador, Armand Gazel.

The library grant was apportioned on a departmental basis, with regard to the size and the special needs of each field of study. The method by which the percentages were arrived at was sometimes questioned by disappointed departmental heads, but on the whole, the system seems to have worked reasonably well. English, the largest department, usually received a good quota; its members were also allowed the privilege of keeping the *Oxford Dictionary* in their own offices! Other departments were not neglected, however. The Department of Law was allocated the largest percentage in 1948 and two years later, the Department of History was given a special grant to buy the Van Riebeeck Society's publications and the works of Sir George Cory and George McCall Theal. The first grants to departments for the purchase of periodicals gave to each the sum of five rands! If more journals were required, departments would have to dip into their book allowances.

The question of examinations directly concerned the newly appointed lecturers of the Division of External Studies. With so many different groups of students in 1947, it is small wonder that difficulties arose in this connection – difficulties which were increased by uncertainty over the status and even the permanency of the new section and by doubts about the untested calibre of most of its staff. There were, in the first place, the constituent college students who would be examined by the university until the end of the federal period in 1951. For them, a system of internal and external examination had long obtained. Then there were the students at the South African Native College – "externals" who enjoyed special "internal" privileges. Those whom the university examined, but did not teach formed a third group. These included fee-paying students at commercial correspondence colleges, those studying for degrees at institutions of less than university college rank and the "lone wolves" who sought no outside instruction. Finally, there were the Director's own charges. In this diversification lay an excellent reason for keeping control of examinations in the hands of the Registrar and his subordinates.

Nevertheless, the Director and his colleagues might reasonably have expected, like the staff of the South African Native College, to "brand their own herrings". What had to be avoided, however, was the imputation of unfairness in any form to other external students. One method of avoiding this accusation had been suggested by Jan Hofmeyr early in 1946. This was the use of numbers instead of names on examination scripts. The Registrar's office was not enthusiastic about this plan, but Professor van der Walt and his lecturers were much in favour. The reason is not far to seek. If candidates were to hide behind the mask of anonymity, then there was no reason why the staff of the Division of External Studies should not correct all examination scripts, including those of candidates who had prepared under the tuition of the rival commercial firms. Within a decade, when the university's new teaching section had become firmly established, the use of numbers was, in fact, introduced. The more recent retreat from student anonymity in examinations has not been universally approved.

The Senate Executive Committee of the University of South Africa came up with a rather complicated scheme for the examination of external students early in 1947 and this, in due course, was accepted, with minor additions, in full Senate. While the rights as examiners of members of the Director's staff were confirmed, it was made clear that they were not to mark any scripts but those of their own students. The system adopted involved the use of three examiners, only one of whom was to be a member of the Division of External Studies. He was to be responsible, in collaboration with the other two, for the setting of any papers to be taken by his own students. For marking purposes, he would only be employed to examine scripts submitted by students of the Division of External Studies, with one of the other men as second examiner. The scheme had one merit, for it enabled a

250

single paper to be set for all students, whether or not they obtained their tuition with the university. It did not, however, prevent some variations in the standard of marking. From 1948 onward, past papers became available for the guidance of students. They could be obtained from the university and could also be consulted at centres throughout South Africa and in Southern Rhodesia and Basutoland.

The system of examination was not entirely satisfactory and, not surprisingly, many alternatives were put forward at meetings of the Director's Advisory Council, the association of university lecturers. This body, however, did not have statutory powers. The main desire was for a scheme involving two examiners only and this was eventually introduced. Further, the whole problem of examinations was closely linked with the status of the university's teaching section. As it grew in size and strength, the examining restrictions placed upon its staff became increasingly irksome. The examiners were appointed by the committees of studies in the faculties concerned, where the Division of External Studies was only represented by one man among many. In addition, staff members were not notified that they had been chosen as examiners until after the information had been passed to the Registrar's office. This procedure, in those days of tension between the sections, was not popular. As early as 1948, there were demands for better treatment for university lecturers. Many felt strongly that the time had come for the teaching arm of the central university, as distinct from the constituent colleges, to have its own Dean – possibly the Dean of the Faculty of Arts, since most of the departments fell into that category. Such a move would give Professor van der Walt and his colleagues greater standing in university circles. In 1951, came a call to upgrade the heads of departments to professorial rank.

In two ways, the Director came to exercise a strong influence over students and thus to strengthen the position of the Division of External Studies in relation to the correspondence colleges. In the first place, the University of South Africa provided an

One member in this photograph of the FIFTH COUNCIL of the University of South Africa represents a link with the former University of the Cape of Good Hope.

The Rev. Leo Sormany was appointed by the Governor-General as a representative of Natal in 1916. He served the examining university until its dissolution two years later and was then nominated by the Council of the Natal University College to the governing body of its successor. He retained office until March, 1949, when the college became the independent University of Natal.

Council 1947

Front row (l. to r.): T.P.C. Boezaart; Dr S.H. Pellissier; Dr Anna J.D. de Villiers; Prof. F. Postma; Mrs M.A. Malan; Prof. J. Smeath Thomas; R.A. Banks.

2nd row (l. to r.): W. Orban; Prof. W.F.C. Arndt; Dr A. Kerr; Dr P.C. Schoonees; Dr R.B. Denison; Dr E.G. Malherbe; Langham D. Murray (Registrar).

3rd row (l. to r.): Prof. H.J. Chapman; Dr S.P.E. Boshoff; Dr A.J.R. van Rhijn; Rev. H.J.R. du Plessis; Prof. A.J.H. van der Walt; Prof. J.P. Duminy; P.A. Taljaard (Asst Registrar).

Insert: Prof. H. v.d. M. Scholtz; Dr W. de V. Malan; Rev. Dr L. Sormany; Prof. I.S. Fourie; J. Cowie; Dr H.H.G. Kreft (Vice-Chancellor).

advisory service which was available to all, wherever they chose to study. Prospective candidates for degree examinations could consult the Director in order to discuss suitable courses in the light of their needs, interests and aptitudes.

In the second place, the Division of External Studies decided to hold an annual Vacation School from 1948. This has undoubtedly become one of the University of South Africa's most successful ventures. It was, from the outset, open to all students and many of those who attended were under the tuition of the correspondence firms. Throughout the last years of the federal period in the university's history, two separate schools were arranged. That for European students was held at the Pretoria Technical College, while non-Europeans made use of the facilities made available at the former Methodist Church institution at Kilnerton near the city. The University of South Africa was able to provide accommodation for the latter group, a circumstance which, together with the need for greater personal supervision in their studies, contributed to the larger numbers attending the Kilnerton school. Most of these students were from the various African ethnic groups, but there were also Coloured and Indian students. Loans and bursaries were offered to help the needy to attend. The schools were held in July and their growing popularity may be gauged from the steady increase in attendance figures. 160 students enrolled for the first one, 84 of them non-Europeans; by 1951, the numbers attending had increased to 253, including 135 non-Europeans. At this period, some 14% of the African, Coloured and Indian students enrolled with the Division of External Studies made use of the schools and about 7% of the Europeans.

Arrangements for the Vacation School were made by the university's Organizer and in every year, a representative committee of the students in each group was chosen to assist in planning social events and to form a link with members of staff. Visits to such places of interest as the Union Buildings, the veterinary station at Onderstepoort and the Voortrekker Monument took place; there were also film shows, musical evenings

254

and additional lectures, including one by Guy Butler on the South African poet, Roy Campbell, and others on African literature and cultural development.

For a brief spell each year, the university was seen in tangible form as a corporation of teachers and learners and for many students, the Vacation School provided a unique opportunity of meeting the tutorial staff to discuss special difficulties encountered in their work. It also did much to break down racial prejudice. The first school was held in a period of political change which saw the success of the National Party in the election of 1948 and some hostility was displayed by African students in that year towards a predominantly Afrikaans-speaking lecturing staff. Antagonism was short-lived, however, when it became apparent that the lecturers of the Division of External Studies were prepared to assist students of all races in every way possible with their courses of study.

Another method of helping students and at the same time of making the student body a more intimate part of the university was suggested at the first Vacation School. This was the formation of study groups in various centres, a task undertaken by the Organizer, A. J. Vorster. These began with centres for European students on the Rand and in Pretoria and for non-Europeans at Dundee in Natal. The number of groups increased and within a few years, others had been established in cities as far apart as Port Elizabeth in the Eastern Province and Salisbury, Rhodesia. However, the movement cannot be regarded as an unqualified success, although it continues to be used in an effort to conteract student isolation. Inevitably, some groups suffered from a lack of continuity as members completed their courses or ceased to study through the university. Arranging the groups took up a great deal of time and they needed the constant encouragement of the Director and his staff. They flourished, however, where local enthusiasm ran high.

One study group in the Eastern Province came to regard itself as the nucleus of something greater. In December, 1950, a musical function was arranged by it in the East London City

The first Vacation School White group, Students and Lecturers, 1948

The first Vacation School Non-white group, 1948

Winter VACATION SCHOOLS were first held in 1948 and provided students with an opportunity to meet their tutors and to discuss special problems with them. They proved immensely popular and became a permanent feature of the academic year. The first function for European students was held at the Pretoria Technical College; that for African, Coloured and Indian students was arranged at Kilnerton, on the outskirts of Pretoria.

Hall. The entertainment was attended by A. S. Roux of the Department of Psychology and his wife. There, the work of the Division of External Studies was highly praised in a speech which contained a short history of its inauguration. Early in 1951, Mary McMillan, the Honorary Secretary of the East London group, wrote to the Secretary for Education, Arts and Science to ascertain the minimum requirements for founding a university college in the city and the degree of assistance which might be expected from the University of South Africa. She was told, however, that government could not contemplate any such extension of higher education in South Africa for many years to come.

Some departments of the Division of External Studies gave excellent advice on how to run a successful study group. In this connection, that offered by Theo van Wijk of the Department of History served as a model for A.S. Roux when he discussed the formation of new groups in the 1951 issue of *Student*. However, it was only in Pretoria and on the Witwatersrand that university lecturers could really give personal attention to group discussions. Bringing the student body into the university community was from the beginning a difficult problem. Certainly, the poor response to questionnaires sent out by the Director – unless on topics of immediate concern to students – seemed to indicate a lack of interest on the part of many. As there were then no compulsory exercises to submit in courses of study, some students did no more than read through the lectures sent to them and made no personal contact with the lecturing staff. Many hoped optimistically – as, perhaps, many still do – that a nodding acquaintance with the university's tutorial matter would be sufficient to ensure at least a pass in any course.

Graduation Day ceremonies would have been an excellent way of bringing the work of the Division of External Studies before the public and of fostering a sense of corporate pride in the university's new role. However, during the last years of the federal period, degrees continued for the most part to be presented at the constituent colleges and at the college for non-

258

Europeans at Fort Hare. In addition, some small ceremonies were held in the university offices in Pretoria following special examinations for wartime students. At all these ceremonies, both collegiate and external students were capped. Several honorary degrees were also conferred, among them a D.Phil. to Mabel Palmer of Durban in 1947, a D.Litt. to D.F. Malherbe of Bloemfontein in 1949 and, in the same year, a D.Ed. to Ferdinand Postma of Potchefstroom. All had done much for higher education in South Africa and for candidates for the university's examinations in particular. It had been Ferdinand Postma who had encouraged the Director to undertake his task in 1946.

An attempt was made to provide alternative functions for non-European students in 1948. There was not a sufficient response to justify holding a Graduation Day for them in Pretoria, but one was arranged at Paarl by the staff of the Huguenot University College. However, there was opposition to this move by some who favoured racially integrated functions of this kind. Protests came from individuals and also from the Coloured Advisory Council and the experiment was not repeated. However, despite opposition at the Cape, there was continued support for the idea among African students in the north. Nothing, however, was done until the last of the constituent colleges had left the federation in 1951. In the following year, two ceremonies were held in the Pretoria Technical College, both of which were presided over by the Vice-Chancellor at that time, Professor S. P. E. Boshoff. In 1953, the non-European function was transferred to Kilnerton and for some years, at the request of students, Degree Day coincided with the Vacation School.

In 1948, permission was given for the lectures of the Division of External Studies to be used by instructors at two non-profit making institutions: Helderberg College in the Cape, the Seventh-day Adventist Church foundation, and Adams College in Natal, the institution for African students over which Edgar Brookes had long presided. At the same period, certain lecturers with the Division of External Studies were giving their services on a part-time basis to the *Kolege ya Bana ba Afrika* in Atte-

The publication of an A N N U A L M A G A Z I N E has for many years enabled the university to keep in closer contact with its scattered student body.

A roneoed *Newsletter* was issued in 1947 and proved such a success that a magazine, *The External Student,* was published in the following year. Two numbers appeared in 1949, but from 1950, the journal appeared annually. It was renamed *Student* in that year and *Unisa* in 1955.

At present, *Unisa Bulletin* is published as the prestige journal of the university.

Cover of first Magazine

DIE EKSTERNE · THE EXTERNAL
STUDENT

SPES IN ARDUIS

1948
ANNUAL
JAARBLAD

ridgeville, Pretoria. These collegiate links, tenuous enough in the early years, foreshadowed later developments.

The first of these came in 1951, when an agreement was reached with the Transvaal Department of Education to bring the Heidelberg Teacher Training College in the province into a special relationship with the University of South Africa. Under this arrangement, some college lecturers were recognized as university teachers working in collaboration with the various heads of departments in the Division of External Studies. The Director and his staff had, in turn, rights of inspection over the work done at the Heidelberg institution. As a result, prospective teachers were able to study for a degree while completing their teaching certificate course. This permitted the college to become, in the words of its Principal, G. J. Jordaan, an institution "waar akademiese studie geïntegreer kan word met die vorming van die onderwyser as mens en as opvoeder". It was a step forward in South African teacher training.

The inauguration of the Division of External Studies also raised again the question of academic training in technical institutes. The Northern Cape Technical College in Kimberley spoke of the possibility of preparing students for external degrees through the facilities now offered by the University of South Africa. It was tempting to see further development along these lines, but it had long been university policy in South Africa to resist the claims of technical colleges to a higher status. Such expansion was not, therefore, encouraged, although the question was to be raised once more at a later period.

Finally, the break between the university and the Huguenot institution at Wellington was not a complete one at the end of 1950, for in the following year there were still 60 candidates for the B.A. degree at the Huguenot Missionary College which had taken the place of the university college. These students were working through the Division of External Studies.

Professor A. J. H. van der Walt and his colleagues had achieved much by 1951, when the last two constituent colleges at Grahamstown and Potchefstroom became independent universities. At the end of that year, the Division of External Studies was supplying courses for 2 215 undergraduates. More than 1 500 of them were of European descent, of whom some 900 were Afrikaans-speaking. In addition, there were more than 400 African students, 175 Asians and nearly 100 Coloured students. Post-graduate work, too, was not neglected and if most of the students in this category were studying for the Bachelor of Education and honours degrees, there had been a steady increase in the number of masters' dissertations and doctoral theses in preparation.

The Director and his staff were providing opportunities for large numbers of people to obtain university degrees who would otherwise have been unable, for a variety of reasons, to do so. When a survey was made in 1950, it was found that more than 90% of the students attached to the Division of External Studies were above the normal age for attending a university; several, indeed, were more than 50 years of age. Again, more students came from rural areas than from urban districts. Although the vast majority lived in South Africa, with the heaviest concentration in the Transvaal, the university was showing itself to be an institution catering for the needs of the whole of southern Africa, as, indeed, had always been the case throughout its history. More than 5% of the student body lived beyond the national borders, most of them in Rhodesia. Several were studying overseas.

The B.A. degree was the main objective, although other degrees, particularly those in commerce and economics, were popular. Teachers and instructors far outnumbered those in other occupations among the students of the Division of External Studies. A striking variety of vocations was, however, represented. Among the student body were clerks, housewives, farmers, businessmen, diplomats, army officers, motor mechanics, secretaries, engineers and ministers of religion. The list for 1950 also enumerated eleven caretakers, a licensed victualler and an entomologist!

However popular the Division of External Studies had become with those seeking graduate qualifications, it did not enjoy the same enthusiastic support in the academic world of South Africa. The progress which has been charted in this chapter was achieved under considerable difficulties and at no time in the first five years in the career of the university's new venture was it certain of becoming a permanent feature of the higher educational scene. The University of South Africa was, until 1951, primarily a federation of constituent colleges and to many people it was inconceivable that the infant teaching unit should inherit the family home when the last college had reached maturity and embarked upon an independent life. For was not the Division of External Studies what it had so often been called in parliament and outside, a mere correspondence school – and an extraordinarily costly one at that?

10 *An uncertain future*

The development of the Division of External Studies and the future of the constituent colleges were not the only concerns of the University of South Africa during the five years which ended with the resignation as Chancellor of N. J. de Wet in 1951 and the election of Judge President G. J. Maritz to succeed him.

The administrative section of the university retained its function as an examining body in a variety of fields. The examination for the Junior Certificate attracted several thousand entries annually. However, the need for this test of scholastic ability gradually diminished as alternative examinations were introduced by various authorities. In time, it was made use of almost entirely by non-European candidates and was finally abolished in 1960. The responsibility for the administration of the Joint Matriculation Board, however, continued to devolve upon the Registrar and his staff. The other conjoint board, which controlled examinations in law and surveying, was becoming an anachronism by the early fifties and ceased to exist at the end of the decade. It was replaced by a Board for the Recognition of Examinations in Law, no longer the administrative concern of the university, although it is represented upon it. The largest number of candidates for examinations conducted by the university came forward in the field of music.

Although relations with the Associated Board in London had been severed at the end of the war, the question of control of examinations in music had not really been finally settled. There were still many people in South Africa who would have pre-

GERHARDUS JACOBUS MARITZ was born on 7 December, 1889 at Klerksdorp. He received his early education in Pretoria and Stellenbosch and after studying at the Victoria College, obtained the B.A. degree in 1908. A Rhodes Scholar, he qualified in 1912 at Trinity College, Oxford, for the Middle Temple in the Honours School of Jurisprudence.

When the first World War broke out, he was practising in Pretoria. He decided to join the abortive rebellion, but was captured and interned. He returned to the law after his discharge and built up a flourishing practice. President of the Income-tax Court in 1926, he was appointed a judge in the Transvaal Provincial Division four years later and Judge President in 1947.

Chosen as Chancellor of the university in 1951, he resigned this office in 1957.

Judge President G.J. Maritz died in Pretoria on 16 July, 1964.

Judge President the Hon. Gerhardus Jacobus Maritz, B.A., Q.C.
Chancellor 1951–1957

267

ferred a return to the old system of examiners from abroad, as was evident when the 25th Annual Conference of the South African Society of Music Teachers met in 1946. Two years later, the Associated Board showed interest in the renewal of co-operation and the appointment of examiners on a fifty-fifty basis. It could also offer a diploma which obtained world-wide recognition. The University of South Africa intimated that it was prepared to consider the matter, but that there was now a fully representative national advisory committee in music, which would have to be in agreement with any changes made. By 1949, however, a final split with the Associated Board had taken place and the following year, in answer to demands from music teachers, the London body began to hold its own examinations in South Africa, in competition with its former associate.

The work of the Registrar's office, which Langham Murray continued to keep strictly apart from that of the teaching section, was largely centred upon this diversity of examination work. By 1951, when the Assistant Registrar, Petrus A. Taljaard, summed up the duties of the department, there were nearly 10 000 entries for music examinations – more than twice as many as there were for degree examinations from students of the Division of External Studies and others. In addition, the two school examinations brought in some 6 000 more entries and there were then about 1 000 for the professional examinations. All this threw a great burden upon the shoulders of the administrative staff. There were notifications to be sent to examiners and moderators, centres to be provided – and already there were more than 1 200 of these in South Africa and elsewhere – and papers to be printed and distributed. The scripts which poured into the university office after the examinations had taken place had then to be despatched to the examiners. Finally came the collating of marks, the notification of results and the preparation of certificates.

That candidates who had enrolled with the Division of External Studies were dealt with in this respect in entirely the same way as those who had studied with the commercial colleges was in keeping with the promises made by Jan Hofmeyr in 1946. The University of South Africa was at all times careful to avoid giving offence to the correspondence firms. Moreover, it was always ready to consider their ideas on the syllabuses for external students.

The university was not prepared, however, to extend official recognition to the colleges individually, nor did it accept that their association had unlimited rights to criticize. The Regulations for External Students which appeared in the annual *Calendar* stated firmly in a preamble that the University of South Africa was not associated in any way with outside bodies or institutions preparing students for its examinations and added, in less emphatic print: "Enrolment in the Division of External Studies is optional".

Relations with the commercial undertakings were, from the outset, far from cordial. Complaints were frequent and the Secretary of the Association of Correspondence Colleges, L. J. Erasmus, listed some of them in a letter to the Registrar in June, 1947. He contended that the very mention of the Division of External Studies in the *Calendar* constituted unfair competition; that arbitrary changes in regulations and syllabuses made the work of the colleges more difficult; that there was a growing fear among external students working through the firms belonging to his association that marks were to be awarded on the year's work of those who studied through the university.

It is true that the Director and many of his staff were greatly in favour of this last course. It would stimulate study and help to close the gap between lecturer and student. However, the University of South Africa was well aware that, in the circumstances, it could not introduce the system, unless means could be devised to extend it to all. One alternative was tried in 1952 at the Vacation School. This was the institution of Progress Record Tests which, since the function was not restricted to students of the Division of External Studies, were considered to be fair to everybody. It was also hoped that such a scheme would encourage a larger attendance at the Vacation School. Few stu-

269

dents, however, were prepared to attempt the tests, even though the idea had first been mooted by candidates for the university's examinations. In the 1953 edition of *Student,* B. M. Allpass (significantly named!) explained why. Many felt, he argued, that "a test for which they were, in July, ill-prepared, was no gauge of their pass-worthiness in November"; moreover, the mark awarded could not only help a border-line student to pass; it could emphasize his lack of ability.

Complaints continued to reach the university, both from the colleges in association and from individual students. Even as late as 1955, there were allegations of discrimination – dismissed as "nonsense" by the Registrar – against candidates unconnected with the Division of External Studies. The Association of Correspondence Colleges dearly wanted closer links with the University of South Africa and the appointment of a second examiner nominated by it. The university, on the other hand, wished to keep the association at arm's length and it is significant that in December, 1947, when the Registrar was invited to the first meeting of the Board of Control of the Association of Correspondence Colleges, Langham Murray promptly declined the invitation.

The commercial undertakings based some of their arguments upon their numerical strength, so far as student enrolment was concerned. However, in this respect, their case was not so good as they made out. This is clear from a detailed memorandum compiled by the Director in December, 1948. There were, it is true, more than 2 500 students who were not enrolled with the Division of External Studies in that year, forming much the larger group. However, 640 of the independent students worked entirely on their own. This still gave the colleges a slight numerical advantage, but there were many institutions in competition with each other. At some – among them the Lyceum College of Johannesburg – students working for degrees formed only a small part of the total enrolment. Four institutions dominated in the university examination field : Transafrica, the Rapid Results College, Union College and the *Volkskorrespondensie*

Kollege. The first named had 572 students, 320 of whom were working for the B.A. examination. Rapid Results gave tuition to 529 men and women, 286 of them studying for the B.Com. degree. The Union College provided tuition for 270 students, 175 of them taking the B.A. course, while the *Volkskorrespondensie* institution's 156 university students were mainly enrolled for the B.A. and B.Com. degrees in almost equal numbers. These two degrees were the most popular among students of the Division of External Studies, with more than half studying for the B.A. and some 17% enrolled for the B.Com. degree. There was some truth in the comment made at this time that most of the commercial firms did not make much money from their degree courses, but kept them for reasons of prestige.

When it came to finance, the correspondence colleges were on firmer ground. However excellent the tuition offered students by the University of South Africa, however laudable the whole concept of university training by correspondence, there is no doubt that the venture failed hopelessly where it was confidently expected to succeed! It had been argued that, since the commercial undertakings could make a reasonable profit on all their operations, the Division of External Studies should be able to do the same. In that way, it would neither become a charge upon the university nor upon the state. It was therefore financed quite separately from the administrative section of the University of South Africa so that its expenditure could be adequately controlled.

Alas, the Division of External Studies soon showed an alarming propensity to swallow up money at a faster rate than anybody – the directors of correspondence colleges excepted – had ever imagined! It began with a small enough deficit – just under R3 167 on 31 March, 1947. By the following year, this had increased to the alarming figure of almost R36 000 and in 1949, to a staggering R61 330. Langham Murray complained that the university's reserves could not meet deficits of this kind, the more so as the government grant for administrative purposes, together with fee income and other sources of revenue, fell very far short of the university's needs. There were deficits here of more than R40 000 in 1947 and of R20 000 in 1948. The University of South Africa was, as a result, requested to make economies. In 1950, some fees were increased, the minutes of meetings were published in alternate years in English and Afrikaans and certain handbooks were issued less frequently.

The situation for the Division of External Studies was a serious one – far more so than most members of the teaching staff realized. Professor van der Walt's section had, however, some support. J. P. Duminy, for example, was able to tell the government's University Advisory Committee that the losses incurred by the teaching division were beyond its control and the committee went so far as to record the encouraging minute that the new venture provided a "service of national importance". The Director tried to keep costs down by cutting back expenditure on such items as library books, in view of the "ernstige finansiële posisie waarin die Afdeling verkeer". However, in the early months of 1949, the bottom had been scraped out of the financial barrel.

On the morning of 7 March, the Director sent an urgent telegram to the Secretary for Education : "Finansiële posisie van Universiteit uiters sorgwekkend. Onmoontlik om enige verdere verpligtinge na te kom sonder versekering van uitbetaling van gevraagde staatshulp vir afgelope twee jaar. Addisionele bankkrediet nie verkrygbaar. Telegrafeer onmiddellik wat die posisie is". The following afternoon, a second appeal was addressed by Professor van der Walt to the Vice-Chancellor, Dr van Rhijn, then in Cape Town : "Universiteit kan nie funksioneer sonder onmiddellike hulp. Alle uitbetaling reeds in Februarie gestaak terwyl salarisse hierdie maand reeds al nie uitbetaal kan word. Verdere bankkrediet onmoontlik".

With bank credit exhausted and no money with which to pay the staff, the position was indeed precarious. The Treasury, which was awaiting the views of universities in general on their financial needs, had already displayed some irritation about the poor showing of the new venture in comparison with the presumed financial stability of the private firms. Now it was distinctly annoyed. A cheque for more than R90 000 was hastily sent to cover the deficit, but a letter written on behalf of the Secretary for Finance, Dr J. E. Holloway, clearly indicated that the matter was regarded in that department in a very unfavourable light. "Die Tesourie beskou dit . . . baie onbevredigend", it stated, "dat so 'n groot tekort afgeloop het en hy voor 'n voldonge feit geplaas is".

However, a departmental committee of W. V. Robertson and P. J. Olckers had recently recommended that the university's Division of External Studies should receive an annual subsidy to a maximum of R56 000. The report was accepted, but the financial position remained difficult for some time to come. On 13 August, 1949, the Director wrote to H. S. van der Walt, who had just succeeded A. A. Roberts as Secretary for Education. He pointed out that the Division of External Studies was still relying on heavy overdraft facilities and asked for a temporary subsidy to relieve a burden which was "reeds weer vinnig besig om te versleg". Assistance was given, but the Secretary for Finance took the opportunity of expressing his dissatisfaction that "hierdie diens aansienlik hoër uitgawe meebring as wat die Kabinet oorspronklik verwag het". The teaching section could not expect to be subsidized at so high a rate in future, nor would the University of South Africa be placed upon a formula basis for an annual grant. Not surprisingly, Dr H. G. Luttig, Member of Parliament for Mayfair (Johannesburg) and Managing Director of the Transafrica Correspondence College, brought up the question of the government subsidy to the Division of External Studies in the parliamentary session of 1950.

There is no reason to impute extravagance to the Director, or to consider that the large deficits were entirely the result of a lack of business acumen, although that is what the commercial firms thought. The whole problem of university finances was investigated by a government commission of enquiry which was appointed in 1951 under the chairmanship of Dr J. E. Holloway, Its report of May, 1953 indicated clearly the special difficulties

The major problems facing S E N A T E in this period were the institution of the Division of External Studies and the coming of age of all the constituent colleges, with the exception of that at Wellington.

The transition from a federal to a purely teaching university with a specialized function took place during the chairmanship of Professor W.F. Barker. It was during his second term that his own college became the independent Rhodes University.

In 1952, the Director of External Studies (later the Principal) became Chairman of Senate. The office has been held by the Principal since that time.

Chairmen of Senate, 1944–1952

274

*Right: Prof. J.C. van Rooy
(Potchefstroom University College)
1944–1946
(Photo: Potchefstroom University)*

*Below: Prof. H. v.d. M. Scholtz
(University College of the
Orange Free State)
1946–1948*

*Below right: Prof. W.F. Barker
(Rhodes University and
University College), 1948–1952
(Photo: Rhodes University)*

of the University of South Africa in financing its Division of External Studies. In the first place, lecturers had to be paid salaries similar to those received by their colleagues of equal rank elsewhere in the South African university world. Secondly, the library cost money to staff and to stock and office accommodation in Pretoria was particularly expensive.

Whatever the reasons for the failure of the teaching venture to pay its way, there is no doubt that its financial problems embarrassed its supporters and delighted those of the correspondence colleges. Governments of all political persuasions dislike spending public moneys unnecessarily. Jan Hofmeyr, the United Party's Minister of Education and Finance in 1946, had seen the possibility of making one small saving when the university scheme was launched. To avoid having to subsidize two institutions working in the same field, government cut the grant made to the Witwatersrand Technical College, which handed over its correspondence courses – some of degree level – to the Division of External Studies.

The economy effected here, however, was more than offset by the seemingly insatiable demands of the new infant, to the dismay of the Nationalist government which took control of the Union's higher education in 1948. A measure of its concern is the injunction given to the Governor-General's nominees to the university Council to pay special attention to financial matters in debate.

The heavy deficits came to light at the very time when the whole future of the Division of External Studies – and, indeed, of the University of South Africa itself – was in jeopardy. Professor A. J. H. van der Walt was doing his best to give his section the standing of a university, but to many, it fell short of the university ideal. It was argued that, if external degrees were really necessary, a joint board could well control them. Alternatively, perhaps the older universities – or the new ones, then emerging from the federal chrysalis – might like to take over the existing external work. On the other hand, the actual teaching could, perhaps, be left to the correspondence colleges which,

276

at all events, were no drain on the national exchequer.

It had been evident when the Brookes Commission on the University of South Africa had reported in 1947, that the government of the institution would have to be drastically revised after the departure of the constituent colleges. It was felt then, and for some years to come, that the university in its new form as a teaching foundation for external students would have insufficient experience to control its own affairs alone. Moreover, there was the question of public trust. The University of South Africa would be regarded with more assurance if it were made evident that its standards were being maintained in the new circumstances. It was therefore suggested by the Brookes Commission that as each college representative left Council when the constituent nominating him achieved independence, a new member should be appointed by the Governor-General on the advice of a "Universities Co-ordinating Board". He would be chosen specifically to represent one of the conventional teaching universities. If possible, something similar should be done on Senate, although it was recommended that, as in wartime, the Senate Executive Committee should control affairs in any transition period. Once the university had lost all the constituent colleges, Senate could be reconstructed on the basis of equal representation for the Director and five selected members of his staff, with' six nominated members chosen on the advice of the proposed co-ordinating board.

As the date approached when reconstruction of the university would have to take place, the commercial institutions, emboldened now that they had successfully combined in a powerful association, began to press for a greater share in the affairs of the university. At the 3rd Annual Conference of the Association of Correspondence Colleges held in Johannesburg in September, 1950, tributes were paid to the sterling work of the private firms by several speakers, among them Councillor C. F. Beckett, the city's Deputy Mayor. It was asserted that the time had come for the commercial colleges to be represented on the governing body of the university and conversely, for the university to have a nominee on the Board of Control of the association. It was also alleged at this period that the Registrar's office was guilty of trying to coerce students to enrol with the Division of External Studies. Great indignation was expressed that an institution heavily subsidized by the state should be allowed to compete in such an unfair manner with commercial undertakings.

The Association of Correspondence Colleges submitted a memorandum to the University of South Africa in December, 1950, asking for representation on the governing body. Council was, however, opposed to this, although it was anxious to know in greater detail exactly what the colleges wanted. Accordingly, a meeting was arranged between Vice-Chancellor van Rhijn and members of the Board of Control of the association at the University of Cape Town on 12 January, 1951. Among those who took part in the discussions was Dr Luttig of Transafrica. Again, the desire for Council membership was voiced. What the members of the Association of Correspondence Colleges really hoped for, however, was for the university to revert to its old examining form and for the Division of External Studies to be severed from it and made a member of the association, on the same basis as the commercial forms. To all this, Dr van Rhijn presented an immovable front. He was, however, prepared to listen to the views of the colleges on a change of name for the university, although he did not much like their suggestion of a "South African Universities' Examining Board". In place of this, he put forward the title "University of South Africa for External Studies", a name which had the support of others in the world of South African higher education at that time. If the Association of Correspondence Colleges wanted any further changes, however, it should apply to the Director himself!

In discussions on the future of the Division of External Studies, Professor A. J. H. van der Walt and his colleagues were in no position to play a decisive role. At meetings within the University of South Africa they were always outnumbered and although the Board of Tutors fought hard to become the legally constituted channel for the expression of the views of the teaching staff,

278

it was never listened to by Council with the respect which that body accorded the opinions of Senate. The Board of Tutors remained no more than a staff association.

Nor was the Director given full recognition. At meetings of all the South African universities, his situation was an anomalous one. The body which had for long been accepted as the joint consultative board for the nation's universities was the Vice-Chancellors' Committee. However, Vice-Chancellors were not always Principals and what was important for a representative association of this kind was that it should be fully capable of making decisions on academic matters. Accordingly, a new body, the Committee of University Principals, was set up in 1949. Here, the University of South Africa was in a difficult situation. It had no Principal. Although the Director and the Registrar were invited to attend meetings of the new committee, the university's official representative was declared to be the Chairman of Senate. Professor Barker, who held this post throughout these years of uncertainty over the future of university training by correspondence, was keenly interested in the affairs of the Pretoria institution, but he had greater loyalties. This was also the period in which his own college, Rhodes, achieved full independence.

While the Committee of University Principals came in 1950 to accept that the University of South Africa's teaching function should continue after the withdrawal of the constituent colleges, it felt that the other universities should retain what it described as "dominant and actual control". This opinion reflected the widespread hostility to the work of the Division of External Studies among many academics, not only in the independent universities, but also in the colleges which were moving in that direction, but which were still represented in force in the Senate of the University of South Africa. The Huguenot University College considered that, in any reconstruction of the federal university, Senate would have to be so constituted that it would command respect for external degrees. This would mean, in effect, that a majority of its members would have to be drawn

279

from the nation's other universities. Professor A. J. H. van der Walt has stated that the widespread insistence upon the safe-guarding of standards in this manner was dictated by a fear that the staff of the Division of External Studies might be in-clined "om die Akademiese peil na benede te dwing om sodoende meer studente te trek". It was also dictated by a quite under-standable hesitation about handing over control to an untried staff and thus running the risk of debasing the value of a South African degree.

Some institutions, indeed, wondered whether it was wise to leave affairs in the hands of the University of South Africa at all. The University of the Witwatersrand suggested a joint board with power to confer external degrees in 1949, a proposal which at that time attracted Langham Murray. The Registrar again took the opportunity of stressing his opposition to any fusion between the examining and teaching sections of the university. The University College of the Orange Free State argued that other universities should be given the chance to undertake ex-ternal teaching. To the newly independent University of Natal, the system was inevitable, but regrettable. It suggested that the best way to mitigate the evils of a university activity of question-able standing would be to vest control of it in two other universi-ties. It felt that the most suitable would be the Universities of Pretoria and the Witwatersrand, if they were prepared to under-take the unenviable task. Self-interest was apparent in the debate and two proposals are worthy of note in this connection. From Bloemfontein came a plea to restrict external work to first degree level, while the University of Pretoria, with its flourishing extra-mural activities, wanted students living within 24 kilometres of a conventional university to be debarred from registering for external degree courses.

On the initiative of the Joint Committee of Council and Senate for External Studies, a smaller committee was set up in 1949 within the University of South Africa to look into the future of the institution. It consisted of the Vice-Chancellor, Dr van Rhijn, the Director, the Registrar, a representative of each constituent college, another for the education departments and three members of the federal Senate. The Senate members were Professor Barker, who acted as Chairman, Professor Gerrit Dekker of Potchefstroom, Dean of the Faculty of Arts, and Professor C. van H. du Plessis of the Bloemfontein college, who was Dean of the Faculty of Commerce and Administration. The committee came to the conclusion that external study should continue and that the University of South Africa was the best body to undertake it.

Various ideas on the most effective method of implementing this decision were considered. The Registrar, Langham Murray, despite his known reservations on the subject of external study, always placed the interests of the university first. If, he concluded, the system were to be perpetuated and the University of South Africa to enjoy a new lease of life as its guardian, then its standing should not be lowered by vesting control of its governing and academic bodies in other institutions. He therefore proposed that representatives of the so-called residential universities should be excluded from Council membership, except possibly as nominees of the Governor-General. Senate, however, should include, he considered, additional members from other universities, but only as a temporary measure until the staff of the Division of External Studies had been built up through new appointments.

The Director saw the force of the arguments in favour of Senate supervision by the other universities, if only as a sop to public and – particularly – to academic opinion. The memorandum which he submitted therefore took care to incorporate the representation of outside professors on the academic body. He considered that, in the nature of the case, he should act as Chairman of Senate. However, although the University of the Witwatersrand was prepared to agree with him over this, others differed sharply. Most felt that Senate itself should, as in the past, choose its own Chairman. It is easy to read an attitude deliberately obstructive into this hesitancy to accord the Division of External Studies full control. However, the teaching section was still small, nor was it the only body responsible for the tuition of external students in South Africa.

The Council of the University of South Africa submitted a memorandum to the Committee of University Principals in 1950, outlining a system of government for the reformed institution which would allow a measure of outside direction. The university was then asked to collaborate with the Department of Education, Arts and Science in drawing up a draft bill. A committee of Council and Senate, consisting of J. P. Duminy, S. P. E. Boshoff, W. F. Barker, Ferdinand Postma and the Director was formed to assist in this. The legislation proposed then went before the Committee of University Principals in January, 1951, where, with a few changes, it was accepted. The Director's position at meetings of the Principals remained an anomaly to the end. Council considered that he should, on this important occasion, represent the university, but the Chairman of Senate had already been invited. Both attended, but Professor A. J. H. van der Walt's role was much that of an interested onlooker, for Professor Barker had the vote.

It seems curious, in retrospect, that the Director's power was still circumscribed in the ensuing legislation which transformed the University of South Africa. He would seem to have been the obvious *ex-officio* choice as the representative of the teaching section on Council. However, Act 30 of 1951 merely specified that a seat on Council was to be offered to a member of the Division of External Studies chosen by Senate. Subservience was thus perpetuated and, in this instance, with little justification.

One of the last suggestions made by the Senate of the expiring Huguenot University College was that the Registrar should be given a voice in Council deliberations. Others felt that he should be there to guard the interests of those students who were not enrolled with the Division of External Studies. However, Council membership was not extended to the university's chief administrative officer. In view of the changes which were soon to take place in the structure of external studies, the decision was probably a wise one.

282

Transvalia Building, Pretoria 1948

The Division of External Studies expanded rapidly and early in 1948, additional accommodation was found in TRANSVALIA BUILDING, on the corner of Central and Pretorius Streets, Pretoria. The University of South Africa acquired 22 offices and took possession before the completion of the new block.

"The Act to amend the University of South Africa Act, 1916, and to provide for matters incidental thereto", to give it its official designation, came into force on 1 August, 1951. To J. R. Sullivan of Durban, it was the fulfilment of his dream of a people's university. Act 30 was, however, something less than a higher educational Magna Carta for external students, although the University of South Africa would henceforth devote all its energies at degree level to their needs. It also retained its subsidiary functions with regard to school and music examinations and continued to administer the affairs of the Joint Matriculation Board and the Joint Committee for Professional Examinations.

Provision was made for certain members of Council to complete the unexpired portions of their terms of office in 1951. The last delegates from the constituent colleges had disappeared from the scene in March of that year, but their places were taken by the Principals of the nation's universities, or by those appointed to represent them. The Governor-General's nominees – six at first, with two more appointed later – included two persons selected to speak for Convocation. One of these was chosen specially to safeguard the interests of African, Coloured and Indian students. Elections for Convocation members were therefore abolished. South West Africa and Rhodesia would cease to be represented when their present members of Council had completed their terms of office. In addition to the representative of the Division of External Studies, the Chairman of Senate was also made a member of Council. The Vice-Chancellor continued to take the chair.

The new Senate was to consist of two members of Council, the Director of the Division of External Studies in an *ex-officio* capacity, all lecturers who were heads of department and such professors who might at a future date be appointed to the teaching staff. From the other universities came two representatives of each of their Senates, together with eight additional professors or lecturers. This was to give outside universities an immediate numerical advantage on the academic body. Their position was

284

further strengthened, since the persons who were Deans of the various faculties when the legislation came into force, as well as the Chairman, Professor Barker, remained as Senate members for a further period. The power of the Division of External Studies was also limited on boards of faculties and committees of studies, for there a university lecturer never acted alone and was usually outnumbered by at least two to one in the composition of these bodies.

The Board of Tutors did, however, gain statutory recognition as a kind of lesser Senate, to which authority it was able to make recommendations. It also continued to serve the Director in an advisory capacity. Despite the small concession, the Division of External Studies was kept firmly in its place in the Act of 1951. It has been said that the representatives of the other universities feared the creation in Senate of a power bloc composed of members of the University of South Africa's teaching staff. This may have been true, for there were some at Senate meetings who treated the Division of External Studies with a condescension born of conscious superiority and had no wish to see its lecturers in a dominant position. Nevertheless, Professor van der Walt and his colleagues had friends among the outsiders there – men of the calibre of that noted linguist, G. P. Lestrade of the University of Cape Town, and S. J. H. Steven of the University of the Orange Free State.

The Director and the University of South Africa would meet with further opposition in their moves to gain wider recognition, but as it grew in stature and gained in experience, the Division of External Studies would eventually silence its many critics. By 1951, at least, early uncertainties had vanished and the youthful teaching venture could begin to make progress along the road to future greatness.

11 *A new university takes shape*

Professor A. J. H. van der Walt regarded the Act of 1951 as "an experiment in the field of higher education in South Africa". The novelty of the new legislation lay, as he told students in the university's annual journal for that year, in the organization of the University of South Africa, rather than in the nature of the work which it undertook. As he pointed out, nobody then questioned "the long-accepted principle of external university studies".

Although it was true enough that the principle of external study was no longer in question, it was by no means universally accepted that the University of South Africa should be the only institution to provide the tuition. Nor did everyone consider it to be the best. The commercial colleges still smarted over the terms of the original legislation which had placed a state-aided competitor in the market beside them. For some years, they and their supporters continued to snipe at the university and the government which helped to finance it, although by 1955, students were coming to see that enrolment for tuition with the University of South Africa had certain advantages. By that date, more than 75% of the 5 586 prospective candidates for its examinations were also making use of the tuition offered by it.

What the correspondence colleges still hoped for was representation on Council in the name of the students enrolled with them and representation on Senate by eight members, selected from a list to be submitted by them to the governing body of the university. They also pressed for a more equitable method of examining students and had come to see certain advantages in the use of numbers instead of names on scripts. Changes in the examining system were, in fact, brought about by the university Senate, but not as a result of pressure from the commercial firms. As for the other demands of the correspondence undertakings, both the Director and the Registrar were, for once, in complete agreement.

"The implicit assumption", said Langham Murray, "that the Division is just another correspondence college, of the same clay as the members of the association (of colleges), is an impertinence". The commercial firms did not represent students, let alone a majority of them, as they claimed, but merely themselves. Professor van der Walt was equally opposed to allowing the colleges any official part in university affairs. Commercial gain could not be recognized in academic circles!

Members of the House of Assembly made what political capital they could out of the case. Among those who spoke out for the commercial firms were Dr A. H. Jonker of the United Party and his colleagues Mrs Margaret Ballinger and P. A. Moore. They attacked the University of South Africa on the ground that it was only a correspondence college itself, competing unfairly for students against other institutions which were in the field as business houses. It was alleged, not without justice, that it had never been government's intention to allow the Division of External Studies to survive, unless it proved capable of paying its own way. And now the state was footing an increasingly heavy bill, while the new teaching section and the University of South Africa were almost synonymous. Why, the institution was not a university at all, in any recognized sense! It should at the very least bear the title of the "University of South Africa for External Studies", as had earlier been proposed.

The title had not only been suggested by Dr van Rhijn, but also by Professor E. G. Malherbe, Principal and Vice-Chancellor of the University of Natal. Moreover, it had a good measure of support from the staffs of the other residential universities. Langham Murray was strongly opposed to any change of name and in February, 1951, demolished the arguments put forward in favour of a new designation at the previous meeting of the Committee of University Principals. There, Professor H. R. Raikes of the University of the Witwatersrand – in general, a supporter of the Division of External Studies – considered that the existing name of the university was misleading and gave the impression to the uninitiated that it was the foremost institution of learning in the country. To which the Registrar replied that, in many ways, it was! Professor Malherbe's view was that the reformed university had no right to inherit the proud traditions of the federal University of South Africa which, after all, was really made up of its constituent colleges. But, said Murray, what of the external students, whose numbers were not so insignificant, even in federal days? Some of them – and, inevitably, he included Senator Brookes in a short list – had made the most valuable contributions to South African life. He further questioned the right of the Principals to voice any opinion on the subject and reminded them that many graduates who could in 1918 and again in 1930 have joined the Convocation of other universities, had elected to stay with the University of South Africa.

Professor van der Walt was equally determined to defend the old name, but Council initially accepted the need for change. As Professor Malherbe said in 1953, "in university circles generally, particularly overseas, it is regarded as anomalous even to give the name 'university' with power to grant degrees, to an institution of this type". The University of South Africa, shorn of its constituents, was no longer akin to its sister in New Zealand, then in its last years. Neither had it been designed to answer the demands of those who, like Professor P. R. Skawran of the University of Pretoria, wanted a post-graduate institution, on the lines of the Australian National University in Canberra, as originally conceived in 1946. It was, to many, quite inappropriate that a mere correspondence school should bear a national title.

However, much the same hostility had been shown when the

federal university was first named and government decided that the opinions of University of South Africa graduates should be sought before any change was made. Letters were therefore sent to a selection of them and replies were received from rather more than half of those approached. Most were against the substitution of a new title and the matter was accordingly dropped. The hostility died hard. As late as 1957, Professor W. G. Sutton, then Principal of the University of the Witwatersrand, expressed the view that correspondence tuition for degrees was not genuine university education and that it was doubtful whether qualifications earned in this way through the University of South Africa had the same value as those obtained at the nation's other universities. It must be confessed that even the most enthusiastic supporters of the Division of External Studies had usually taken the line that external students missed the many advantages of community life in a residential university. However, the assumption that degrees awarded by the University of South Africa were inferior incensed the Director and his staff. The representatives of the other universities on Senate were always there to prevent any lowering of standards. Moreover, Professor van der Walt had assembled a team of high quality to take charge of the various departments of study and the care with which lecturers continued to be selected contributed greatly to the success of the university's teaching section.

Many of the newcomers were to play a prominent part in the affairs of the University of South Africa and of other universities in the country. To the Department of Bantu Languages came the Stellenbosch graduate, J. A. Louw, and D. Ziervogel, with a doctorate from the University of Pretoria. The latter at length became head of the department. G. van N. Viljoen returned to the Department of Classics on a permanent basis, replacing O. von Weber as departmental head. T. A. van Dyk, who subsequently moved to Potchefstroom University, joined the Department of Psychology, while B. S. van As was appointed as the first permanent lecturer in the Department of Native Administration, of which he later became head. The Department of

Sociology, then still allied with Social Work, gained the services of H. L. Crause, who in time migrated to the University of Port Elizabeth. Rhodesian-born J. A. Cilliers worked with L. M. du Toit in the Department of Accounting and E. H. Venter came from the Free State to the Department of Education and was later appointed to the Chair of Empirical Education in the Faculty.

F. van den Bogaerde, who received his early education in the Netherlands and Switzerland, arrived from the University of Stellenbosch to join the Department of Economics of which he subsequently became head. B. J. van der Walt and D. F. I. van Heerden were appointed to the Department of Mathematics and Applied Mathematics. The former was long to remain with the university; the latter moved to the University of the Orange Free State. Another lecturer appointed at this time – D. E. Nel of the Department of Geography – also went to the Bloemfontein university. His successor, M. J. Louw, later joined the staff of the institution which became the University of the North.

Expansion also necessitated the creation of new departments. There was, for example, a demand for a properly constituted department to provide courses in German. The second World War was then a recent memory and fears were expressed in the English language press in 1951 that a permanent lectureship in that field might be offered to Erich Holm, who had been an announcer on Germany's short-wave radio transmissions during the late global conflict. However, this appointment was not made and the post was at length filled by B. A. T. Schneider, who was born in Berlin and subsequently came out to South West Africa. He obtained a doctorate from the University of Stellenbosch and later became head of the Department of German. Dr Schneider had lecturing experience at both the University of Stellenbosch and the University of Cape Town.

Another development at the end of the Van der Walt period in the history of the modern university was the institution of Departments of Bibliography and Librarianship, later amalgamated as the Department of Library Science. The courses offered were arranged by the head of the Department of Philosophy, Dr H. J. de Vleeschauwer, and the Librarian, H. Zastrau. The library itself was steadily expanding and by 1953, had over 45 000 items on its shelves. A comparison was made at this time with the Merensky Library of the University of Pretoria. This indicated that students and staff of the University of South Africa made rather greater use of the facilities offered there than did their counterparts at the neighbouring university. Staffing, however, remained a problem for many years and, as the Librarian said, "die afdeling het hulpeloos te min personeel". It was nevertheless growing slowly and among the newcomers in the last period of Professor van der Walt's leadership was H. F. van Broekhuizen, who at the time of his retirement in 1972 was in charge of the documentary and special collections.

The creation of professorships would considerably enhance the status of the Division of External Studies, but despite a growing demand in the early fifties from the teaching staff, the representatives of the other universities on Council and Senate showed great hesitation in approving the step. Even so good a friend of the university as G. P. Lestrade was not at all in favour of professorial appointments within the University of South Africa. He agreed that the lecturers might well be given some sort of title, but "Professor", never! Financial considerations also delayed the introduction of higher posts for the teaching staff for some time, since this was the period when the Holloway Commission was investigating university finances in general. However, in 1954, fourteen professorships were created, of which nine were filled immediately. Six of those appointed had been among the first lecturers of 1946 and early 1947. These were D. H. Cilliers, Edward Davis, D. J. de Villiers, C. F. J. Muller, A. S. Roux and H. J. J. M. van der Merwe. The other three had come a little later: H. J. de Vleeschauwer, F. E. Rädel and Dirk Ziervogel. There were six southern Africans by birth, together with a Belgian, an Englishman and a German who had made their homes in this country.

Even before these posts had been approved, the lecturing staff had been accorded a further mark of confidence. In 1951, the Dean of the Faculty of Law, Advocate H. F. Sampson of Rhodes, resigned and his place was taken by Advocate Dawid de Villiers of the Division of External Studies. This appointment was soon followed by that of D. H. Cilliers as Dean of the Faculty of Education in succession to J. Chr. Coetzee of Potchefstroom University for Christian Higher Education. Shortly afterwards, J. A. van der Walt of the Department of Sociology replaced Professor D. C. S. du Preez of Potchefstroom as Dean of the Faculty of Social Science. The time was not far distant when all Deans would be members of the university staff. Gradually, too, the Division of External Studies provided the Chairmen of the various committees of studies.

These were small gains in a university still dominated by the representatives of the more orthodox institutions of higher education in the country. Professor A. J. H. van der Walt's standing was not yet as high as many people felt it should be. To them, it was illogical that the most important figure in what had become a teaching university in the fullest sense was not automatically the leader of the academic Senate, even though that body and its Executive Committee were controlled by other universities. Such a move, however, aroused strong opposition from those who regarded it as an attempt to wean the University of South Africa from outside control. This hostility had by no means been overcome in April, 1952, although in that month, sufficient support for the Director was forthcoming to ensure his election as Chairman of Senate in succession to Professor Barker. Another milestone in the development of the university had been reached.

Further reorganization took place after the retirement of Langham Murray as Registrar at the end of March, 1953. He had carried out his duties in an exemplary manner throughout a long and difficult period and it was not surprising that he should have been asked to give his services to another university institution in a similar capacity. This was the University College of Rhodesia and Nyasaland, today the University of Rhodesia.

292

Langham Murray had, however, always insisted in Pretoria that the administrative and teaching sections of the University of South Africa should be kept entirely separate. With his departure for Salisbury, Council could consider again whether a system which prevented the staff of the Division of External Studies from seeing the Registrar's records and the Registrar from advising students was, in fact, really necessary.

The Assistant Registrar, Petrus A. Taljaard, was chosen from 87 applicants for the Registrar's post. Langham Murray welcomed his successor in a valedictory which appeared in the 1953 edition of the journal, *Student*. "I have stepped down", he said, "from the platform; but Amurath to Amurath succeeds and the mantle of Elijah (a black silk gown, with a narrow facing of scarlet silk down each side in front – *Calendar* – 'Academic Dress') has fallen upon a worthy Elisha". The gown of office was not long to drape the new Registrar's shoulders. Later in 1953, Petrus Taljaard became a member of the Transvaal Provincial Council and was given leave of absence by the university until the end of 1954, by which time he was due to retire.

The Secretary of the Division of External Studies, B. F. J. van Rensburg, was appointed Registrar in an acting capacity and his duties as Secretary were taken over by the Chief Clerk, L. G. van der Merwe. These posts were made permanent in January, 1955, while two years later, the Secretary became the Assistant Registrar. The examining section, in deference to the views of the commercial colleges, was kept separate under the supervision of J. J. Brits. His task was an arduous one, as his colleague, A. J. Vorster, pointed out in an article published by *Student* in 1954. The previous year's degree examinations had involved the handling of about 30 000 scripts from more than 4 000 students writing at 550 centres in southern Africa and overseas.

The Director attended a conference on correspondence education in the United States of America in 1953. Soon after his return, he reached the then retiring age of 60. His services, however, were so valuable that Council persuaded him to remain

PETRUS ARNOLDUS TALJAARD was born on 2 December, 1894 on the farm Uitval in the Wepener district of the Orange Free State. He first attended school in the Bethulie concentration camp, continued his education in Wepener and matriculated at Grey College, Bloemfontein in 1915, winning a Thomas Robertson bursary. He obtained the B.A. degree at Grey University College in 1918 and the LL.B. at the Transvaal University College two years later.

He entered the service of the Department of Union Education in 1919, but six months later joined the small administrative staff of the federal university. Accountant in 1927, he became Assistant Registrar in 1934. He succeeded Langham Murray as Registrar in 1953, but was not active in the post, as he became a member of the Transvaal Provincial Council. He retired at the end of 1954, but returned to administrative duties with the university in a temporary capacity until his final resignation in 1969.

P.A. Taljaard was for many years active in local government. Four times Mayer of Hercules, he was also Deputy Mayor of Pretoria.

His death occurred in Pretoria on 8 September, 1970.

Petrus Arnoldus Taljaard, B.A., LL.B.
Registrar 1953–1954

294

with the university for a further period. The old title by which he had been known since the establishment of the Division of External Studies was replaced by that of Principal, so that Professor van der Walt was at last able, in his new capacity, to draw together the administrative and teaching sections, so long divided. He was also enabled to meet his colleagues on equal terms at meetings of the Committee of University Principals.

By this time, tuition was being offered in a wide range of subjects, although not all those in which the university provided examinations figured on the list. The sciences in particular were severely restricted. Students, naturally enough, had to show that they had carried out adequate practical work before they were admitted to examinations; there were, however, no departments offering tuition and Senate control was in the hands of outside advisers. Barker of Rhodes assisted in this way during the early fifties; so, too, did S. F. Bush of Natal. The Dean of the Faculty of Science throughout this period was Professor D. J. du Plessis of Potchefstroom. The question of courses in pure science was to be raised again.

Already there was a demand for degrees in pharmacy and the technical colleges carrying out diploma work in this field would have been delighted to provide students with graduate qualifications through the University of South Africa. The same was true of engineering and the time was not far distant when a Secretary of Education, J. J. P. Op't Hof, would publicly suggest that the university, like its London counterpart, should again institute degrees in this branch. Such developments would, however, bring to the fore the old problem of the relationship of technical colleges to university foundations and there was still widespread opposition to any blurring of the distinction between them. For the present, the Committee of University Principals merely asked the University of South Africa to help with science examinations while the institution considered future action with regard to courses of its own.

Fine arts, a sub-division of the Faculty of Arts, was also restricted. O. J. P. Oxley, Professor of Fine Arts at Natal until

296

1952, was the first Chairman of the University of South Africa's Committee of Studies in that field and afterwards acted in an advisory capacity. There was also a Committee of Studies in Music, under the chairmanship of Professor P. R. Kirby of the University of the Witwatersrand, but no separate Faculty of Music was ever created and the subject remains a division of the Faculty of Arts.

Divinity degrees were in abeyance, although a number of relevant subjects, among them systematic theology and Hebrew, were listed in the *Calendar* as examination options in the requirements for an arts degree. There was a Committee of Studies in Semitics under Professor A. van Selms of the University of Pretoria. However, the early Committee of Studies in Divinity under the chairmanship of Professor S. du Toit of Potchefstroom was replaced by an adviser, the Rev. W. Cosser of Rhodes University.

The possibility of obtaining an external degree undoubtedly attracted an increasing number of students of all races to register with the University of South Africa. By the end of the Van der Walt period, the institution had outstripped all its competitors so far as student numbers were concerned. It is not surprising, therefore, that a feeling arose that the university was not adhering closely enough to the obligation laid upon it in Act 18 of 1946. This stated that the University of South Africa was to satisfy itself that, when a student applied for registration, there existed "sufficient reasons preventing him from attending a university institution". Council, in order to silence complaints on this score, began to refer consideration of doubtful applications for registration to the other universities in 1953 and 1954. The changed procedure immediately laid a heavy burden upon university administrations; moreover, it occasioned angry comments from prospective students, who began to appeal to the Minister of Education, Arts and Science himself. Not every university in the country insisted on its rights in this matter. The University of Natal, for example, was quite prepared to leave all doubtful cases concerning registration to the University of South

Africa. Problems arose, however, in connection with the extra-mural courses offered by the University of Pretoria, for many there considered these entirely adequate to meet the needs of students living in the immediate neighbourhood. The Minister, J. H. Viljoen, found himself in a difficult position. It was, perhaps, undemocratic to refuse a suitably qualified student who was prepared to pay the University of South Africa's fees, simply because he might be able to attend some other institution. It was finally decided to return to the old system in the course of 1954 and thereafter the University of South Africa again selected its own students.

Financial difficulties continued to beset all universities in the post-war years and the Holloway Commission of 1951 decided to gain first-hand information concerning the problem by visiting the various institutions, including the college at Fort Hare. A memorandum was compiled by the University of South Africa in February, 1952 and presented to the commission in the name of the university Council. The memorandum took the opportunity of stressing one fact which it thought should be given serious consideration. It was felt that the University of South Africa could only do its work efficiently if the students who registered with it for examination purposes were compelled, except in special circumstances, to receive tuition with the university or with an approved teaching institution "wat voltydse of deeltydse mondelinge klasonderrig verskaf". This would have the effect of driving the commercial correspondence colleges out of the field of undergraduate instruction and would enable the University of South Africa to demand higher standards of its students by compelling them to complete obligatory assignments of work.

The memorandum went on to suggest that compulsory enrolment with the Division of External Studies would not lead to increased government grants, since the cost of the extra staff required would be balanced by the additional income deriving from a larger student body. This was, perhaps, wishful thinking, but it was also argued that more money could be raised by increasing the fees. At that time, it was alleged, fees were kept down in order to compete on favourable terms with the commercial firms. Such a policy, however, was expensive, as the university, unlike its rivals, had particularly heavy commitments. The University of South Africa considered that an adequate subsidy formula would have to be found for the Division of External Studies and suggested a sliding scale based upon income. This would provide state aid of R3 for each R1 on the first R10 000 of income, diminishing to 24 cents for each R1 in respect of income above R80 000. The university felt that the "token grant" of R4 000 for administrative purposes was quite unrealistic; losses had been incurred there for several years as a result of this parsimony on the part of government.

In connection with the whole question of subsidy, the memorandum drew the commission's attention to the fact that, with eight nominees of the Governor-General on its Council, "kan die Universiteit redelik verwag dat die Staat se belangstelling meer prakties getoon sou word". In addition, it reminded the members that the University of South Africa undertook certain functions in the public interest. It sought, against competition from overseas, to introduce " 'n eg Suid-Afrikaanse gees in die S.A.-se musieklewe" and had also, partly at the request of government, initiated a series of examinations in speech training.

When the commission reported in 1953, an entire chapter was devoted to the problems of the University of South Africa. So far as compulsory enrolment was concerned, the members were not, for the time being, in favour. They considered that the high standard maintained by the lecturers of the Division of External Studies had an excellent effect upon the work of the commercial colleges. Moreover, there was good reason, they felt, to wait until a greater proportion of students chose to study through the university.

In tracing the history of the separate subsidy for the Division of External Studies, the commission recalled that, at the beginning, it had been thought that government aid would not long be needed. This expectation had never been realized. While the

University of South Africa could, to some extent, help itself by raising its fees, a satisfactory subsidy formula would nevertheless have to be found. The commission's suggestions here were not unreasonable, if perhaps somewhat stringent so far as the administration was concerned. A shorter sliding scale was recommended: R2 for each R1 on the first R20 000 of student fees, including registration, followed by a rand for rand subsidy for the next R20 000 and thereafter, 50 cents for each R1 of income received. The scale would include the administrative subsidy and it was expressly recommended that, as examinations should pay for themselves, no part of the sum allocated to the Division of External Studies should be used to make good any deficit incurred on them.

The University of South Africa was not yet to be treated on the same basis as the other universities for subsidy purposes, but at least, with the acceptance of the Holloway Commission's proposals, the financial outlook appeared brighter. There would be five-yearly revision of the subsidy and the Committee of University Principals, which completely took over the functions of the moribund Vice-Chancellors' Committee in 1955, was to be represented on the government's University Advisory Committee. More money would always be welcome – especially to finance such schemes as the provision of additional adult education and the founding of a publications series. However, with fee revenue of nearly R240 000 in 1955 – to which the state added about R160 000 – the University of South Africa enjoyed a very satisfactory surplus of some R24 000 in that year.

In other ways, too, as Professor van der Walt's period in office drew to a close, things went well for the university. The Vacation School continued to flourish and was able to make a modest profit each year. There was – exceptionally – a small decline in the attendance figures for 1954, when for the first time students from the European race group were in the majority. However, 393 prospective candidates for the university's examinations attended in the following year, of whom 206 were Europeans and 187 were from the other race groups. More significantly, the statistics show that more than 19% of the non-European students enrolled with the Division of External Studies made use of the Vacation School – more than three times the proportion of European students.

Graduation ceremonies were also held each year as in the past. The former Kilnerton Institution continued to be used for African, Coloured and Indian students, but in 1955, the Degree Day function for Europeans was transferred to the Pretoria City Hall, where, on the occasion, the congregation was addressed by the Superintendent General of Education for the Cape Province, Dr J. G. Meiring, a member of the university Council.

The University of South Africa also assumed new responsibilities. The question of higher education for non-Europeans was made the subject of a government commission appointed in November, 1953. Its members were Dr Holloway, Professor Malherbe of the University of Natal and Professor R.W. Wilcocks of the University of Stellenbosch. The *Kolege ya Bana ba Afrika* was discussed in the commission's report, in part with reference to the University of South Africa's desire to see the two institutions develop in association. However, the college had never prospered and was far from providing education at undergraduate level. Nevertheless, the connection between college and university was a pointer to the possible direction higher education for non-Europeans in South Africa might take. Public opinion was by no means unanimous that a policy of separate development should be applied to university training by the creation of institutions reserved for specific groups of peoples. The Natal Indian Congress reacted to the possibility by condemning it; so, too, did the Convocation of the University of Natal. Moreover, the Principal of the University of Cape Town, Professor T. B. Davie, indicated that American universities were moving away from the practice of segregation in higher education.

However, if that was to be the pattern for the future, there were those ready to sponsor new foundations. The Town Clerk of Benoni spoke up for the creation of a non-European university at Daveyton and the University of Pretoria was prepared to take an African university college in the north under its wing. There was undoubtedly a growing need for more facilities for non-Europeans and, as the Secretary for Native Affairs, Dr W. W. M. Eiselen, commented in 1956, the University of South Africa could play " 'n baie geskikte moeder- of voogdyskapsrol". It had a long tradition of association with colleges and, until the University College of Fort Hare had linked its fortunes with Rhodes University in Grahamstown, had enjoyed a special relationship with the one institution of standing in the short history of higher education for non-Europeans in South Africa.

An opportunity for the University of South Africa to show that it was capable of playing this role again came in 1955. The Catholic university college at Roma in Basutoland had been taken over by the Oblates of Mary Immaculate, an order which had created the bilingual University of Ottawa in Canada. This Canadian institution helped to staff the Basutoland college, later named in honour of Pope Pius XII. Students there, mainly African, had been allowed the privilege of sitting as external candidates for the examinations of the University of South Africa. Now, after the South African Department of Education, Arts and Science and the British government had given their approval, it was proposed to bind the two institutions closer in a loose association. As a first step towards enhanced status, the Pius XII Catholic University College was permitted, in September, 1955, to hold its own graduation ceremony at Roma. Finally, on 27 September, an agreement was signed between the Rector, Father R. Guilbeault, and the University of South Africa, whereby the university was to have two representatives on the governing body of the college, with reciprocal arrangements for assessor members from Roma to attend academic meetings in Pretoria. The scheme did not work without friction, nor was it of long duration. It was important, however, as a move in a new direction. As Professor van der Walt said at the time : "Hiermee is myns insiens die grondslag gelê van 'n beleid wat in die toekoms van groot betekenis mag word in verband met die organisasie en ontwikkeling van hoër onderwys vir die nie-blankes van ons land".

Hard on the heels of this new development came another which, despite the claims of the protagonists, was neither in the best interests of South African university education as a whole, nor in those of the University of South Africa. A private foundation, created under the Companies Act of 1926, was proposed at the beginning of 1956. It was to be called the *Vrye Christelike Universiteitskollege* and was to be registered at an address in Bureau Lane, Pretoria. Its main purpose, according to the draft constitution setting out its intended functions, seems to have been the granting of degrees in divinity, but the door was left open for other degrees to be conferred as well. It was also prepared, if the occasion presented itself, to teach students of all race groups, although it was to be founded in the first instance for Europeans. The new institution hoped to provide both conventional lectures and tuition by correspondence.

This proposed development, as the Registrar pointed out, was "in direkte botsing met die huidige wetlike posisie, waarvolgens die Universiteit van Suid-Afrika die enigste inrigting is wat eksterne studie mag eksamineer". It seems that, in 1956, the college had already started operations, but the Department of Education, Arts and Science did not recognize the graduate qualifications it was offering. However, what was then described as " 'n gevaarlike ontwikkeling" was arrested by a general disinclination to allow its pretensions. The Committee of University Principals insisted that its wings be clipped by compelling those who wished to register it as a company to delete all references to "university" and "higher education" in its draft constitution. As for the subject for which it was primarily intended, the University of South Africa pointed out that the introduction of a full divinity course in the Division of External Studies was only a matter of time.

In 1953, the University of South Africa at length came into possession of a home of its own. On the morning of Saturday, 21 March, a ceremony took place at which the new three-

The ADMINISTRATION BUILDING in Skinner Street, Pretoria was constructed to provide an expanding university with a home of its own.

The foundation-stone was laid by the Chancellor, Judge President G.J. Maritz, on 21 March, 1953. The Division of External Studies moved into the new building on 1 June and the Registrar's section, housed since 1949 in Kerry Building, opposite the State Library in Vermeulen Street, joined the teaching staff in September of the same year.

Later, an adjoining block of flats was purchased and an extra storey added to the main structure.

Administration Building, 263 Skinner Street, Pretoria

storied building, approaching completion, was given an official blessing. The Vice-Chancellor, S. P. E. Boshoff, welcomed those present at 263, Skinner Street, Pretoria and the Director – not yet at that date the Principal – outlined the history of the university's accommodation in the past. Professor Steven of the University of the Orange Free State, Dean of the Faculty of Arts, conveyed the good wishes of the other universities. Others who addressed the gathering were H. S. van der Walt, Secretary for Education, Arts and Science, Jan H. Visse, Mayor of Pretoria, and W. D. Terry of the Heidelberg (Transvaal) Training College, a former student of the university. Finally, the architect, C. S. Lodge, handed Judge President G. J. Maritz, Chancellor of the university, the traditional silver trowel with which to lay the foundation stone.

At last, the University of South Africa was under one roof and the new building was even able at first to provide the facilities for the European Vacation School. A. J. Vorster described the many activities in each of the departments in an article entitled "Ons nuwe gebou", which appeared in the journal *Student* for the following year. *Student,* however, carried an editorial warning. Already, after only eighteen months, the building had become too small for an ever-expanding university. Soon, Edward Mansions next door would have to be taken over and a fund was also established to provide additional office and library accommodation. The City Council made a substantial donation to this and by the end of August, 1955, the sum of' more than R42 000 had been promised or contributed by public bodies, staff, students and well-wishers.

By this time, the University of South Africa had made remarkable strides. Although it had not yet been completely accepted as an equal by the nation's other institutions of higher education, much had been achieved. The Division of External Studies enjoyed better representation on Senate than had been the case four years before. Council, too, continued to play its part in a wider sphere by appointing delegates to such bodies as the Joint Matriculation Board. It also nominated members of other associations, among them the National Road Safety Organization and the South African Council for the Advancement of Music. For some years, Council, with praiseworthy impartiality, appointed a representative to two antagonistic bodies – the South African Institute of Race Relations which it had long supported and the rival South African Bureau of Racial Affairs. However, in 1962, it decided to withdraw from both associations. The governing body was also represented on the Council of the *Kolege ya Bana ba Afrika* by the Principal.

As a teaching institution, the University of South Africa had finally proved its worth. The tangible effect of this was seen in the passing of Act 54 of 1955, which was approved on 20 June. By this legislation, known as the University of South Africa Amendment Act, 1955, the Principal of the university became the Vice-Chancellor and the Division of External Studies simply a division of studies. Leadership in Council devolved upon an elected Chairman.

Professor A. J. H. van der Walt therefore succeeded Professor Boshoff as Vice-Chancellor, the latter being chosen to lead Council. It was as Vice-Chancellor and Principal that Professor van der Walt retired at the end of March, 1956 in favour of Professor Samuel Pauw, formerly Director of the Bureau of Social and Educational Research of the Department of Education, Arts and Science. Professor van der Walt's achievement had been a remarkable one. He had given to a small offshoot of a university's activity a standing which few in 1946 ever expected it to attain. He had shown tenacity in the face of much opposition and had skilfully taken every opportunity to advance the cause of the university's teaching section without exposing it to risks which might well have resulted in its disappearance from the higher educational scene.

Professor van der Walt prepared the defensive lines, giving to the Division of External Studies a firmly entrenched position. By 1956, the University of South Africa could go forward under new generalship, strong enough to move over to the offensive, to pioneer new ventures, to experiment and to make itself felt

SAMUEL PAUW was born at Elsburg, Transvaal on 25 August, 1909. After matriculating in 1925, he trained as a teacher at the Pretoria Normal College and in 1930, obtained the degree of B.Sc. at the University of Pretoria. An M.A. in sociology of the University of South Africa in 1939, he was awarded the D.Phil. degree by the University of Pretoria in 1946.

A teacher in Springs and Germiston from 1931 until 1936, he subsequently worked in Cape Town with the Juvenile Advisory Board. In 1940, he joined the lecturing staff of the University of Pretoria, becoming Associate Professor of Sociology in 1948. In the following year, he was appointed Professor and head of the Department of Sociology at the University of Stellenbosch. In 1955, he became Director of the National Bureau for Educational and Social Research, a post which he held until he succeeded Professor van der Walt as Principal of the University of South Africa on 1 April, 1956.

Professor Pauw built upon the firm foundations laid by his predecessor and under his guidance, the university expanded rapidly, acquiring a new standing among the nation's higher educational institutions. He retired from office on 31 March, 1972.

Professor Samuel Pauw, B.Sc., M.A., D.Phil.
Member of Council 1956–1972
Principal 1956–1972

in every aspect of national life. However, the university would never have been able to do this had it not been for the dedication of its first Principal. It was in recognition of his invaluable services that, at the graduation ceremony in 1956, Professor van der Walt was awarded an honorary doctorate in literature by a grateful university. He remained a loyal supporter of the institution which he had done so much to create and for fifteen years more gave its governing Council the benefit of his wise advice in the many problems which faced it. His death on 16 August, 1972 was greatly lamented by all those still in the service of the university who had helped him to establish the teaching

12 *The pace quickens*

The second Principal, Professor Samuel Pauw, took office on 1 April, 1956. The University of South Africa stood on the threshold of a period of development unparalleled in its history.

The new Principal spoke in his first year of the university's need to advertise itself. Its growth to that date suggested that, so far as attracting students was concerned, it already enjoyed wide public recognition. There were, however, other reasons for making itself better known. To provide an even more efficient service, funds were required. As Professor Pauw was to point out in the following year, the amount of money privately donated in more than eighty years of South African university extension had been pitifully small.

The Principal also emphasized in 1956 the vital importance of fostering a group spirit within the university. There was still too slender a link between teacher and taught, and to many students, the University of South Africa was merely a means to an end, a shadowy, unsubstantial foundation with which they had little personal contact. To those who lived far from Pretoria, it was, as Professor Pauw described it, "onsigbaar"; not all would then have agreed with him, however, when he called it " 'n lewende werklikheid".

Nevertheless, it was accomplishing much and if compulsory enrolment could only be introduced, still more could be done to strengthen the ties between the lecturing staff and the candidates for university examinations. Ministers of Education, however, were hesitant to give the University of South Africa the control it asked for. The commercial firms could not be left out of the reckoning and whenever they felt that their rights were imperilled, they could threaten legal action and enlist the support of those able to make political capital out of any interference with private enterprise.

Yet the correspondence colleges were attracting a smaller percentage of the total registration each year. By 1960, when the number of students registered with the University of South Africa had topped the 10 000 mark, more than 90% of them were enrolled with the division of studies – a designation for the teaching branch which, incidentally, lingered on for a number of years in university legislation, but which was already falling into disuse. The annual growth rate of the university exceeded 10% and there was no doubt that the institution was proving most valuable in exploiting the nation's untapped intellectual potential. Expansion in one small department of study is an indication of that of the whole. The Department of Anthropology had some 240 students in 1955; four years later, it had almost three times as many.

Post-graduate work was also increasing in volume. The large number of candidates for the Bachelor of Education degree shows how popular the facilities offered were to teachers in service, but higher degrees in other fields – especially psychology and English at this period – were much sought after. There was no lowering of standards to sugar the pill for external candidates. Matriculation requirements for entry to a degree course were of the same nature as at the residential universities; moreover, despite the size of the registered student body, the number of degrees conferred annually by the University of South Africa was on a par with the yearly output of graduates at the Union's smaller institutions – the universities at Potchefstroom, Grahamstown and Bloemfontein.

Although external study for a degree presents special difficulties, the failure rate was excessively high. The examination results of unattached candidates were often deplorable, but even among the university's own students, the level of academic attainment left much to be desired. The introduction of compulsory assign-

312

ments on which a year mark could be based would undoubtedly effect an improvement in this regard, but the correspondence colleges were strongly opposed to this innovation, unless means were devised to extend it to all students. There were also frequent cancellations and withdrawals in the course of each year. In 1958, for example, it was estimated that almost 40% of the registered students fell away before the examinations were held. Many students were unsuccessful in their first year of study, but this was – and is – a common feature of the South African university scene. One possible solution was debated by the Transvaal Department of Education at this period – the lengthening of the school course to provide a higher standard of entry to university. The suggestion had more than once been made in the past, but had always – regrettably, in the eyes of many – been rejected. It met with no better fate on this occasion.

Significant new developments took place during the first seven years of Professor Pauw's leadership, both in the nation and in its oldest university. By the time South Africa had become a republic and had left the British Commonwealth, the reconstituted university which bore the national name had also moved far along the path which would lead to full academic independence. Its growth in these years was phenomenal. Student enrolments increased rapidly and many additions were made to the teaching staff in order to keep pace with the demand for tuition. Some came with reputations already established in the world of learning; others filled junior posts and remained to gain distinction in their fields and to play leading roles in the life of the University of South Africa. For several, too, the university was the workshop in which they learned their craft, before moving on to make their mark elsewhere. Among those, for example, who lectured under the guidance of Professor Muller in the Department of History in the early years of Professor Pauw's principalship were M. J. Swart, who became Professor of History at the University of Port Elizabeth, B. A. le Cordeur and Arthur M. Davey, today with the University of Cape Town, and G. N. van den Bergh, now at Potchefstroom University.

The professoriate was greatly expanded in this period, both in the established departments and in the new ones which were brought into being. The Department of *Afrikaans en Nederlands* gained the services of the distinguished writer, Professor P. de V. Pienaar, who joined the staff from the University of the Witwatersrand. Professor Pienaar subsequently left to accept a position at the University of Pretoria. A. C. Myburgh, formerly with the government's Department of Native Affairs, was appointed Professor of Anthropology. A graduate of the Universities of Stellenbosch and Pretoria, he had begun his career with the University of South Africa in 1956 as a member of the Faculty of Law. Professor Georg Marais, a Ph.D. of the University of Wisconsin with wide experience of South Africa's industrial problems, joined Professor Rädel in the Department of Business Economics.

C. P. T. Naudé was promoted to a professorship in the Department of Classical Languages. Formerly on the staff of the University of the Witwatersrand, he had completed his academic training at Oxford and Leiden. Professor D. C. Krogh became head of the Department of Economics. Subsequently appointed Director of the Federated Chambers of Industry of South Africa, he had lectured at the Universities of the Orange Free State and Pretoria and had been made Assistant Economic Adviser to the Prime Minister early in 1961.

Professor C. J. D. Harvey of the University of Natal joined Professor Davis in the Department of English, but soon left to become head of this department at the University of Stellenbosch. Professor Davis resigned shortly afterwards, but his successor, Professor D. R. Beeton, formerly Librarian and Research Officer with the Council for Scientific and Industrial Research, was already on the staff of the university. Professor Beeton had studied at the University of Pretoria. Professor J. H. Moolman, who had long been attached to the Division of Planning of the Natural Resources Development Council, was appointed to the vacant Chair of Geography.

The Department of History, the largest of its kind in the

country by the early sixties, gained the services in 1958 of the well-known writer and historiographer, Floris A. van Jaarsveld. Subsequently promoted to a professorship, he was one of the many newcomers who brought to the university a wealth of experience in the school teaching field. With several other members of the staff, he later moved to the Rand Afrikaans University in Johannesburg, where he became head of the Department of History. He holds this post now at the University of Pretoria.

An outstanding scholar who joined the Department of Mathematics and Applied Mathematics at this period was Professor Hanno Rund. In the course of a brilliant career, he had held appointments at the Universities of Freiburg, Bonn and Toronto, before returning to South Africa as head of the Department of Mathematics at the University of Natal. A member and prize winner of the *Suid-Afrikaanse Akademie vir Wetenskap en Kuns,* he had made many valuable contributions in his field.

Professor A. M. T. Meyer came to the Department of Philosophy from the neighbouring University of Pretoria, where he had received his doctorate in 1949. Professor Meyer had also studied at the University of the Witwatersrand and in the Netherlands. The author of several publications, he had carried out research in London on English philosophical thought. F. W. Blignaut joined Professor Roux on the permanent staff of the Department of Psychology in 1957 and subsequently obtained a professorship. A graduate of the University of South Africa, he achieved distinction for his investigation into the effects of alcohol on mammals undertaken under the auspices of the National Council for Social Research.

It was in the early years of Professor Pauw's term of office as Principal that the subdivision of unwieldy departments began. The single department in the Faculty of Law was first divided into two : Roman-Dutch and Mercantile Law. At a later stage, Private and Public Law Departments were added, while more recently the departmental system has been further remodelled.

The extension of legal studies brought new men to the staff and led to the creation of additional professorships between 1959

315

and 1961. N. J. van der Merwe, who came to the university in 1957 from the University of the Orange Free State, was the first Professor of Mercantile Law; he was succeeded as head of this department by M. L. Benade, a graduate of the Universities of Stellenbosch and the Orange Free State who was appointed to the vacant Chair in 1965.

Professor Willem A. Joubert joined the university from the University of the Orange Free State, where he was Dean of the Faculty of Law. An LL.D. of the University of Stellenbosch who had also studied at London, Heidelberg and Zürich, he had begun his university teaching as a lecturer at Potchefstroom. Professor Joubert was appointed head of the Department of Private Law and long served as Dean of the Faculty. His colleague for a number of years was Professor P. M. Nienaber, who was born in Belgium where his father was then studying. Professor Nienaber, a Ph.D. of the University of Cambridge, came to the Department of Private Law from the University of Pretoria.

Also born in Belgium was Willy J. Hosten, who was appointed to the lecturing staff in 1957, later becoming Professor of Roman Law and Comparative Law and head of the department. He attended school at Middelkerke and Ostend before emigrating to South Africa, where he graduated at the University of Stellenbosch. Professor S. A. Strauss took charge of the Department of Public Law. A graduate of the Universities of Stellenbosch and the Orange Free State, he had also studied at Yale and Heidelberg. Professor Strauss had previously been attached to the university in Bloemfontein.

Shortly after this subdivision of the single department in the Faculty of Law, Professor D. H. Cilliers requested a similar separation between the various fields in the Faculty of Education. The single department at length became four: Method and Administration, Philosophy of Education, Empirical Education and History of Education. The first two have since been given new designations and a fifth has been added: the Department of Orthopedagogics.

In 1960, Professor O. C. Erasmus was appointed as head of

316

the Department of Philosophy of Education. A Doctor of Education of the University of Pretoria, he brought considerable teaching experience in South Africa, South West Africa and Swaziland to the service of the university. Professor I. S. J. Venter was promoted to a professorship in the following year as head of the Department of History of Education. He obtained his doctorate in education from the University of the Orange Free State in 1956, resigning as Vice-Principal of a Bloemfontein high school to join the teaching staff of the University of South Africa in 1957. Professor Cilliers remained head of the Department of Method and Administration – later Didactics and Comparative Education – until his retirement in 1972.

Appointments were also made to provide study courses in fields which eventually became autonomous departments within the various faculties. An offshoot of the Department of Mathematics was that of Mathematical Statistics, of which Professor H. S. Steyn became head in 1959. Professor Steyn received his early university education in Bloemfontein, subsequently obtaining doctorates from the Universities of Edinburgh and Pretoria. He lectured at the latter institution and at the University of Natal and immediately prior to his acceptance of a post at the University of South Africa, was in charge of a department in the Council for Scientific and Industrial Research.

The Departments of Criminology and Social Work separated themselves from that of Sociology. Both Professor P. J. van der Walt of the Department of Criminology and Professor I. J. J. van Rooyen of the Department of Social Work began their careers with the University of South Africa in the parent department. Professor van der Walt, a Doctor of Philosophy of the University of Pretoria, has been Mayor of Pretoria for two successive terms and has travelled extensively in Europe and the United States, where he has made a close study of the problem of juvenile delinquency. Professor van Rooyen graduated at the University of South Africa and was Secretary of the National Council for the Care of Cripples in South Africa. He later accepted a post at the Rand Afrikaans University.

The small Department of French of the early days blossomed into a Department of Romance Languages. A suggestion was made early in 1958 by the Board of Tutors that a lectureship in Portuguese should be instituted in order to strengthen the ties binding South Africa with neighbouring territories and in so doing, to extend the usefulness of the university. In the following year, Professor Marius Valkhoff of the University of the Witwatersrand, whose wife then lectured in French at the University of South Africa, kindly offered to undertake tuition in that language and in Italian. However, it was not until the arrival of P. Haffter in 1960 that further expansion became possible. Born in Switzerland and a Doctor of Philosophy of the University of Zürich, he came to the university with experience in both language teaching and journalism. He was appointed to a professorship in 1962 and under his skilful and energetic direction the Department of Romance Languages has made great strides. His journalistic experience, too, has assisted the university in a number of directions and he has been a valued Chairman of the Publications Committee. For some years, only Italian was offered, in addition to French, but in course of time, lectureships were founded in both Portuguese and Spanish. The department has pioneered the use of modern teaching methods in language tuition.

Another recommendation put forward by the Board of Tutors was implemented in 1960, when Mrs E. Foxcroft joined the staff to found a Department of Russian, the first to be established in South Africa. Mrs Foxcroft, born in pre-revolutionary Russia, had escaped as a child from her native land and had at length reached England, where she took her degree at Oxford. The department has remained a small one, but of the greatest importance in the field of international affairs. The success of Mrs Foxcroft's Russian Evenings has also done much to awaken a wider interest in the culture of her country of origin.

Several other departments date from the early period of Professor Pauw's principalship. A Department of Music, now known as the Department of Musicology, was founded under Professor

D. J. Roode, who for twelve years had been in charge of that subject at the University of the Orange Free State. Professor Roode, who retired in 1966, also became the university's Director of Music. The Department of History of Art and Fine Arts made a modest debut in 1961 with the appointment of Karin M. Skawran, a graduate of the University of Pretoria who also studied in Munich. Miss Skawran was promoted to a professorship in 1972.

At the beginning of 1961, A. H. van Zyl of the University of Pretoria became the first Professor of Semitic Languages. It was not his first contact with the University of South Africa, for he had worked there for a term in 1954 and three years later, had been appointed an examiner. An active Faculty of Divinity was brought into being in 1960, with the Rev. Cosser of Rhodes University as Dean. In that year, Professor J. A. Lombard joined the staff. A Doctor of Divinity of the University of Pretoria, Professor Lombard had studied in Europe as well and had worked under the distinguished theologian, Karl Barth. Towards the end of the following year, he was joined by Professor I. H. Eybers, another Pretoria graduate who had also obtained a doctorate at Duke University in the United States. The tutelage of an outside Dean was clearly no longer necessary and was soon brought to an end. The Faculty of Divinity was ultimately expanded into three departments.

The absence of tuition in science subjects resulted in an exceptionally low standard of attainment by candidates at the university's examinations. This was particularly marked in the field of chemistry. There were strong arguments, therefore, for the founding of a Department of Chemistry to provide the necessary instruction, in conjunction with practical work at approved centres with adequate laboratory facilities. Opposition was strong, particularly when it appeared that tuition implied research laboratories. It was thought that the Council for Scientific and Industrial Research in Pretoria already provided research facilities and that, if the University of South Africa were determined to enter the science teaching field, it should restrict its activities to diploma

319

courses. Teletuition was still in an experimental stage and it might be academically unsound and harmful to the best interests of the South African university world for an institution primarily concerned with the advance of the humanities and social sciences to extend its functions in this manner.

So the arguments ran, but the university, encouraged by support from industry and basing its case on the irrefutable logic of statistics, stood firm. Finally a department, experimental at first, was set up under Professor G. W. Perold, a Doctor of Science of the University of Pretoria who had studied at Zürich under the Nobel Prize winner, Leopold Ruzicka. For ten years, he had been in charge of research at the Pretoria headquarters of the Iron and Steel Corporation. The department prospered, the research laboratories which had caused so much contention were constructed and tuition in physics was introduced, at first under the aegis of the department. No teaching has been offered in other science subjects and the courses of study in biology, zoology and other fields have remained in the care of committees of studies under the chairmanship of scientists from sister institutions.

The introduction of tuition in physics in this manner had its parallels in other departments. The study of astronomy, for example, had been earlier introduced by the Department of Mathematics and in the Department of Anthropology, archaeology found its place. An anthropological museum was also set up in the latter department. The tendency, too, was to drop subjects for which syllabuses, but no tuition, were provided, if no adequate demand existed. For this reason, courses in certain African languages spoken outside South Africa were at length withdrawn from the curriculum of the department concerned at the request of Professor Ziervogel. Tuition, however, was retained in all the important African languages of South Africa.

The University of South Africa was reaching out to a wider circle and making an increasing impact upon national life in many spheres. One of its most successful ventures was the founding in 1960, through the initiative of Professor Rädel of the

320

Department of Business Economics, of the flourishing Bureau of Market Research. Its primary purpose was to provide information for commerce and industry, to analyse market structure and trends and to place its conclusions at the service of the government in the planning of national economic policy. Financial support came from the university, the National Council for Social Research and the private sector. The Bureau of Market Research has published a series of valuable surveys on consumer purchasing and has conducted seminars in many centres throughout the country. The work of its first Director, Professor Rädel, in this and other spheres, was recognized by the university in the presentation to him of the first Council Award for outstanding achievements.

A Committee for Academic Interests was established in this early period of Professor Pauw's leadership. This brought to the University of South Africa a steady stream of scholars from home and abroad to participate in seminars and to deliver papers. Among those who lectured in 1958 and 1959 were Dr J. T. Robinson of the Transvaal Museum, Professor P. M. Endt of the *Rijksuniversiteit,* Utrecht and Professor B. Lamar Johnson of the University of California in Los Angeles.

The university also undertook to promote academic publications. A *Communications* series was inaugurated which, for a number of years, enabled lecturers and students to publish the results of their researches. A new series, *Studia,* was later introduced. In addition, the journal *Mousaion* for library science, under the editorship of Professor de Vleeschauwer, was taken over as a university publication. The Faculty of Law's *Codicillus* was a worthy and widely circulated forerunner of several journals published by various departments, while the inter-faculty journal, *Acta Classica,* owed much to the initiative of the teaching staff of the Department of Classics. Professors and lecturers also played a large part in the founding of scientific institutes. Among these may be mentioned the South African Mathematical Society and the later South African Historical Society.

Continued rapid expansion soon made the administration building too small for the needs of the university.

On 27 June, 1958, the Chancellor, Dr F.J. de Villiers, laid the foundation-stone of the LIBRARY BUILDING on the south-east corner of Skinner and Van der Walt Streets. The library and offices were occupied in the following year. Before long, it became necessary to add another wing in what proved to be an unsuccessful effort to keep pace with the growth of the university.

Library Building

The inadequacy of the new administrative building in Skinner Street to house an expanding staff made it imperative to speed the pace of fund raising in order to construct additional accommodation. The first member of the administrative section to devote himself to this task on a full-time basis was G. C. Kachelhoffer, but in 1957, the university appointed H. P. Dekker, for many years Assistant Registrar of the University of Stellenbosch, as Public Relations Officer. Shortly after his arrival, he conducted a nation-wide tour and through his efforts and those of his predecessor, funds soon accumulated. Construction of the new library building on the corner of Skinner and Van der Walt Streets began in November, 1957 and the foundation stone was laid in June of the following year. One of the architects of these handsome premises, Brian Sandrock, would play a further part in the physical development of the university. The library and additional office accommodation were occupied in 1959. Once again, the problem of living space had – temporarily, at least – been solved.

The library then possessed some 65 000 books and about 1 200 periodicals and was at last housed in a fitting manner. However, fears were expressed in *Unisa* for 1961 that the section of the building set aside for the library would prove inadequate within five years. The normal annual increase at that time of some 15 000 volumes was constantly being augmented by donations from various sources, among them the American government and the Carnegie Corporation. The accommodation problem did become a pressing one, although an efficient service was maintained. Every effort was made to ensure the prompt delivery of books by post to students living outside Pretoria and post-graduate students were able to avail themselves of the world-wide inter-library loan system.

A start was made in establishing a separate section in the library for Africa studies, but this plan was abandoned in favour of a more ambitious project. The autonomous Africa Institute of South Africa was founded in 1960 by the *Suid-Afrikaanse Akademie vir Wetenskap en Kuns* in co-operation with the university, and its offices and separate library were housed in the new building. Both the Chancellor and the Principal of the University of South Africa played a leading role in the affairs of its governing body, which also included representatives of the nation's other universities. The former Principal, Professor A. J. H. van der Walt, was connected with the Africa Institute in an executive capacity and as editor-in-chief of its publications section until his final retirement from active life. The present Director, Professor J. H. Moolman, was the former head of the Department of Geography; his successor, Professor P. Smit, was for some years a Research Officer with the institute.

The library building also provided many additional departmental offices and a well-appointed conference room, the Pretoria-Philadelphia Hall, named in commemoration of the founding of the city and in thanks to the municipal authorities for their generous assistance in the construction of the building. The staff, however, continued to expand rapidly and although an extra storey was added in 1959 to the administration building in Skinner Street, it became necessary two years later to extend the library premises by building another wing. More property was acquired in 1962, when the university purchased De Doorns Hotel on the corner of Prinsloo and Visagie Streets. This became the home for several years of the Departments of Anthropology, Bantu Languages and Native Administration. A residence was also provided for the Principal in George Avenue, Arcadia.

The steadily increasing enrolment of students necessitated the employment of a larger administrative staff. By 1962, some forty people were at work in the production section alone, under the Manager, S. J. Marais. This department was then almost as big as the entire administration of the University of South Africa of ten years earlier. The production and distribution of tutorial material has always been of the greatest importance to a university which relies so heavily upon the written word in its teaching function. The duties of Miss J. P. Gould and her team of translators in the department which later became known as the Language Bureau were also of vital significance in a bilingual university. An Information Department was opened in 1960 to offer advice and guidance to students in the planning of their courses of study. The new service was placed in charge of G. C. Kachelhoffer, who retained control until October, 1961, when he joined the teaching staff as a Senior Lecturer in the Department of Mercantile Law. The work of the department was continued by Charl Cillié and D. H. van Eeden. The administration suffered a sad loss in 1957 with the death of the Accountant, L. Coetser, but a worthy successor was found in Alewyn J. Vorster.

The other universities still played their supervisory role in the life of the University of South Africa. When Professor Pauw took office, for example, almost two-thirds of the members of the Executive Committee of Senate were outsiders. Inevitably some differences of opinion arose, such as those concerning the introduction of a Department of Chemistry. Representatives of other universities also felt that supervision – if that was what was expected of them – had become redundant. And on Council, under the chairmanship of Professor Boshoff, there was uncertainty as to whether other Principals or their delegates should take part in the deliberations as individual members or as representatives of their own institutions. The University of South Africa was outgrowing the old order of things. When the various legislative measures governing its activities were consolidated in Act 19 of March, 1959, it was clear that the time was fast approaching when the university would have to be granted freedom to develop in its own way, commensurate with that enjoyed by other institutions of similar rank in the country.

By then, another change in the leadership of the University of South Africa had taken place. In 1957, the Chancellor, Judge President G. J. Maritz, resigned and Council selected Dr François Jean de Villiers as his successor. It was a happy choice, for Dr de Villiers was to be the first holder of that office to play an active part in university affairs. The new Chancellor was chosen not only for his ability in the cultural, academic and scientific spheres, but also for his outstanding contributions in the broader aspects of national life. In the course of his career, he had been a leading figure in such bodies as the South African Chemical Institute, the Council for Scientific and Industrial Research, the National Advisory Council for Adult Education and the *Suid-Afrikaanse Akademie vir Wetenskap en Kuns*. Chairman of the Commission of Enquiry into Vocational and Technical Education, he was, at the time of his installation as Chancellor, the Organizing Director of Industrial Development in South Africa.

An important aspect of university expansion concerned finance. Although the report of the Holloway Commission had not placed the University of South Africa on the same subsidy basis as the other universities, the late fifties were not difficult years for the Pretoria institution. By the early sixties, however, the position was no longer as satisfactory and the decade opened with a deficit of some R13 000. A new basis would soon have to be found for the University of South Africa which would bring it into line with its sister universities.

There was also talk as the fifties drew to a close of the further extension of adult education. The university had always shown itself willing to shoulder new responsibilities and in 1956, had gone out of its way to assist the Boksburg municipality with a special course in local government. However, now that it was rapidly acquiring a standing in the country as a true university institution, the suggestion of a national board for extra-mural studies was not altogether welcome. It was considered undesirable in university circles that too many diploma and certificate courses should be introduced; the University of South Africa had already instituted several – among them, those in accounting and library science – and it was felt that any further development should be made primarily with graduate qualifications in view.

The Vacation School continued to attract an increasing number of students of all races. By 1958, the attendance approached 600 and four years later, had almost doubled. It soon became necessary to arrange separate classes for African students at Atteridgeville, on the western outskirts of Pretoria, and for other non-Europeans within the city itself. Graduation Day, too, had become firmly established as an important event in university

Legislation passed in 1959 made the University of South Africa the guardian of five UNIVERSITY COLLEGES for African, Coloured and Indian students. Four of these were to be new foundations; the other, the University College of Fort Hare, was of older date.

All at length gained independence. On 1 January, 1970, the colleges at Alice, Sovenga and Empangeni for African ethnic groups became the Universities of Fort Hare, the North and Zululand respectively. On the same date, the college as Kasselsvlei for Coloured students became the University of the Western Cape. On 1 January, 1971, University College, Durban for Indians was transformed into the University of Durban-Westville.

University of South Africa

Fort Hare

the North

the Western Cape

Durban-Westville

Zululand

life. Among those who addressed the graduands, their families and their friends in the late fifties were the Minister of Education, the Hon. J. H. Viljoen, in 1956 and the Administrator of the Cape Province, Dr J. H. O. du Plessis, in 1959. In the following year, the present Prime Minister, the Hon. B. J. Vorster, spoke of the university's success in justifying its existence and in 1961, His Excellency the Governor-General, the Hon. C. R. Swart, soon to become South Africa's first State President, recalled the time when he had received a University of South Africa degree at the Pretoria ceremony of 1919.

A special function was held in 1959 at Engelenburghuis, Pretoria, in connection with the fiftieth anniversary of the founding of the *Suid-Afrikaanse Akademie vir Wetenskap en Kuns.* Honorary degrees were conferred upon three leading figures in South African and Dutch cultural life. Professor T. H. le Roux, long a tower of strength at the University of Pretoria and a notable contributor to Afrikaans language studies, received the degree of Doctor of Literature and Philosophy. T. E.W. Schumann, the son of a German missionary and an expert in the fields of climatology and meteorology, was awarded a Ph.D. The same degree was conferred upon M. W. Woerdeman, formerly Professor of Medicine at the Municipal University of Amsterdam, of which he was then *Rector Magnificus.* Dr Woerdeman, who had been similarly honoured by the University of Oxford in 1950, was Chairman of the *Koninklijke Nederlandse Akademie van Wetenschappen.*

In the same year, a major development in the provision of higher educational facilities for non-Europeans was made. The association of the Pius XII Catholic University College with the University of South Africa proved to be an uneasy one and the authorities at Roma began to look elsewhere to ensure the future well-being of the Basutoland institution. After an abortive attempt to enter into a special relationship with the University of London, the college succeeded in gaining full independence in 1964. Professor van der Walt had been correct, however, in regarding the brief link between the Catholic foundation and the

University of South Africa as the forerunner of similar affiliations.

There was only one other institution of this type in South Africa in 1958: the University College of Fort Hare, then associated with Rhodes University, Grahamstown. Although it cannot be said that the policy of providing separate higher educational facilities for ethnic groups found universal favour in South Africa, legislation was passed in 1959 which brought the connection between Fort Hare and its neighbour to an end and created four more colleges: the University College of the North at Sovenga in the Transvaal and that of Zululand at Empangeni, Natal; the University College of the Western Cape at Kasselsvlei and the University College, Durban. The first two, like that at Fort Hare, were for African students, the college at Kasselsvlei was for the Coloured population and University College, Durban for Indians. These institutions were all placed under the control of the government departments responsible for the affairs of the race groups concerned.

In terms of Act 45 of 1959, the University of South Africa was made the guardian of the colleges as they moved along the road to eventual independence. It played a part in their government, supervised their academic life, helped to staff them and conferred its degrees upon their successful students. Each year, the college lecturers conferred with the departments of the Pretoria institution on the setting of examination papers and the marking of scripts. At length, on 1 January, 1970, four of the colleges were accorded full university status as the Universities of Fort Hare, the Western Cape, Zululand and the North; a year later, University College, Durban became the University of Durban-Westville.

For a decade, therefore, the university in Pretoria resumed its former federal role, although the relationship with its new charges was not of the same close nature as that binding the former constituents to the parent body. It resembled rather the link between the institution at Fort Hare – then the South African Native College – and the federation.

331

In 1960, the University of South Africa appeared set upon the broad highway of uninterrupted development, with a triple function as examiner, teacher and guardian of students, both internal and external. However, there was already a small cloud on the horizon which presaged a storm of considerable proportions. In May, 1959, the Secretary for Education received a letter from the Town Clerk of Boksburg. The municipality had heard that there might soon be an extension of university education on the Witwatersrand and wished to put forward a case for the building of any new institution on a site within the urban boundary. A few months earlier, a committee seeking improved higher educational facilities for Afrikaners in Johannesburg had written to the Minister of Education in connection with the possible establishment there of a teacher training college for Afrikaans-speaking students.

In his reply to the enquiry from the Johannesburg committee, the Minister, the Hon. J. J. Serfontein, pointed out that the provision of colleges of education was a provincial matter and therefore lay outside his control. In answer to the request from Boksburg, he explained that if Afrikaners on the Rand began to agitate for additional university facilities, the government might well be deluged by similar demands from English speakers in Port Elizabeth, Kimberley or the Free State goldfields area. The cost would be prohibitive, the problem of staffing enormous and the need questionable. South Africa already provided, he said, more opportunities for its citizens of European origin to obtain a university education than any country in Europe. There was therefore little justification for further expansion in that direction. Events would prove that this was not to be the final word. The issue was to be intimately bound up with the future of the University of South Africa.

13 *An unexpected problem*

When the University of South Africa entered the 1960's, the future seemed bright with promise. Student numbers were increasing rapidly, excellent appointments ensured the maintenance of high standards and the university was at last enjoying high prestige both as a teaching institution and as the mother of a new brood of associated colleges. It had not succeeded in gaining full control over all its registered students, but it was already providing tuition for the vast majority of them. It had yet to be treated on an equal footing with the nation's other universities for subsidy purposes, but its finances were reasonably sound. In these respects, however, there seemed every likelihood of early recognition of an enhanced status and Professor Pauw could look back with pride upon great achievements since he had taken office and forward with confidence to the years ahead.

Compulsory enrolment was soon achieved. Ministerial approval, long withheld while the commercial colleges in association were able to carry out a strong rearguard action, was finally given in 1962. From 1964, all students registered for examinations were obliged to receive their tuition through the university. With this amendment to the statute, lecturers were able to bring greater pressure to bear upon candidates for university examinations through the introduction of compulsory assignments of work. Learning could thus be directed to greater purpose and the gulf between student and teacher narrowed. It was a change long overdue.

On the financial side, the University of South Africa had been forced to make economies after incurring the heavy deficit of more than R50 000 in 1961. The following year showed a surplus and, with the help of increased tuition fees, the situation was further improved in 1963, when revenue exceeded expenditure by more than R30 000. Nevertheless, the university was always in an invidious position in comparison with other South African institutions. However, Professor A. C. Cilliers, reporting in 1963 on the quinquennial revision of subsidies, recommended that the University of South Africa, notwithstanding the special nature of its service, should be treated in the same manner as its sister universities for government assistance. The report received official approval and its recommendations were gradually made applicable to the Pretoria institution. By 1966, it was placed fully under the new formula, with certain modifications which concerned its non-residential character. The immediate result was encouraging, but the formula was a fixed one. Not surprisingly, therefore, in an age of spiralling costs, annual deficits began to reappear in the later sixties and strict economy was necessary once again.

At the beginning of the decade, the university was expanding rapidly and had long since outgrown the modest accommodation it had acquired in the city. By 1962, plans were afoot to construct a new building which, it was hoped, would provide an enduring home. In that year, the City Council of Pretoria offered the University of South Africa a site near Klapperkop, a hill on the south-eastern outskirts of the city overlooking Fountains Valley. It was a generous gesture, but when the news was made public, it provoked a sustained outburst of protest from a number of local residents who feared that the natural beauty of Pretoria's environs would be desecrated if a new university building were to be built on the site suggested. However, before the new year was out and before the necessary fund raising campaign to implement the scheme had been set in motion, another development had arisen which seemed to place the future of the university as a Pretoria institution for external students in jeopardy.

The roots of this new problem lay in the agitation of the

middle fifties for improved higher educational facilities for Afrikaners in Johannesburg and the Reef towns. The first success was achieved with the opening in 1961 of the *Goudstadse Onderwyskollege,* an Afrikaans-medium teacher training college. Those of its students who sought graduate qualifications worked to that end through the University of South Africa, but there was a strong desire for a second university nearer at hand. Although government was not at that time in favour of this, a departmental committee was set up in the course of the following year to investigate the question. It reported in December, 1962 and recommended that the University of South Africa should undertake additional functions for the Afrikaners of the Rand. Even before that date – on 12 September, 1962 – the Minister of Education, Arts and Science, the Hon. J. de Klerk, had tentatively suggested to the Principal that the university might move to Johannesburg to begin residential courses there. This was agreed to, on the understanding that such a departure would not encroach upon the University of South Africa's existing and future obligations to its external students. It had to be remembered that a fine reputation in a specialized field had been built up since 1946; moreover, any change of policy such as that contemplated by the Minister would infringe the gentleman's agreement that the institution would never seek to enter the teaching fields of sister universities of the traditional kind.

On 14 February, 1963 the Principal was given to understand that a Cabinet decision had been reached which endorsed the project, but which seemingly ignored the important proviso made by Professor Pauw that external work must continue as in the past. The university felt constrained to reiterate its commitment to the external student. This was done by the Chairman of Council, Professor Boshoff, at the official opening of the academic year on 21 February. He stressed that the university's function of catering for the needs of external students was of "paramount importance and must in no way be prejudiced", since "no additional residential function could be more important than its training of external students". The Cabinet apparently took

335

STEPHANUS PETRUS ERASMUS BOSHOFF was born on 14 July, 1891 in the Senekal district of the Orange Free State. After matriculating at Paarl in 1908, he obtained a Thomas Robertson bursary for further study and graduated in 1911 with distinction at Grey University College, winning the Chancellor's Gold Medal and a Queen Victoria Scholarship. An M.A. in 1913, he continued his studies in Amsterdam.

The outbreak of war brought him back to South Africa, where he took part in the rebellion and was captured. He forfeited his bursary as a result of his involvement in this affair.

After working in an attorney's office, he joined the staff of the Arts Department of the theological school in Potchefstroom, where he became a professor in 1917. He was also able to complete his doctoral studies with distinction in Amsterdam. He became Professor of Afrikaans at the University of Cape Town in 1930 and from 1932 to 1934 was Director of Education for the Transval.

An educationist of note and a writer of distinction, he received honorary doctorates from the University of South Africa and the University of the Orange Free State.

A Council member from 1932 until 1934 and again from 1944 until 1969, he was chosen as Vice-Chancellor from 1952 to 1955. When the Principal was made Vice-Chancellor under new legislation, he became Chairman of Council, a post which he held until his resignation from the governing body.

Professor Boshoff died at Potgietersrus on 30 April, 1973.

Professor Stephanus Petrus Erasmus Boshoff, M.A.,
Litt.D., D.Litt. (h.c.), D.Litt. et Phil. (h.c.)
Member of Council 1932–1934; 1944–1969
Vice-Chancellor 1952–1955
Chairman of Council 1955–1969

note of this unequivocal statement and on 15 March, the Minister of Education informed the Principal that plans to move the university to the Witwatersrand had been shelved.

It seemed that development in Pretoria would continue uninterrupted and that any agitation by the Rand Afrikaans University Committee which had been formed to promote the extension of higher education there would no longer involve the University of South Africa. It was not to be. Negotiations were resumed, and on 13 September, 1963, Minister de Klerk wrote at length to the Chairman of Council on the future of the University of South Africa. Taking note of its phenomenal growth and of its plans to inaugurate a vast building programme and to recruit new staff, he intimated that government thinking on the university question might easily lead the institution into financial difficulties if it expanded on too large a scale. Outlining future possibilities, he pointed out that the associated colleges for non-Europeans would probably become full universities in time. They would be encouraged, together with the existing institutions for European students, to follow the example of the University of Pretoria and establish strong extra-mural divisions. This would cause a drop in enrolments with the University of South Africa, since more than 60% of its student body came from regions where extra-mural study courses could be provided. In addition, other universities would no doubt feel disposed to introduce correspondence methods of tuition as well.

Such a fundamental change of approach would undoubtedly have an adverse effect upon the development of the University of South Africa. Nor was this all, for if it should wish to become a conventional type of university, a Pretoria campus would be out of the question. Government was not in favour of either a second university for Afrikaners in the city, or a new university using English as a medium of instruction. Council would therefore be well advised to proceed with caution in order to avoid shouldering commitments for which the necessary subsidy might not be forthcoming.

The Minister's letter led to renewed correspondence and a

338

series of discussions between him and the Principal in the latter part of September and early October of that year. Professor Pauw held that an extension of correspondence work to other universities would amount to " 'n verbreking . . . van die lank aanvaarde en eerbiedige ooreenkoms in verband met die funksie-verdeling tussen die Universiteit van Suid-Afrika en die residen-siële universiteite". If this agreement no longer held, then the University of South Africa might conceivably be free to enter the residential field. The Minister, however, reiterated his objection to the establishment of a second residential university in Pretoria : the University of South Africa must keep to its existing respons-ibilities.

The range of these responsibilities was however also in doubt. The Minister did indeed admit that the suggestion of allowing other universities to undertake correspondence work was not based upon any predetermined policy decided upon by govern-ment, but he could not guarantee that students of all races would continue to benefit from the services provided by the University of South Africa. From the Minister's reply to further representa-tions it appeared that the government stood firm upon a policy of separate development in university education, even by corres-pondence, and that the University of South Africa would in time lose its non-European students.

It is clear that the question of a university for Afrikaners on the Witwatersrand was not absent from these exchanges on the subject of the University of South Africa's future. The Minister of Education was certainly in favour of such a development, and a possible move to the Witwatersrand was once more a live issue. At a special meeting on 27 and 28 November, 1963, Council decided to appoint a committee to discuss the future of the Uni-versity of South Africa, to review building plans and to ascertain the sort of help which could be provided for any new Rand uni-versity. In addition, Council sought permission to collect devel-opment funds to a ceiling of R500 000.

On the committee, which became known by its Afrikaans name, the *Toekomskomitee,* both Council and Senate were well

FRANÇOIS JEAN DE VILLIERS was born at Paarl on 25 April, 1898. He matriculated in 1917, obtained a B.A. degree at the University of Cape Town and gained further graduate qualifications from the University of California and Cornell University in the United States. He received the D.Sc. degree of the University of South Africa in 1925 and is a Fellow of the British Royal Institute of Chemists. He is also a holder of the Frans du Toit award and the Havenga Prize of the *Suid-Afrikaanse Akademie vir Wetenskap en Kuns.*

Chairman of the Communications Association of South Africa, the National Film Board and the Africa Institute, Dr de Villiers has for many years been active in various fields. A Past President of the Associated Scientific and Technical Associations of South Africa, he has been Chairman of a number of national bodies, among them the *Akademie,* the South African Chemical Institute and the Fuel Research Institute of South Africa.

The Chairman of a number of government commissions, he also played a large part in the founding of the Bureau of Standards and the Council for Scientific and Industrial Research. For 20 years, he was the Industrial Adviser to the Department of Commerce and Industry and became a director of the South African Industrial Development Corporation.

He has contributed much to the expansion of educational facilities. Long a member of the Council of the University of Pretoria, he promoted the establishment of a Faculty of Engineering and of the Instiute for Management and Administration there.

A member of the Council of the University of South Africa from 1954 until 1957, he succeeded Judge President G.J. Maritz as Chancellor in the latter year.

Dr François Jean de Villiers, B.A., M.Sc.,
Ph.D., D.Sc., F.R.I.C.
Member of Council 1954–1957
Chancellor since April, 1957

340

represented. The members of the committee were anxious to find out from the Rand Afrikaans University Committee what that body expected of the University of South Africa. In this matter, the presence of Council member Dr P. J. Meyer on the *Toekomskomitee* was invaluable, since the head of the South African Broadcasting Corporation was also Chairman of the Rand committee. Talks were held with representatives of the Rand committee at which Professor Pauw again explained that whatever role the University of South Africa might play in the founding of the new institution, nothing would be done to affect the important pioneering work for external students. It was, however, a bilingual university, and he intended to maintain that position, both in the existing division and in the proposed residential section, if it were to become a branch of the University of South Africa. The Rand committee accepted the Principal's standpoint, on the understanding that if the University should develop a teaching section for Afrikaners on the Rand, its management must accord with the wishes of the committee. This would necessarily entail a separation of the proposed internal and the existing external divisions of the University of South Africa, and it was along these lines that the *Toekomskomitee* drafted a report which was approved by Council on 11 April 1964. An internal section in Johannesburg was recommended, with the external department remaining in Pretoria.

The proposal, as the *Toekomskomitee* had come to realize, had certain undoubted advantages. The pioneer venture in correspondence teaching was not without value in suggesting new approaches in the work of other universities. Many of the methods of tuition which had been evolved since 1946 could profitably be adapted to meet the needs of internal students. In another way, too, the University of South Africa could prove of immense assistance in controlling a teaching section of the conventional type, designed for Afrikaans-speaking students. Its long tradition of bilingualism could prevent the exclusive use of one language in the new division and at the same time help to foster better understanding between the two language groups.

342

There were, however, serious disadvantages in inaugurating such a new service. There was always the fear that the external section would in time become no more than a secondary function of the university. Moreover, the administrative problems involved in the control of a twin-campus institution would be enormous. Professor van der Walt, the former Principal, made it clear in a report to the *Toekomskomitee* that he favoured the eventual unification of the two sections in Johannesburg. The Prime Minister, Dr Verwoerd, shared this view and suggested on 16 April that the Minister of Education sound out the Principal on the possibility of a complete move to the mining city. Early in May, after Professor Pauw had discussed the university's proposals with him in Cape Town, the Minister wrote to the Principal, stressing the disadvantages of a divided university.

Both the Board of Tutors and the University Senate endorsed Council's opinion that the existing function and bilingual character of the University of South Africa must at all costs be maintained, whatever decision was reached on the question of a move to Johannesburg. On 6 May, the Management Committee of Council – the *Dagbestuur* – decided that a Planning Committee, under the chairmanship of Professor Boshoff, should be formed to investigate the position more closely. It consisted in the main of the members of the *Toekomskomitee,* but included the Registrar and other nominees of the Board of Tutors as well as outside members of the Executive Committee of Senate.

The new committee began its sittings on 14 May, 1964 and in the following weeks made a thorough investigation of the question of the university seat. It was in constant communication with the Rand Afrikaans University Committee and also contacted the City Council of Johannesburg on the subject of a suitable site in the city. The problem of the university's non-European external students had an important bearing on the committee's decisions. It was at length decided that, as government planned eventually to attach them all – either as internal, extra-mural or external students – to the various university colleges, it would be best to retain an office for them in Pretoria

343

BAREND FREDERIK JANSE VAN RENSBURG was born on 15 December, 1910 on a farm in the Brandfort district of the Orange Free State. He matriculated at Boshof in 1928, joined the staff of a bank and was later appointed to the Natal Provincial Administration. In 1933, he served in the Department of Internal Affairs of the Union government, transferring soon afterwards to the Department of Union Education. He graduated in both arts and commerce, obtaining the B.A. degree in 1937 and the M.Com. in 1952.

Appointed to the staff of the university as Assistant Accountant in 1935, he became Secretary of the Division of External Studies in 1946, sometimes helping with the teaching in the early days on a part-time basis. He acted as Registrar during P.A. Taljaard's absence, succeeding to the permanent post at the beginning of 1955. Like his predecessors since 1918, he also undertook certain other duties, among them the secretaryship of the Joint Matriculation Board.

Barend Frederik Janse van Rensburg, B.A., M.Com.
Acting Registrar 1 October, 1953 – 31 December, 1954
Registrar since 1 January, 1955

344

until the official policy was implemented. For the rest, the committee's final report of September, 1964 recommended that the whole university should move to Johannesburg, but without relinquishing its correspondence function and bilingual character. The only difference of opinion lay in the choice of a site.

The Planning Committee investigated the relative merits of two localities. The first, Emmarentia, in the western part of Johannesburg, was felt to be more suitable for a purely urban university. The second site at Bruma, close to Bedfordview on the opposite side of the city, had decided advantages as the campus for a university which was intended to serve the entire Witwatersrand and adjoining regions of white population. The Rand Afrikaans University Committee was nevertheless strongly in favour of Emmarentia and Council therefore set up a Site Committee to study the problem more closely.

The new committee began its investigation on the basis of certain general principles. In the first place, it was assumed that the university, as a conventional teaching institution, would cater in the main for the Afrikaners of the Witwatersrand, Vanderbijlpark and Vereeniging region. Secondly, no site should be chosen which did not allow for future expansion. In the third place, the campus would have to be easily accessible both as a seat of learning and as a cultural centre. Finally, the housing needs of the existing lecturing and administrative staffs would have to be given special consideration.

After a close study of the two localities, in which Professor J. H. Moolman and his Department of Geography played an important part, the Site Committee strongly recommended the choice of Bruma, a decision which was endorsed by the Director of the Natural Resources Development Council. The City Council of Johannesburg was also in favour and was willing to help the university to acquire the necessary land there. On the other hand, the Rand Afrikaans University Committee remained firmly attached to Emmarentia.

By the end of 1964, the University of South Africa was pressing government to come to a decision on the question of the move to Johannesburg. However, the Minister of Education would not proceed until the site question had been finally settled. On that unresolved issue a Department of Education committee rejected Emmarentia, although a minority report gave its support to the Rand Afrikaans University Committee's choice. The Minister also approached Professor A. C. Cilliers, Chairman of the University Advisory Committee, to look into the financial aspects of moving the University of South Africa to Johannesburg. Here, another drawback to any change of seat became apparent. In his report, Professor Cilliers gave his opinion that the scheme would cost even more than the establishment of an independent University of Port Elizabeth on the foundations of the Rhodes University branch which had been operating in the coastal city.

By this time, too, there were increasing demands from Afrikaners in the political and commercial fields on the Rand for an independent, unilingual Johannesburg university to cater for the needs of that community. The newspaper *Dagbreek en Sondagnuus* stated categorically that the general dissatisfaction on the Rand over the whole issue stemmed from the University of South Africa's insistence on bilingualism if it opened a branch there. It was not, therefore, just the question of a site which was proving a stumbling-block. The *Afrikaanse Sakekamer,* too, wanted to see the creation of a unilingual Johannesburg university for Afrikaners, with a flourishing extra-mural section. It was, however, prepared to accept a bilingual division for external students, but not for non-Europeans.

The tide was running strongly in favour of a separate university when on 19 March, 1965 Professor Pauw wrote again to the Minister, asking for a speedy solution to the problem to dispel the cloud of uncertainty which was hanging over the University of South Africa. He stressed again the university's firm decision to maintain its bilingual character in all departments, even though Afrikaners would certainly form a majority in the proposed new section.

However, the growing demand for a Witwatersrand university where Afrikaans would be the sole medium of instruction weighed

347

heavily with the Cabinet when it again examined the university question. Finally, on 28 April, 1965, the Minister of Education informed the University of South Africa that if it moved to Johannesburg, it would be compelled to use Afrikaans alone in its internal teaching. Only in its external function, eventually to be restricted to European students only, would the use of both official languages be permitted.

This ran counter to the Pretoria institution's declared policy and on 26 June, Council, on the recommendation of both the Senate and the Board of Tutors, expressed its regret that it could no longer entertain the idea of establishing itself in the neighbouring city. However, if the next move proved to be the founding of an independent university there, the University of South Africa would do everything possible to assist the newcomer.

This was, in fact, to follow. On 4 August the Principal was informed that the Cabinet had decided upon the opening of a second Johannesburg university, in which Afrikaans would be used for instructional purposes. In his letter the Minister thanked the University of South Africa for its offer to help in this connection and added that he could state "duidelik en ondubbelsinnig" that "u toekomstige taak net korresponderend en vir so lank as wat nodig eksaminerend sal bly".

It was the end of a protracted period of strain – "one of the tensest epochs in the annals of the University", as the Principal later described it. Had the move taken place, it might have been, in Professor Pauw's words, "the biggest event in the history of South African higher education". On the other hand, the demand for unilingual instruction might have become too strong to withstand, and the fine traditions built up in twenty years by the University of South Africa might have been lost as the correspondence section became increasingly a secondary function of the university. Most members of staff and students hailed the end of the period of uncertainty with relief, for the proposed move was not generally popular. One former student of the University of South Africa spoke for many when, in March, 1965, he begged the Prime Minister to veto the whole idea of a transfer to Johan-

348

nesburg. It would be, he argued, an unnecessary tragedy, for the university, as constituted in Pretoria, performed an outstanding service to the entire community.

The Rand Afrikaans University duly came into being and the University of South Africa gave its assistance to the new-comer in generous measure. Professor G. van N. Viljoen of the Department of Classical Languages, who had played no inconspicuous part in the lengthy debate over the proposed move, became the first Rector of the new institution. Those of his colleagues in Pretoria who accompanied him on a permanent or a temporary basis, brought with them to Johannesburg many of the ideals which had contributed to the success of the older university, now free at last to begin a fresh period of expansion in its own field.

14 *The clear road ahead*

Plans for the future could at last be made without the fear of a possible veto from above. The university was to remain in Pretoria and its position as a recognized national institution was assured. It could, indeed, be considered an international university to an even greater degree than ever before, since its student body, although as always predominantly South African, was drawn from many distant countries. It suffered, however, from one grave drawback – the lack of adequate accommodation.

The proposals for a new building had been shelved during the uncertainties of past months, but with the removal of the prospect of a transfer to Johannesburg, the matter became at once the most pressing problem for the immediate future. The properties in Skinner and Prinsloo Streets were no longer sufficient to house the entire lecturing and administrative staffs and additional units had to be rented in other buildings. The old Land Bank in Paul Kruger Street was taken over, primarily for the production department, and offices were also made available in President Centre, Pretorius Street and, later, in the Ada Bisschop homes adjoining the library in Skinner Street. Accommodation for the Department of Musicology was found in premises next to De Doorns and in the early seventies, the University of South Africa also overflowed into the Bourke Trust building in Andries Street. This dispersion of staff hampered the university's effectiveness; moreover, by 1968, the annual rental of additional accommodation exceeded R72 000.

Conference and seminar rooms were also required. Not only

350

were many more departmental and inter-disciplinary seminars taking place at the university, but the teaching staff was also playing an increasingly important role in the founding and development of national associations in various fields, meetings of which were often held in Pretoria. Limited facilities existed for tutorial study groups and seminars, but for such larger gatherings as the annual Vacation School, which by 1971 was attracting more than 3 000 students, accommodation had to be sought outside the university. The Pretoria College of Education and African and Indian high schools provided the lecture rooms for these winter vacation courses. However, in 1973 – the centenary year – the University of South Africa moved out of the northern capital to meet some of its widespread student body in other centres, arranging schools in both Cape Town and Durban, as well as in Pretoria.

In the same year, graduation ceremonies were also held in these cities for Coloured and Indian students, although this was no more than the further extension of a policy already decided upon. Degrees and diplomas were conferred annually at the associated colleges while the university retained academic responsibility for them; graduation ceremonies for European students, however, were always held until the late sixties in the Pretoria City Hall. The accommodation problem became so acute that restrictions had reluctantly to be placed upon the number of friends and relatives admitted. In 1969, the annual function was held in the Civic Theatre, Johannesburg, where closed circuit television had to be used to allow all present to follow the proceedings. By 1971, it had become necessary to hold two ceremonies for European students. In that year, one took place in Pretoria and the other in the City Hall, Germiston. Graduation Day for Europeans returned to Pretoria in 1972, with two ceremonies in the City Hall, while another was held at Laudium in the capital for members of the Indian and Coloured communities. Degrees were conferred upon African students at Ga-Rankuwa.

By that time a new building had almost been completed on

De Doorns

Shortage of accommodation compelled the University of South Africa to rent many offices in central Pretoria.

In addition, the DE DOORNS boarding-house on the corner of Prinsloo and Visagie Streets was acquired in exchange for other property owned by the university in Skinner Street.

At a later stage, CLOGHEREEN, formerly the home of the Bourke family, provided a welcome addition to the premises owned by the University of South Africa. This house with its delightful gardens adjoins the university's present hill-top home.

Cloghereen

Muckleneuk Ridge above Fountains Valley, with splendid views over the city to the distant Magaliesberg beyond. The project was an ambitious one and was expected to cost seven and a half million rands, an estimate which, in an era of rising costs, erred on the conservative side. A national fund raising campaign was launched in November, 1965 and an initial target of three and a half million rands was set. The University of South Africa Foundation was established, with a membership consisting of university representatives and prominent leaders in commerce and industry. One of the latter, Jan S. Marais of the Trust Bank, became Chairman of the Board of Trustees. The campaign began in Pretoria, where the local Chairman, Reuben Rutowitz, played a valuable part. It soon spread to Cape Town and Johannesburg. Between 1966 and 1970, regional campaigns had been inaugurated in the Eastern Province, the Kimberley area, the Witwatersrand, the Vaal Triangle and the Orange Free State. In terms of Act 13 of 1964, Council membership was broadened to include representatives of the donors and of the City Council of Pretoria.

The Principal and other members of staff travelled extensively in order to stimulate interest in the scheme and in 1966, the small Public Relations Office under A. B. Cloete became an active Department of Development, whose informative periodical, *Unisa Bulletin,* gave the university wider publicity. The first Director of Development, L. C. Malan, was succeeded soon afterwards by A. P. Schutte and the department is now headed by J. E. M. Verwey. As in Pretoria, the success of the regional campaigns owed much to the enthusiasm of leading businessmen. Theo Rood, who became a representative of the donors on Council, was active in the Vaal Triangle and later, in succession to Derek Scorer, in Johannesburg. The former Gloucestershire and England cricketer, Wally Hammond, was Chairman of the Kimberley committee. Others prominent in the various campaigns included F. van Kraayenburg in the Orange Free State, J. D. Wrigley and J. M. Christopher in the Cape Province and Chris. Saunders in Natal. Commercial undertakings responded

354

generously, as did industrial concerns, municipalities and the general public. By the end of 1969, promises totalled more than three million rands, with about R1 500 000 immediately available for building purposes.

Staff and students contributed substantial sums. In 1965, a Students' Association was formed in Johannesburg under the chairmanship of C. A. Jurgens and soon had branches throughout the republic and South West Africa. Some members of the teaching staff visited Windhoek to lecture to the members there. The religious and cultural leader, Dr William Nicol, who received the degree of Doctor of Literature and Philosophy *(honoris causa)* at the graduation ceremony in 1966, accepted the honorary presidency of the association. He was succeeded by Major-General Sir Francis de Guingand, the first honorary Vice-President. At the Vacation School in 1968, the Samuel Pauw Student Fund was established, to which past and present students of the university contributed. The Chancellor, Dr F. J. de Villiers, himself an old student of the University of South Africa and generous supporter of the development campaign, made a liberal donation to the Student Fund.

Another valuable contribution to the university came from South West Africa, where a fund was inaugurated in memory of Professor J. P. verLoren van Themaat, the brilliant jurist who played so important a part in presenting South Africa's case in the South West Africa question at the World Court in the Netherlands. At the time of his death in 1966, Professor verLoren van Themaat was a member of the university's Department of Public Law. Control of the fund was vested in a board under the chairmanship of Mr Justice V. G. Hiemstra and it was planned to provide a Centre of International Law in the new university building. The centre was first established under the aegis of the Institute of Foreign and Comparative Law, founded at the university in 1964.

Although the building programme progressed at a steady pace, there was a certain insecurity in other aspects of university finance. The Cilliers Report had placed the University of South

355

Africa on a subsidy basis similar to that of other universities, but the rejection of its author's subsequent report on the 1969-1973 quinquennium ushered in a period of marked financial uncertainty. This was intensified by the rejection in 1969 of the interim report of the Commission of Enquiry into University Affairs. This commission, under the chairmanship of Mr Justice J. van Wyk de Vries, was aided in its deliberations by Professor H. S. Steyn of the university's Department of Mathematical Statistics, who was seconded to it as a professional adviser and later became a full member.

This was not the only outside field in which members of the university's staff were active. In 1966, Professor M. L. Benade of the Department of Mercantile Law was appointed to the Commission of Enquiry into Company Law and Professor F. E. Rädel of the Department of Business Economics to that which investigated the fishing industry. Two years later, members of several departments served on the government commission appointed to enquire into fiscal and monetary policy. They included Professor D. C. Krogh of the Department of Economics and Economic History, his colleague from the Netherlands, D. W. Goedhuys, and A. F. van Niekerk of the Department of Mercantile Law. These two associates of Professor Krogh on the commission were subsequently awarded professorships by the University of South Africa.

Early in 1970, a group led by Professor W. F. J. Steenkamp left for Australia to study methods of cargo handling, with special reference to containerization. Shortly after his retirement in 1971, Professor Steenkamp received an honorary doctorate in commerce from the university, with whose Departments of Economics and Business Economics he had been associated for some years. The same award was made at that time to Professor S. P. du Toit Viljoen, who had also been attached to the Department of Economics. Professor Marius Wiechers of the Department of Constitutional and International Law was among others who distinguished themselves in wider spheres. Following in the footsteps of his mentor, Professor verLoren van Themaat, he was chosen as a member of South Africa's World Court team in 1970.

Several won recognition for outstanding contributions to academic life. These included Professor W. A. Joubert of the Department of Private Law and G. van N. Viljoen, then still with the university in the Department of Classical Languages. They were presented with Council Awards for leadership and advancement of their subjects at the graduation ceremony of 1966. Others honoured for their achievements included Professor B. A. T. Schneider, awarded a silver medal by the Goethe Institute of Germany in 1965 for his work in the field of German studies, Professor C. J. H. Schutte of the Department of Chemistry, a Raikes Medallist in 1968, and Professors Benade of the Faculty of Law and H. S. Cilliers of the Department of Accounting, who gained the Toon van den Heever Prize of the *Suid-Afrikaanse Akademie vir Wetenskap en Kuns* in the following year. The *Akademie's* Stals Prize went to Professor F. W. Blignaut of the Department of Psychology in 1965 and to Professor P. Smit of the Department of Geography in 1972. The mathematical statistician, Professor H. S. Steyn, was awarded the Havenga Prize offered by the *Akademie* in 1970. In that year, Professor A. S. Roux was elected President of the Institute of Psychology, Professor D. R. Beeton, President of the English Academy of Southern Africa and Professor J. H. Moolman, President of the South African Geographical Society. Professor P. J. van der Walt had the unusual distinction of being chosen an active member of the American Society of Criminology, although not resident in the United States.

Many members of staff attended congresses at home and abroad. Among them was Professor B. S. van As of the Department of Native Administration, who gave the opening address at the Wilton Park International Conference on Development Aid, held in Sussex, England in 1970. Five years earlier, Dr J. F. Heyne was the guest of the Law Faculty of the University of Tokyo, where he delivered several lectures on South African mercantile law. Professor A. M. T. Meyer of the Department of Philosophy, who has recently accepted a permanent post in the

357

Netherlands, was a visiting professor in 1970 and 1971 at the *Rijksuniversiteit,* Utrecht.

The founding of the Rand Afrikaans University was not the only cause of a drain of staff to fill positions elsewhere in South Africa. Professor Rund of the Department of Mathematics obtained a Chair at the University of the Witwatersrand and Professor M. H. H. Louw of the Department of Political Science was appointed to the vacant Jan Smuts Chair of International Relations at the same university. Another who achieved distinction abroad was Vincent Brümmer of the Department of Philosophy, who became a professor in the Faculty of Divinity at the *Rijksuniversiteit,* Utrecht. Professor Brümmer is the son of N. J. Brümmer, long Professor of Philosophy at the Victoria College, later the University of Stellenbosch, and the grandson of Professor J. I. Marais of the neighbouring seminary. Both his father and his grandfather had served the old examining University of the Cape of Good Hope.

The continuing expansion of the University of South Africa and the departure of senior members of staff led to many new appointments at all levels. A large proportion of those who became senior lecturers and professors in the university were already in its employ. The University of South Africa was also fortunate in obtaining the temporary services of distinguished academics from other institutions. These included Professor D. W. Krüger, one of South Africa's leading historians, who joined the Department of History after his retirement from Potchefstroom University. He subsequently became editor-in-chief of the *Dictionary of South African Biography.* Professors J. Chris. Coetzee of Potchefstroom and C. K. Oberholzer of the University of Pretoria assisted the Faculty of Education and Professor J. H. van den Berg of the *Rijksuniversiteit,* Leiden was the guest of the Department of Psychology. Professor G. Cronjé joined the Department of Criminology in the centenary year, together with Professor J. C. de Wet of the Faculty of Law. Professor Cronjé, as head of the Department of Sociology at the University of Pretoria, had introduced courses in criminology there in 1949. A man of remarkable versatility, he subsequently held the Chair in the field of dramatic art at Pretoria. Professor de Wet brought his considerable attainments and long experience at the University of Stellenbosch to the service of the Faculty of Law as Professor Extraordinary.

One appointment to the teaching staff deserves special mention. General J. P. Gous, who had received his university training at the University of Stellenbosch, enlisted in the South African Police in 1932 and rose to become Commissioner. In 1972, soon after his retirement, he joined Professor P. J. van der Walt in the university's Department of Criminology. General Gous had long fought to raise the professional status of the police force; the key lay in better educational qualifications for its members and it is fitting that his assumption of his new duties should coincide with the introduction of the degree of Bachelor of Arts in Police Science, the only one of its kind to be offered in South Africa.

Many visitors from the world of higher education in other countries came to lecture or to forge contacts with the University of South Africa. Among them were Professor M. R. Bonvalet, Principal of the University of Madagascar, Professor Kathleen Atkinson, the classicist from Queen's University, Belfast, Professor H. M. H. N. Irving of the Department of Inorganic Chemistry at the University of Leeds and Dr Charles Malik of the American University in Beirut, formerly the Lebanon's Minister of Foreign Affairs and Chairman of the General Assembly of the United Nations Organization.

Several took a closer look at the work of the university. In April, 1969, Dr J. H. Barclay, Director of Adult Education at the University of Edinburgh, called in the course of a world tour which brought him into contact with a large number of higher educational institutions. He paid the achievements of the University of South Africa high tribute and gave his opinion that its standards compared very favourably with those of other universities of repute. In the course of the following month, Dr Walter Perry, Vice-Chancellor of Britain's Open University, then in the formative stage, visited Pretoria with his Registrar, A. Christo-doulou. His purpose was to study the University of South Africa's methods of tuition with reference to the programme planned by his own institution. Dr Perry confessed that he had learned much and was particularly impressed by new develoments in business economics and by the excellence of the library. In 1972, the Director of External Studies at the University of New England in Australia, Howard C. Sheath, was able to share his experiences in the field of teletuition with the Principal. He complimented the university on its efficient organization and upon the advances made in the use of modern teaching techniques.

Another visitor from overseas spent three months at the University of South Africa in 1967. The report which he subsequently compiled was of the greatest significance, both for its careful and objective evaluation of the work being accomplished by the university and for its detailed recommendations. Professor Charles A. Wedemeyer, the William H. Lighty Professor of Education in the extension section of the University of Wisconsin, was invited by Professor Pauw and the governing Council with the main object of studying "the effectiveness of our methods, procedures and organization" and of giving his considered opinion on the desirability of introducing "modern media of communication and education".

Professor Wedemeyer had much to say that was highly complimentary to the university, with particular regard to the comprehensiveness of its service and to the high standards maintained. He praised the leadership of the first Principal and his successor, for the university was, as he put it, "the very special creation of two dedicated men". His lengthy report, however, pointed to certain deficiencies and suggested ways of remedying them. He felt that the university's teaching publications, for example, could scarcely be said to attract the reader, however sound the material they contained. Much could be done to improve their appearance which, in design, lay-out and quality of paper, fell far short of that of the glossy annual house magazine, *Unisa*. At the same time, Professor Wedemeyer appreciated that the issue of teaching material on so large a scale involved high production costs and was quick to note that the University of South Africa operated on a sub-economic budget.

He also recognized the problem of vacation courses then limited to a single series each year held in one centre only. He commented, too, upon the difficulties encountered by the library in its contacts with distant students – difficulties which, he readily admitted, the staff sought constantly to overcome. Much, he considered, could still be done in the whole field of relations between student and lecturer in order to provide that extra counselling and assistance which the external student so often requires. Professor Wedemeyer was, however, of the opinion that continued growth would see the evolution of new approaches in correspondence tuition and in that connection, recommended the introduction of a programme of study by the university.

It would have been unhelpful to those whose lives were dedicated to future planning had Professor Wedemeyer's evaluation been wholly eulogistic. Many of the points he raised were already matters to which the university authorities had devoted much thought; all were examined in detail. Much has been achieved since his visit. The use of tapes for tuition purposes, to supplement the written word, is one example of the modern techniques adopted. 4 000 were sent to students in 1968; well over 100 000 were despatched in 1972. Since Professor Wedemeyer's visit, too, a Bureau for University Research has been established under Professor G. H. A. Steyn to investigate student problems and the in-service training of lecturers. It was, however, encouraging to know that, despite all strictures, an impartial observer with wide experience in the field could conclude his observations on the university of 1967 by stating that it was "one of the foremost institutions for the independent learner in the world" and potentially, if not at that date actually, the greatest of them all.

Meanwhile, the work of the university was carried on with undiminished vigour by a staff steadily increasing in numbers beyond the thousand mark. There were, inevitably, losses which brought more than a moment of sadness. In February, 1969,

ABRAHAM JOHANNES KOEN was born on 6 July, 1903 at Brandfort in what was then the Orange River Colony. He received his early education in the Klerksdorp district of the Transvaal and matriculated at Grey College, Bloemfontein in 1922. After farming for a year, he trained as a teacher in Potchefstroom, where he also obtained the B.A. degree in 1928. He added to his graduate qualifications by gaining a B.Ed. degree in 1942.

A.J. Koen taught at Paardeplaas and Lagersdrift, before accepting the headship of the high school at Hartebeesfontein which he had attended as a boy. He later became Headmaster of the Helpmekaar Hoër Seunskool and in 1955, formed part of a mission sent to study differentiated secondary education overseas. In the following year, he was appointed Chairman of a commission to investigate and plan educational services in South West Africa.

Deputy Director of Education in the mandated territory in 1957 and 1958, he moved to the Transvaal in the same capacity, becoming Director of Education there in 1963.

A man of wide interests, he has served on a number of bodies, among them the Board of Education, Science and Technology. He is also Chairman of the Advisory Board for Nature Conservation and of the Board for National Zoological Gardens.

Appointed to the university Council in June, 1963, he has been its Chairman since February, 1969. He was awarded an honorary doctorate in education by the University of South Africa in 1973.

Dr Abraham Johannes Koen, B.A., B.Ed., D.Ed. (h.c.)
Member of Council since 29 June, 1963
Chairman of Council since 8 February, 1969

Professor S. P. E. Boshoff retired, thus severing a long connection with the university Council. Professor Boshoff, who died at Potgietersrus on 30 April, 1973, had been publicly acclaimed by the University of South Africa in 1963 when, together with the distinguished Belgian writer, Frank Lateur (Stijn Streuvels), the honorary degree of Doctor of Literature and Philosophy was conferred upon him. His place as Chairman of Council was taken by Abraham Johannes Koen, a past Director of Education in the Transvaal who was awarded an honorary doctorate in education by the university in 1973. This was one of several honorary degrees presented to persons of all races in the centenary year.

In 1967, the death in an aircraft disaster of Professor J. P. van S. Bruwer of the University of Port Elizabeth deprived the governing body of the services of another valuable member. Four years later, one of the donors' representatives, Dr G. S. J. Kuschke of the Industrial Development Corporation, died in Johannesburg shortly after his resignation from Council.

The teaching staff, too, lost several outstanding members. J. W. Loubser of the Department of Accounting died in an airliner crash at Windhoek in April, 1968 and the death occurred in May, 1971 of Dr H. T. Gonin, a former missionary then lecturing in the Department of Mathematical Statistics. Two more deaths took place later in 1971 : that of Professor B. J. Roux, head of the Department of Political Science and Public Administration in November, and of Dr J. F. Heyne, Senior Research Officer with the Institute of Foreign and Comparative Law in the following month.

The unexpected death of Alewyn J. Vorster in September, 1967 was a grievous loss to the administrative section. The Chief Accountant had been in the service of the university since March, 1945 and had been closely connected with the development of the teaching branch in a number of capacities. P. J. Viljoen took over his duties and a new post, that of Finance Officer, was created to co-ordinate the work of the accounts section. This was filled by the former Director of Development, A. P. Schutte.

The change was part of the continuing expansion and reorganization of the complex administration of the university. The functions of the Information Department were greatly extended and placed in charge of J. J. Brits, who retired in 1972 as Chief Adviser on Students' Affairs. An additional senior position was then added and the service directed by M. B. Ferreira and M. H. Stockhoff. New techniques necessitated the establishment of new sections. A Computer Centre was founded under D. Scheepers and programming divisions formed. This important aspect of the university's work is now in charge of Professor R. H. Venter. A Language Laboratory was instituted in connection with the introduction of modern methods of tuition and placed in the care of Professor H. J. J. M. van der Merwe of *Afrikaans en Nederlands*.

S. J. Marais was first succeeded by A. P. Schutte as Production Manager, before the appointment of the present head of this section, J. J. Verheem. The department not only kept pace with the increasing demand from students for study material, but also undertook the printing of other university publications. By 1971, it was producing more than 30 million pages of lectures and 10 million pages of tutorial letters annually. M. G. van Niekerk's despatch section was responsible for the mammoth task of sending these out to destinations all over the world.

The University of South Africa retained its administrative responsibility for the examinations of the Joint Matriculation Board and for those in music, with the Registrar, B. F. J. van Rensburg, as Secretary and W. H. le Roux as Under-Secretary of this joint section. A standing committee of Council, with outside representatives, controlled the music examinations and another, assisted by assessor members, regulated speech training. In 1967, on the retirement of Professor Roode as Director of Music, H. J. Joubert, one of South Africa's most talented musicians, was appointed in his place. Hennie Joubert, held in high esteem as an accompanist, teacher and performer on both organ and piano, had for long been one of the university's music examiners. The work of the university in the field of general music examinations – quite separate from the academic teaching in the

Department of Musicology under its new head, Professor Bernard van der Linde – was of particular value to music teachers, for whom annual courses were arranged.

Throughout the years of Professor Pauw's leadership, student numbers continued to grow. By 1968, the 20 000 mark had been topped and four years later, nearly 30 000 men and women had enrolled for courses. In the same period, there was a steady rise in the numbers of those seeking post-graduate qualifications and by 1971, over 15% of the registered students were taking advanced degrees. Moreover, the University of South Africa was becoming increasingly a "university for seniors", as the Principal put it. In the same year, some 3 000 of those studying for general degrees in the various faculties already possessed graduate qualifications obtained elsewhere. The upward trend in enrolments continued and the student body numbered some 32 000 in the centenary year.

Although efforts to extend the university's teaching function to localities outside Pretoria were no more than sporadic before 1973 and limited to occasional lectures and seminars in other towns and cities, certain administrative contacts were established. In 1966, a branch library was opened in Windhoek and in the following year, the university returned to its old home when it set up a regional office in Cape Town. A. T. Laubscher was placed in charge and on his return to Pretoria as Committee Clerk, Charl Cillié took over his duties. A library was also opened in the Cape Town office for the convenience of students and contact with the main library in Pretoria was maintained by telex.

A number of important developments took place in the later period of Professor Pauw's principalship. One of the greatest success stories was the founding of the School of Business Leadership. The initiative came from the private sector and in 1963, discussions were held between the University of South Africa and certain national commercial and industrial organizations. In these negotiations, the Chancellor, Dr de Villiers, the Principal and Professor Rädel of the Department of Business Economics played

Teaching Staff 1947

*1st Row (seated, l. to r.): E. Davis, M.A.; J. Alb. Coetzee, M.A., D.Phil.;
P.J. Coertze, M.A., D.Phil.; A.J.H. van der Walt, M.A., D.Phil. (Direc-
tor); B.F.J. van Rensburg, B.Com., B.A. (Secretary); H.J.J.M. van der
Merwe, M.A., D.Litt.; D. de Villiers, B.A. (Hons.).*

*2nd Row (l. to r.): C.B. Smit, M.A.; L.J. le Roux, B.Com., M.Sc.; K.D.
Venter, M.A.; D.H. Cilliers, M.A., M.Ed.; C.F.J. Muller, M.A., D.Phil.;
J.H. van der Merwe, M.Sc.; A.S. Roux, MA.; H. Hofmeyr, C.A.(S.A.),
A.C.W.A.; J.A. van der Walt, M.A.; E.F. Potgieter, B.A.*

Rear: F.M.P. Oosterhof, M.A.

Above:
At the beginning of 1972, there were more than 500 lecturers and professors on the ACADEMIC STAFF of the University of South Africa (picture above). Several were among the original 16 who formed the teaching section of the Division of External Studies at its inception.

Below:

When the University of the Cape of Good Hope was founded in 1873, the ADMINISTRATIVE STAFF consisted of the Registrar and a messenger. Growth was very slow until the creation of the Division of External Studies in 1946. At that time, the Registrar's section numbered 29 persons, with 13 more in the Director's division.

At the beginning of 1972, there were 584 members of the administrative staff (picture below).

a prominent part. Professor Rädel's colleague, Georg Marais, was sent on an extensive tour of Europe and the United States to investigate the possibility of introducing a successful leadership programme under university auspices. As a result of his favourable report, it was decided to begin a course of training within the Department of Business Economics in 1964. However, at the beginning of 1969, the School of Business Leadership became an autonomous body within the Faculty of Commerce and Administration, with Professor Marais as its Director. It has its own Council, upon which both the university and the business world are represented.

Professor Marais was assisted from the start by a carefully selected staff of wide experience and special methods of instruction were devised to meet the problems of learning in this field. The School of Business Leadership worked in close association with similar organizations abroad, lecturers from overseas were invited and seminars were held as far from Pretoria as Swaziland. Masters' and doctoral degrees were instituted and in 1970, an Advanced Executive's Programme was launched.

Among the new departments formed in the more recent years of the university's history was that of Communication, under Professor F. W. Blignaut, formerly of the Department of Psychology. The Department of Communication came into being after government's acceptance in 1968 of the report of an investigating committee under the chairmanship of the Chancellor, Dr de Villiers. Professor Blignaut was a member of this committee of enquiry. His unexpected death at the end of February, 1972 was a grave loss to the department which he had done so much to create.

It was in the previous year that the Faculty of Social Science, of which Professor Blignaut was then Dean, was merged into the Faculty of Arts, thus ending a separate existence of more than a quarter of a century. A general streamlining of the faculty system occasioned the change. The six Faculties of Arts, Science, Law, Education, Divinity and Commerce and Administration were retained, with sub-faculties where necessary. Departmental business was first considered at sub-faculty meetings, before being discussed at full faculty level.

Other new departments included Computer Science under Professor R. H. Venter, Industrial Psychology, in charge of Professor I. van W. Raubenheimer, and Linguistics, closely associated with *Afrikaans en Nederlands* and under the guidance of Professors H. J. J. M. van der Merwe and F. A. Ponelis.

The creation of new departments and the extension of work in others led to the introduction of more degrees and diplomas. Additional degrees in library science, theology, operations research, law and accounting science were instituted, together with those in business leadership and police science. New certificates and diplomas were awarded in librarianship, criminology, social work and education. Fresh ground was continually being broken. In the Faculty of Education, for example, a diploma in nursery education was introduced and a course in special education offered. The latter was undertaken by V. H. Vaughan of the Department of Orthopedagogics. His work for the physically handicapped had already won him international recognition and a further honour was bestowed upon him in 1973 when the University of South Africa awarded him the degree of Doctor of Education *(honoris causa)* after his retirement.

Other departments continued to flourish and if the accent here falls upon the projects they inaugurated, it should be remembered that their main concern was always to improve the quality of their teaching in the interests of the students enrolled with them. It was essentially in this area that they made their greatest impact and it was through the efforts of many dedicated members of the academic staff that the work of the university came to be appreciated not only in South Africa, but also beyond the borders. An instance is provided by the Department of Semitics under Hungarian-born Professor J. J. Glück. The excellent course in modern Hebrew offered by this department even attracted students from Israel itself.

Departmental and inter-disciplinary seminars were held with increasing regularity within the university and several new de-

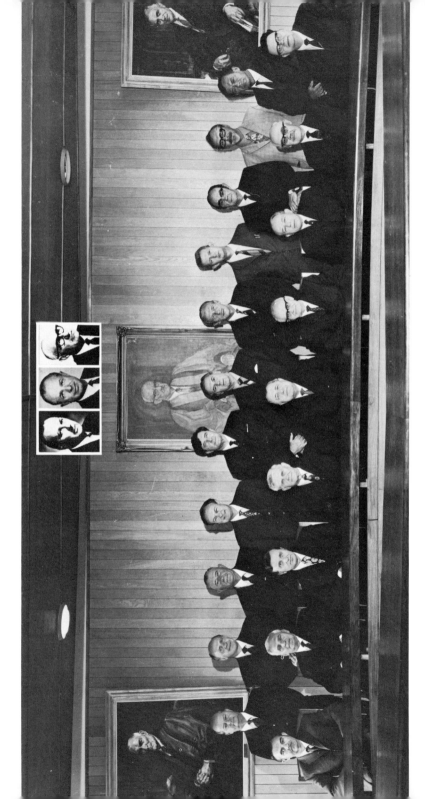

The tenth COUNCIL of the University of South Africa (1970-1974) consisted in 1971 of ten members appointed by the State President, four representatives of the university Senate, two Principals of other South African universities nominated by the Committee of University Principals, two representatives of Convocation and two of the donors, two members nominated by the City Council of Pretoria and the Principal of the university.

Since then, another amendment to the University Act has resulted in the elimination of the two representatives of other universities.

University Council 1971

Front row (l. to r.): Rev. G.J. Davidtz; Dr J. Hurter; Dr J.S. Marais; Prof. H.J.J. Bingle; Mr A.J. Koen (Chairman); Prof. S. Pauw; Mr Justice V.G. Hiemstra; Mr I.T. Meyer; Prof. C.M. v.d. M. Brink.

Back row (l. to r.): Prof. W.A. Joubert; Mr L.F. Rive; Gen. H.B. Klopper; Dr J.P. Kearney; Prof. O.P.F. Horwood; Mr Theo Roodt; Prof. T. van Wijk; Prof. J.H. van der Merwe; Mr J.H. van Dyk; Prof. H.J.J.M. van der Merwe; Dr E.F. Potgieter.

Inset: Prof. G.R. Bozzoli; Mr H. Goldberg; Dr A.D. Wassenaar.

partmental journals made their appearance. *Unisa English Studies* was first published in 1963 under a slightly different title and was followed in 1964 by *Dynamica,* the journal of the Department of Business Economics. In the following year, the Department of Fine Arts issued the pilot number of *De Arte,* a magazine of high scholarly standard and aesthetic appeal which has appeared regularly since 1967. This publication owed much to the enthusiasm of Professor Walter Battiss, the head of the department from the end of 1964 until his retirement in 1972. He was awarded an honorary doctorate in literature and philosophy by the university in 1973 for his outstanding contributions to South African art. Other journals followed in the late sixties: *Limi* of the Department of Bantu Languages, *Mercurius,* issued by the Department of Economics, the Department of History's *Kleio* and *Ars Nova,* published by the Department of Musicology. The first number of *Theologia Evangelica,* produced by the Faculty of Divinity, appeared in April, 1968.

In addition, members of the Faculty of Law formed the editorial board of the *Comparative and International Law Journal of Southern Africa* and the Bureau of Market Research has recently commenced publication of *Research for Marketing.* Other publications, not specifically departmental, were sponsored by members of the teaching staff. Professor H. J. J. M. van der Merwe played a large part in the launching of the linguistic journal, *Taalfasette,* while Professor Glück and Professor I. H. Eybers founded the annual, *Semitics.* These, and the university's own publications, obtained a circulation which extended far beyond the confines of the Pretoria institution.

Departments also undertook work of international significance in their fields. In 1966, the Department of History provided a valuable guide for historical research by publishing its *Select Bibliography of South African History.* This compilation, edited by Professors C. F. J. Muller, F. A. van Jaarsveld and Theo van Wijk, made extensive use of the knowledge of specialists in various subject areas, both inside and outside the republic. Before the publication made its appearance, plans were formulated to bring it up to date with supplementary issues. Other projects include the work of Professor Beeton and Helen Dorner of the Department of English in compiling an *Index of English Usage in Southern Africa* and the joint venture of the Departments of Romance Languages and *Afrikaans en Nederlands* in the production of a Portuguese and Afrikaans dictionary.

The library continued to expand and in little more than ten years from the date of its transfer to the new building on the corner of Skinner and Van der Walt Streets had acquired some quarter of a million items. Its staff, under H. Zastrau and his successor, S. I. Malan, was able to build up a number of special collections, among them a record library, a variety of material in micro-reproduction form and an extensive series of government publications from many parts of the world. As in the past, gifts augmented annual purchases. These included a collection of German-Africana donated by Dr A. O. Hesse, the genial member of the Department of German who retired in 1972, books presented by Professor S. P. E. Boshoff and others donated by the governments of Spain and the Argentine Republic. In addition, the Pretoria bookseller and bibliophile, J. L. van Schaik, bequeathed his valuable library to the university in 1965. Legal works were housed separately in the care of the Faculty of Law and the Institute of Foreign and Comparative Law. This collection was also enriched through generous gifts. The donors included the Portuguese Law Society and the French and Japanese governments.

A complete separation was at length effected between the library and the Department of Library Science. Professor S. I. Malan, who had been head of both library and department, handed over control of the former to J. Willemse, retaining responsibility for the academic work. In July, 1973, the university presented an honorary doctorate in library science to Professor Herman Jan de Vleeschauwer, who had done so much to bring the department into being.

The close of the Johannesburg university debate had been followed by several years of intense activity which placed a heavy

THEO VAN WIJK, son of the Rev. A.J. van Wijk and grandson of the Rev. Charles Murray, was born at Kuilsrivier, Cape Province on 12 November, 1916. He received his early education at the high school in Franschhoek and later attended Rhodes University College. He obtained the B.A. degree with distinctions in history and German in 1937, a first-class University Education Diploma in 1941 and the M.A. *cum laude* in history in 1945.

In 1939, he became the first permanent archivist in Windhoek, South West Africa and between 1942 and 1945, held several teaching posts before accepting a lectureship at Rhodes University College. He joined the staff of the Division of External Studies in this capacity in 1948, became a senior lecturer in 1954 and was promoted to a professorship in 1961. In 1969, he acted as Principal.

Professor van Wijk has specialized in European history and has considerable research experience in London, Paris and The Hague. He is at present investigating the place of the Cape in European politics between 1780 and 1806.

Appointed a member of Council on 1 April, 1969, Professor van Wijk became Principal of the University of South Africa on 1 April, 1972.

Professor Theo van Wijk, M.A.
Dean of the Faculty of Arts 1966–1970
Member of Council since 1 April 1969
Principal since 1 April, 1972

burden upon the Principal's shoulders. He not only had to supervise the day to day running of a giant institution, but also to devote much time and energy to the task of keeping the university well before the public gaze as its new home on Muckleneuk Ridge took shape. Professor Pauw was afforded a measure of relief when it was decided that from 1969, a member of the teaching staff was to be seconded on an annual basis as an assistant to the Principal. Professor S. I. Malan undertook this duty for the first year; his successors were Professor Marinus Wiechers of the Faculty of Law and Professor J. C. G. Janse van Vuuren of the Faculty of Education.

In 1967, the "new" University of South Africa – the teaching university for many thousands of scattered students throughout the world – came of age. It had already achieved wide renown and recognition of its standing from the Committee of University Principals. For in 1966, Professor Pauw had been chosen as Chairman of that body, a position which he held for two years. At this period, too, the Registrar became its Secretary. It was time to bring the old system of guardianship to a close, for the members of the university no longer needed the imposition of outside experts to guide them at meetings of Council and Senate.

A new dispensation was therefore granted the university by Act 53 of 1967. No longer would all the other university Principals or their representatives take their seats in Council. Instead, the Committee of University Principals would appoint two of their number to a reconstructed governing body. Within a few years, even this degree of control was to fall away. So far as Senate was concerned, the University of South Africa would in future be free to choose its own outside advisers to assist, where necessary, the university professors and heads of department. One further link with the past was also broken by this legislation. The University of South Africa was now in every sense a teaching university and the phrase "division of studies" no longer had meaning. It was therefore dropped from the Act.

In 1971, Professor Pauw decided to retire as Principal and in February of the following year, Council appointed Professor

378

A campaign, inaugurated by Professor Pauw, at length enabled the University of South Africa to construct the UNIVERSITY BUILDING on Muckleneuk Ridge, overlooking the city of Pretoria and the wooded Fountains Valley.

Occupation began in June, 1972. The first meeting of Council in the new premises was held on 17 June of that year and that of Senate on 1 September.

University Building, Muckleneuk Ridge, Pretoria (see overleaf)

Theo van Wijk of the Department of History and a former Dean of the Faculty of Arts to succeed him. Professor Pauw stepped down at the end of March, 1972 and the third Principal of the University of South Africa took office on 1 April.

A few months later, Council appointed two Vice-Principals to assist him on a full-time basis. Professors F. E. Rädel of the Department of Business Economics and H. S. Steyn of the Department of Mathematical Statistics assumed duty in their new roles on 1 August.

By that date, the university had taken possession of its imposing new home on Muckleneuk Ridge, for the first departments had vacated their old quarters in central Pretoria in the previous June. The building, designed by architects Brian Sandrock and T. Neethling, includes comprehensive office accommodation, a magnificent auditorium, together with other conference and seminar halls, and a fully computerized library. In addition, a roof top observatory provides facilities unique in South African universities for the study of astronomy. The most striking feature of the new structure is the long projection from the brow of the hill, supported by a giant steel girder resting on a massive column. This stage of the construction work was inaugurated at a special ceremony held on 28 November, 1968, when the Prime Minister, the Hon. B. J. Vorster, unveiled the column.

A further welcome accession to the complex was made in the following year, with the purchase from the Bourke Trust of the adjoining property, Cloghereen. This delightful hill-side house, with its cool rooms and wide verandah overlooking grassy lawns, is surrounded by the finest garden of indigenous trees and shrubs in the province. It was the former home of the Pretoria director of companies, Myles Esmond Bourke, and his wife, Marguerite, and has since been transformed into a worthy residence for the Principal.

The university's new building was officially opened on 14 April, 1973 by the State President, the Hon. J. J. Fouché, and an extensive programme of concerts, exhibitions and congresses was arranged to mark the centenary year. It was altogether

382

appropriate, too, that at a time when the University of South Africa remembered its small beginnings in a colonial past, it should choose to confer an honorary doctorate in administration upon a descendant of its first Vice-Chancellor, Sir Langham Dale. The recipient had, however, a more personal claim to be so honoured, for Langham Dale Murray had served the university with devotion for many years and had guided it wisely as Registrar when the Division of External Studies was emerging from the federal chrysalis.

One hundred years ago, the University of the Cape of Good Hope was founded as an examining board, invested with the trappings of a university. It had no home of its own until the evening of its days; it spoke no language but English for most of its life; it asked many questions, but provided no answers. Once only in each year, it emerged from obscurity to appear before an admiring public. Then, it conferred with due solemnity its degrees and certificates upon those who had triumphed over the inquisitors hired to test the knowledge they had acquired elsewhere. Its Council consisted of government nominees and the representatives of its graduates, its Vice-Chancellor was a part-time official and its administration was for long in the hands of a single officer, the Registrar.

Fifty years ago, its successor in Pretoria was the nucleus of a group of colleges, in which its intellectual life was concentrated. From the viewpoint of the rented rooms in which it carried out its business, it was still very much an examination factory, although its administrative functions had been expanded. The Vice-Chancellor did not yet devote all his attention to its affairs, but a small clerical staff assisted the Registrar in his duties. Its governing Council was, however, a more widely representative body and it possessed an academic Senate and a faculty system. English was no longer the university's only tongue, for it had come at last to recognize the equal claims of Dutch and Afrikaans. But to most of its students it was an abstraction. They owed their allegiance to its colleges, moving slowly forward along the road to independence. Only the scattered external students were directly attached to it, but the university taught them nothing and regarded them as unwelcome intruders upon the higher educational scene.

Today, the University of South Africa looks out from its commanding new seat upon a vast student body in all parts of the republic and far beyond its borders. No longer an examining machine, it has become an association of learners and teachers, dedicated to the advance of the frontiers of knowledge through study and research in a multitude of disciplines. In little more than a quarter of a century, it has been transformed from the insignificant centre of a dissolving federation of constituent colleges into an institution with a unique function and a permanent place in the society which it serves. It has become, at last, a university indeed.

Two men of vision made the University of South Africa great. Andries Jacobus Hendrik van der Walt saw the possibilities and with characteristic thoroughness and resolution, confounded his many critics by making external university study a reality for thousands. With the willing help of a handful of dedicated scholars, he laid the foundations of a teaching university in the Division of External Studies. Samuel Pauw built on. He won for the university more than grudging acceptance, but whole-hearted recognition; he fought to maintain its position as a bilingual institution for students of all races; he made it, through his drive and determination, a national university of the first rank. In the new home which his unstinting efforts have provided for it, the University of South Africa, under the guidance of his successor, Professor Theo van Wijk, will continue with confidence to meet the challenge of the years which lie ahead. In so doing, it will justify the faith of its founders, who never lost hope for the future in difficult yesterdays.

384

Index

385

386

389

390

392

394

Marais, J.I.   24, 36, 37, 86, 98, 123, 173, 359
Marais, J.S.   354
Marais, S.J.   325, 365
Marchand, B.P.J.   69, 131
Maritz, G.J.   265–267, 306, 326
Maritzburg College   84, 101
Market Research, Bureau of   321, 374
Martin, J.   56, 105, 106
Marwick, J.S.   220
Mary Immaculate, Oblates of   302
Mary, Queen   50
Mathematical Society, South African   321
Mathematical Statistics   317, 356, 357, 364, 382
Mathematics and Applied Mathematics   2, 4, 14, 15, 18, 22, 37, 42, 57, 62, 102, 229, 234, 290, 315, 320, 359
Matriculation   15, 23, 27, 37, 42, 51, 54, 56, 57, 62, 63, 82, 92, 96, 110, 112, 129, 137, 151, 212, 312
Matthews, A.   56
Matthews, Z.K.   169
Mauritius   22
Mayfair, Johannesburg   273
Maynard, J.M.   50
Maynard Scholarship   50
Medical education   23, 27, 63, 95
Medicine, Faculty of   95, 155, 330
Meiring, J.G.   301
Melbourne, University of   68
Mercantile Law   356
Mercurius   374
Merensky Library, University of Pretoria   291
Merriman, J.X.   24, 43, 74, 83, 84, 87, 88, 98, 99, 103, 112
Metaphysics   2
Method and Administration, Department of   229
Methodist Church   254
Meyer, A.M.T.   357
Meyer, P.J.   315, 342
Michaelhouse   158
Michaelis, M.   68
Michell, L.L.   122
Micro-reproduction   375
Middelburg, Transvaal   180
Middelkerke, Belgium   316
Miles-Cadman, C.F.   220

Milner, Alfred, Viscount   50, 96, 97
Milner Art Scholarship   50
Milner Park, Johannesburg   136
Mining engineering   42, 91, 95, 96, 99, 100, 102, 173, 212
Minnesota, University of   101
Minos, P.J. Oliver   69
Mirrielees, Margaret, Lady   68
Moçambique   212
Modern languages   37, 56, 62, 100, 113, 117, 196
Molteno, Elizabeth M.   68
Molteno, J.C.   25, 31
Montagu, J.   3
Moolman, J.H.   314, 325, 346
Moore, P.A.   287
Moorrees, A.   36, 37, 123, 131, 176
Morrison, J.T.   62, 103, 105–107
Mousaion   321
Muckleneuk Ridge, Pretoria   354, 375, 378–381
Mudie, C.J.   107
Muir, T.   51–53, 56, 82, 89, 99, 107, 122
Muller, C.F.J., Prof.   51, 227, 228, 233, 291, 313, 374
Muller, C.F.J., Rev. Prof.   36, 37, 50, 51, 131, 134
Muller, H.   228
Muller, T.B.   50, 51, 112, 229
Munich, University of   319
Murray, A.   15, 19, 74
Murray, C.   27
Murray, J.   19, 25
Murray, Langham D.   159, 184, 185, 192, 198–199, 213, 216, 217, 221, 224, 234, 236, 243, 268, 270, 271, 280, 281, 287, 292, 293, 383
Murray, W.G.R.   132, 133, 140
Music degrees, Cape University   42, 69
Music, Director of   365
Music examinations and courses   42, 43, 90, 91, 116, 137, 158, 159, 188, 255, 265, 268, 284, 297, 299, 365
Music, South African Council for the Advancement of   307
Music Teachers, South African Society of   268
Musicology   318, 349, 366, 374
Myburgh, A.C.   314

397

401

No. 16—1873.]　　　　　AN ACT

To Establish and Incorporate a
　　　　　　　　　　Cape of Good H

WHEREAS it is expedient, for
　　　　ment of sound learning
of Her Majesty's subjects in this
and incorporate an University a
Hope, and thereupon to dispen
of the existing Board of Public
enacted by the Governor of the
with the advice and consent
Council and House of Ass
follows :—

I. An university, consisting
vice-chancellor, a council, and
established at the Cape of Cood
a body politic and corporate by
University of the Cape of Good
name shall have perpetual su
adopt and have a common seal,